LEARNING THE LAW

LEARNING THE LAW

BY

GLANVILLE WILLIAMS, Q.C., LL.D., F.B.A.
*Rouse Ball Professor of English Law in
the University of Cambridge*

"A man has but one youth, and considering the
consequences of employing that well, he has reason
to think himself very rich, for that gone, all the
wealth in the world will not purchase another."
Sir R. North, *On the Study of the Laws.*

TENTH EDITION

LONDON
STEVENS & SONS
1978

First Edition	...	...	...	...	1945
Second Edition	...	...	...	...	1945
Second Impression Revised			...	1946
Third Impression		...	...	...	1948
Third Edition	...	...	...	...	1950
Fourth Edition	...	...	...	...	1953
Fifth Edition	...	...	...	...	1954
Sixth Edition	...	...	...	...	1957
Seventh Edition	...	...	...	...	1963
Second Impression		...	...	...	1966
Third Impression		...	...	...	1967
Fourth Impression		...	...	...	1968
Eighth Edition	...	...	...	...	1969
Ninth Edition	...	...	...	...	1973
Second Impression		...	...	...	1974
Tenth Edition	...	...	...	...	1978

Published by
Stevens & Sons Limited of
11 New Fetter Lane, London
and printed in Great Britain by
Richard Clay (The Chaucer
Press) Ltd., Bungay, Suffolk

ISBN Hardback 0 420 45130 7
Paperback 0 420 45120 X

PREFACE TO THE TENTH EDITION

Earlier prefaces have made acknowledgment for much kind assistance, and I should like on the present occasion to add my grateful thanks to the following for suggestions and advice: Mr. Bernard Downey, Mr. Gordon Borrie, Mr. Philip Gaudin, and my colleagues Professor J. A. Jolowicz, Mr. M. J. Prichard and Mr. P. T. Wallington.

June 20, 1978   G.L.W.

CONTENTS

Chapter 1

THE DIVISIONS OF THE LAW

But in these nice sharp quillets of the law,
Good faith, I am no wiser than a daw.

—Shakespeare, *King Henry the Sixth,*
Part 1, II, iv.

CRIMES AND CIVIL WRONGS

ONE of the layman's inveterate errors is to suppose that the lawyer is largely—even exclusively—concerned with criminal law. A venerable legal chestnut that will probably be inflicted upon the reader before he has proceeded far with his studies (so why not by me?) concerns an old lady who was being given a glimpse of the Court of Chancery. She peered round and asked where was the prisoner. (According to a gloss on the tale, someone then explained to her that a Chancery judge did not try anybody except counsel.) In fact the law is divided into two great branches, the criminal and the civil,[1] and of these much the greater is the civil. Since the nature of this division must be grasped at the outset of legal studies, I shall try to give a simple explanation of it.

The distinction between a crime and a civil wrong, though capable of giving rise to some difficult legal problems, is in essence quite simple. The first thing to understand is that the distinction does *not* reside in the nature of the wrongful act itself. This can quite simply be proved by pointing out that the same act may be both a crime and a civil wrong. Occasionally at a bus station there is someone who makes a living by looking after people's impedimenta while they are shopping. If I entrust my bag to such a person, and he runs off with it, he commits the crime of theft and

---

[1] "Civil law" is a phrase used in several meanings. It may mean, as in the above context, the law that is not criminal law. It may also mean the law of a State as opposed to other sorts of law like international law; or it may mean Roman law. A "civilian" is a person learned in Roman law.

also two civil wrongs—the tort of conversion and a breach of his contract with me to keep the bag safe. The result is that two sorts of legal proceedings can be taken against him; a prosecution for the crime, and a civil action for the tort and for the breach of contract. (Of course, the plaintiff in the latter action will not get damages twice over merely because he has two causes of action; he will get only one set of damages.)

To take another illustration, if a railway signalman, to dumb forgetfulness a prey, fails to pull the lever at the right moment, and a fatal accident occurs on the line, his carelessness may be regarded as sufficiently gross to amount to the crime of manslaughter, and it is also the tort of negligence towards the victims of the accident and their dependants, and a breach of his contract with the Railway Executive to take due care in his work. It will be noticed that, this time, the right of action in tort and the right of action in contract are vested in different persons.

These examples show that the distinction between a crime and civil wrong cannot be stated as depending upon *what is done*, because what is done may be the same in each case. The true distinction resides, therefore, not in the nature of the wrongful act but in *the legal consequences that may follow it*.[2] If the wrongful act is capable of being followed by what are called criminal proceedings, that means that it is regarded as a crime (otherwise called an offence). If it is capable of being followed by civil proceedings, that means that it is regarded as a civil wrong. If it is capable of being followed by both, it is both a crime and a civil wrong. Criminal and civil proceedings are (in the normal case) easily distinguishable: the procedure is different, the outcome is different, and the terminology is different.

In criminal proceedings the terminology is as follows. You have a *prosecutor prosecuting* a *defendant*,[3] and the result of the prosecution if successful is a *conviction*, and the defendant may be *punished* by one of a variety of punishments ranging from life imprisonment to a fine, or else may be released on probation or

---

[2] *Cf. per* Lord Esher M.R. in *Seaman* v. *Burley* [1896] 2 Q.B. 344 at 346.
[3] Formerly called "prisoner" in felonies and "defendant" in misdemeanours; felonies have now been abolished as a separate class. The term "prisoner" is invidious for one who has not yet been convicted. Instead of "the defendant" the expression "the accused" is very commonly used.

discharged without punishment or dealt with in various other ways.

Turning to civil proceedings, the terminology is that a *plaintiff sues* (*i.e.* brings an *action* against) a *defendant*. The proceedings if successful result in *judgment for the plaintiff,* and the judgment may order the defendant to pay the plaintiff money, or to transfer property to him, or to do or not to do something (injunction), or to perform a contract (specific performance). In applications for a writ of habeas corpus or for one of the prerogative orders (mandamus, prohibition or certiorari) the parties are called applicant and respondent respectively. In matrimonial cases in the Family Division the parties are called *petitioner* and *respondent,* and the relief sought concerns dissolution of the marriage, consequential financial arrangements, and the custody of children.[4] (There are also other kinds of civil relief, but they need not concern us here.)

It is hardly necessary to point out that the terminology of the one type of proceedings should never be transferred to the other. "Criminal action," for example, is a misnomer; as is "civil offence" (the proper expression is "civil wrong"). One does not speak of a plaintiff prosecuting or of the criminal accused being sued. The common announcement "Trespassers will be prosecuted" has been called a "wooden lie," for trespass has traditionally been a civil wrong, not (generally) a crime. (There are some statutory offences of trespass, such as trespass on a railway line; and a "squatter" or other trespasser in a house that is occupied or required for occupation generally commits an offence if he fails to leave upon request.)[5]

Again, the word "guilty" is used primarily of criminals. The corresponding word in civil cases is "liable"; but this word is also used in criminal contexts.

Civil and criminal courts are partly but not entirely distinct. The Crown Court has almost exclusively criminal jurisdiction. Magistrates are chiefly concerned with criminal cases, but they have important civil jurisdiction over licensing and family matters. On the other hand, the county court is only civil, and so is the High Court apart from appeals.

---

[4] The petitioner *petitions* for a divorce against the respondent; and the proceedings, if successful, result in a *decree* of divorce.
[5] Criminal Law Act 1977 s. 7.

Magistrates, by the way, are one and the same as justices of the peace. Over most of the country magistrates are lay J.P.s sitting with a clerk; even the court clerk may be legally unqualified. (The "clerk to the justices" is legally qualified, but he is often occupied with administration.) In Central London and some other large towns magistrates' courts consist of a full-time stipendiary magistrate who is a lawyer.[6] Although the names "justice of the peace" and "magistrate" are synonymous, there is a slight tendency to use the former for "the Great Unpaid" and the latter for professional magistrates. Magistrates' courts are alternatively called "courts of summary jurisdiction" and "courts of petty sessions" (though the last phrase is now pretty well obsolete).

COURTS WITH CRIMINAL JURISDICTION

Let us look more closely at the trial of criminal cases. Crimes are divided into *indictable* (pronounced "inditeable") and *summary* offences. Indictable offences are, as the name implies, triable on indictment (pronounced "inditement"). This means that they are the more serious sort of crimes, triable by judge and jury (formerly called a petty jury) in the Crown Court.

Created by the Courts Act 1971, the Crown Court is the successor of the following courts (all of which used to sit with juries):

1. The criminal jurisdiction of assizes (the red-robed High Court judge on circuit);
2. Quarter sessions ("sessions" for short; here the place of the judge was taken by magistrates, or else by a professional recorder);
3. A few Crown Courts having the jurisdiction of assizes.

A session of the Crown Court is normally presided over by a *circuit judge* or *recorder,* who controls the trial and directs the jury; but it may also be constituted with a *High Court judge*.[7] High Court judges are, on average (but only on average), more able or more experienced than circuit judges; and the theory is that they therefore try the more serious and difficult cases. But the

[6] Known in London as metropolitan magistrates.
[7] A judge of the Court of Appeal may sit as a High Court judge.

peregrinating High Court judge is under pressure to be on his way; so while he will try a straightforward case of wounding with intent, which would be within the capacity of any judge, he will often leave a long and complicated fraud case to be tried by a circuit judge. A criminal trial at first instance in the Crown Court is always by jury. The old name "recorder" is preserved for part-time judges who are given the same jurisdiction as circuit judges; they are allowed to continue other occupations such as practice at the Bar or as solicitors, whereas circuit judges are full time. When you visit a Crown Court you will probably see justices of the peace sitting with the circuit judge or recorder. They vote on matters of sentence, but in practice it is the professional judge or recorder who rules on the law and procedure in the course of the trial. The Crown Court sitting in the City of London (off Ludgate Hill) is still known officially as the Central Criminal Court and colloquially as the Old Bailey. Two of its judges (of circuit judge rank) continue to be called the Recorder and the Common Serjeant of the City of London.

The Crown Court sits in various other centres, some of them served only by circuit judges and some also by High Court judges. "Practice directions" set out which indictable offences are normally allocated to a circuit judge ("lower band" offences as they have come to be called) and which require a High Court judge.[8]

Appeal from the Crown Court lies to the *Court of Appeal (Criminal Division)*.[9] The appeal may be on law or fact or against sentence, but only the defendant can appeal—not the pros-ecutor.[10] On a successful appeal against conviction the court will

---

[8] Technically there are four classes, not two. See [1972] Crim.L.R. 14.
[9] Created in 1966 and superseding the Court of Criminal Appeal, which in turn had superseded the Court for Crown Cases Reserved in 1907. The Court of Appeal (Criminal Division) sits in practice in two courts, one composed of the Lord Chief Justice, a Lord Justice of Appeal and a puisne (*i.e.* High Court) judge, and the other composed of one Lord Justice of Appeal and two puisne judges.
[10] Except that when a defendant is acquitted the Attorney-General may refer a point of law involved in the case to the Court of Appeal in order to have a ruling for future cases: Criminal Justice Act 1972 s. 36. The C.A., after giving its judgment, may also refer such cases to the House of Lords. The acquittal will not be affected by the outcome of the reference.

quash[11] the conviction; but it may substitute a conviction of some other offence of which the jury could have convicted.

From the Court of Appeal a further appeal lies (in important cases, with leave) to the House of Lords. At this stage the appeal is open even to the prosecutor. It will be understood that by "the House of Lords" in connection with appeals is not meant the same body as the House of Lords when sitting as part of the legislature. For when it is sitting as an "Appellate Committee" to hear appeals, only the Law Lords take part. The Law Lords (more formally called the "Lords of Appeal") are the Lord Chancellor, the Lords of Appeal in Ordinary (*i.e.* salaried life peers) and peers who hold or have held high judicial office.

Crimes not triable on indictment are known as summary (formerly petty) offences; they are triable without a jury by magistrates' courts. Many crimes, though falling within the class of indictable offences, can be tried in magistrates' courts if certain conditions are satisfied; they are said to be "triable both ways."

Appeal lies from a magistrates' court to the Crown Court. The whole case is reheard; there is no jury, but at least two magistrates sit with the judge or recorder. An appeal on a point of law can also be taken (either direct from a magistrates' court or from a decision of the Crown Court on appeal from the magistrates' court) to a *Divisional Court of the High Court* by a procedure known as "case stated," and a further appeal may be taken from the Divisional Court (subject to restrictions) to the House of Lords. The Divisional Court consists of two or more (generally three) judges of the High Court. A peculiarity of this appeal by way of case stated is that it is open not only to the defendant but also to the prosecutor (whereas in trials on indictment there is no appeal from an acquittal).

The scheme of criminal courts can be represented diagramatically as follows:

[11] Note the word and its spelling (neither squash nor quosh). It is cognate with modern French *casser,* as in *Cour de Cassation.* Note also that lawyers speak of *decisions* of lower courts being "reversed," while *convictions* are quashed.

Summary offences and indictable offences tried summarily	Indictable offences tried on indictment
House of Lords	House of Lords
Divisional Court of High Court (on case stated)	Court of Appeal (Criminal Division)
Crown Court	Crown Court
Magistrates' courts	

The term "indictment" itself needs explanation. Originally an "indictment" was a "true bill" found by a "grand jury," *i.e.* a jury for presenting suspected offenders. The trial upon it at assizes or quarter sessions was by a "petty jury." Nowadays the grand jury is abolished, but we still retain the word "indictment" for the document commencing criminal proceedings that are to be tried by jury. The present-day indictment may be defined as a document preferred by anyone to the Crown Court, and signed by the clerk of the court. Normally there will have been a preliminary investigation of the charge before magistrates (except that the investigation is generally reduced to a formality, unless the defendant asks for a real one), and the magistrates will have committed the defendant for trial. A form of indictment for murder is:

Court of Trial: The Crown Court held at Leeds
The Queen v. *AB*
charged as follows:
Statement of Offence.

Murder.

Particulars of Offence.

AB, on the   day of   , in the county of
, murdered JS.

Date   [Signature of officer of the court]

Prepositions have come to be used rather sloppily in criminal matters. In good usage, one is charged, tried, acquitted, convicted, or sentenced *on* (or *upon*) an indictment or count or charge. One is indicted *on* a charge of theft, or *on* two counts of theft. One is indicted or tried *for* an offence,[12] and the indictment/count/information/charge is *for* the offence.[13] (An information is a document making a criminal charge before magistrates.) One pleads guilty (or not guilty) *to* a count or charge or indictment, or *to* an offence. One is acquitted or convicted (or found guilty) *of* an offence.

COURTS WITH CIVIL JURISDICTION

So much for criminal cases. Turning to civil cases, the courts with original[14] jurisdiction are chiefly the High Court and county courts. High Court judges sit in London and also in the provinces (High Court cases outside London are often taken by deputy High Court judges who are in fact circuit or county court judges or plain barristers).[15]

The High Court is divided into three Divisions: the Queen's Bench Division, the Chancery Division, and the Family Division. The first administers primarily the common law, the second primarily equity. More will be said about this particular distinction in the next chapter. The Family Division was created by an Act of 1970 in place of the previous Probate, Divorce and Admiralty Division—a curious miscellany of jurisdictions (over wills, wives and wrecks, as Sir Alan Herbert put it) which were lumped together for no better reason than that they were all

---

[12] On the other hand, one is charged (verb) *with* an offence.

[13] Some writers misguidedly say "indicted with theft," "indicted with counts of theft and robbery," "convicted of three counts," and so on. Even more horribly, a Lord Chief Justice has used the expression "summonsed for." "Summons" is the noun, not the verb.

[14] *i.e.,* jurisdiction as a court of first instance: jurisdiction other than appellate jurisdiction.

[15] The peregrinating High Court was formerly called the Assize Court. Trials on the civil side of assizes or with a judge and jury in London were formerly said to be *"at nisi prius."* The reason for the phrase was that, when a case arose in the provinces, it was directed to be tried in London "unless before" the trial in London the justice of assize should come into the county to try it.

founded (to some extent) on Roman and canon law. In 1970, wills went to the Chancery Division and wrecks to the Queen's Bench Division.

Appeals from the High Court generally lie to the Court of Appeal (Civil Division)[16] and thence to the House of Lords. Why two appeals should be allowed can be explained only by reference to history. "The institution of one court of appeal may be considered a reasonable precaution; but two suggest panic," said A. P. Herbert. It is a panic that pays no regard to the resources of suitors. By way of alleviation, a civil case may go on appeal direct from the High Court to the House of Lords under the "leapfrogging" procedure introduced by the Administration of Justice Act 1969. This can happen, with the consent of the parties and on certificate from the judge, if the case turns on the construction of legislation or is governed by a previous decision of the Court of Appeal or House of Lords which one of the parties wishes to overturn.

The less important civil cases are tried in the county courts, with appeals to the Court of Appeal and thence to the House of Lords. As noticed before, magistrates also have some civil jurisdiction, chiefly in matrimonial matters, guardianship, adoption, and affiliation (maintenance of illegitimate children).

Neglecting magistrates' courts, the system of civil judicature explained above may be represented thus:

A report of a case will sometimes say that it was decided by a Divisional Court. This consists, as already said, of any two or more judges of the High Court. Formerly the chief importance of

---

[16] Consisting usually of the Master of the Rolls and the Lords Justices of Appeal. Occasionally Law Lords and puisne judges sit to help with the work.

the Divisional Courts in civil cases was that they heard appeals from county courts. Now that such appeals go direct to the Court of Appeal, the importance of Divisional Courts is much reduced. However, they still hear appeals from magistrates' courts (or from the Crown Court on appeal from a magistrates' court) by way of case stated, such appeals in criminal matters going to the Queen's Bench Division and in family matters to the Family Division. Further appeal lies from the Divisional Court to the House of Lords.

The present High Court, and the Court of Appeal on its civil side, were set up by the Judicature Act 1873. The High Court superseded the old courts of Queen's Bench, Common Pleas, Exchequer, Chancery, Probate, Divorce and Admiralty, and a few minor courts. The Court of Appeal superseded the old Court of Exchequer Chamber and Court of Appeal in Chancery. Together the Crown Court, High Court and Court of Appeal make up the Supreme Court of Judicature.

It is an odd fact that the House of Lords, which is the supreme tribunal, is not part of the so-called Supreme Court of Judicature. This was due to a political accident. The Judicature Act 1873, which was passed by a Liberal Government, abolished the House of Lords as a final court of appeal (though not as part of the legislature); but the Act was not to come into operation until 1874, later extended to 1875. In 1874 the Conservatives took office, and, fearing (it is said) that the abolition of the Lords as a judicial body might be the thin end of the wedge, leading ultimately to the abolition of the Lords as a legislative body, they restored the appellate jurisdiction of the House of Lords—but omitted to make it a part of the Supreme Court.[17]

Although, when exercising its appellate jurisdiction, the House of Lords consists exclusively of the Law Lords, it nevertheless sits in the same building as the House of Lords when meeting as a limb of the legislature; but since the last war it has made a practice of sitting in a committee room instead of the House itself (except when the House is in recess).[18] Also, the judgments of the Law Lords are referred to as "speeches" or "opinions." The Court of Appeal sits in the Law Courts in the Strand, which is also the permanent seat of the High Court.

[17] See Robert Stevens in 80 L.Q.R. 343.
[18] For an interesting note, see 118 New Law Journal 1160.

There are many courts and tribunals of special jurisdiction, chief among which are the industrial tribunals administering various legislation relating to employment. Appeals lie from the latter on some questions to the High Court and on other questions to the Employment Appeal Tribunal, with possible further appeals to the Court of Appeal and House of Lords. Then there is the Restrictive Practices Court, which considers agreements that restrict prices or the conditions of supply of goods, and unfair trading practices; again an appeal lies to the Court of Appeal and House of Lords.

The House of Lords is no longer our highest court, because the European Court sitting in Luxembourg adjudicates upon the law of the European Economic Community, and its decisions are binding on British courts by reason of the European Communities Act 1972. The impact of EEC law, though at present somewhat limited, grows continually; it is to be seen in company law, trade marks and other "industrial property," the law of monopolies, the control of aliens, employment law, customs, and some other economic areas. An English court can ask the European Court for a ruling on any doubtful question of EEC law.

The Judicial Committee of the Privy Council is the final court of appeal from the colonies (with remnants also of its appellate jurisdiction from the self-governing members of the Commonwealth). Its composition is much the same as that of the House of Lords when exercising appellate jurisdiction, though certain Commonwealth judges may sit in addition. Cases before it are much less frequent than formerly, but if you have the opportunity you should boldly walk in and listen to one of its deliberations. You will find the highest judges in the land sitting unpretentiously, without robes, in a room in Downing Street, and the cases that they hear are almost always of interest even to a beginner.

The advice to listen to cases in court applies, indeed, to every kind of court. Even when the court-room is somewhat crowded, the police and ushers will generally facilitate the entry of those who announce themselves as law students. The addresses of all courts will be found in Shaw's *Directory of Courts in England and Wales*.

THE CLASSIFICATION OF CIVIL WRONGS

The more important types of civil wrong may be briefly
mentioned. One is the *breach of contract*. This is easy to
understand, and all that the student needs to know at the outset of
his studies is that a contract need not be in a formal document or
indeed in any document at all. You make a contract every time
you buy an apple or take a taxi.

Another civil wrong is a *tort*. This word conveys little meaning
to the average layman, and its exact definition is a matter of great
difficulty even for the lawyer; but the general idea of it will become
clear enough if one says that torts include such wrongs as assault,
battery, false imprisonment, trespass, conversion, defamation of
character, negligence and nuisance. It is a civil wrong independent
of contract: that is to say, it gives rise to an action for damages
irrespective of any agreement not to do the act complained of.
Etymologically the word comes to us from the law-French *tort*,
signifying any wrong, and itself derived from the Latin *tortus*,
meaning "twisted" or "wrung." And the word "wrung" is the
same in origin as "wrong." (It is strange how the notion of wrong
is wrapped up with that of twisting: the opposite of wrong is right,
which is the Latin *rectus*, straight). Nowadays, however, a tort is
not any wrong but only a particular kind of wrong, of which
examples were given above.[19] The adjective from tort is
"tortious": thus one speaks of a tortious act.

A third civil wrong is a *breach of trust*. A "trust" is not a mere
obligation of honour, as the word may seem to suggest; it is an
obligation enforced by the courts. Everybody has a rough idea of
what a trust is; it occurs where a person, called technically a
settlor, transfers property (such as land or shares) to another,
called a *trustee*, on trust for yet another, called a *beneficiary*.
(Actually the same person may combine two or even all three of
these capacities; but this complication need not be considered
here.) Where the trust is created by will the settlor is also called a
testator (the name for anyone who makes a will); and an
alternative name for the beneficiary is *"cestui que trust,"* an
elliptical phrase meaning "he [for] whose [benefit the] trust [was
created]." In this phrase *cestui* is pronounced "settee" (with the

---

[19] For a further discussion see Williams and Hepple, *Foundations of the
Law of Tort* (London 1976), Chap. 1.

accent on the first syllable),[20] *que* is pronounced "kee," and trust as in English. Grammatically the plural should be *cestuis que trust* (pronounced like the singular); but by an understandable mistake it is sometimes written *cestuis que trustent,* as if trust were a verb.[21] The beginner will perceive by this time that several law-French words survive in our law from the time when French was the language of the upper classes. In the case of a charitable trust there need be no definite beneficiary but the property is held on trust for the public as a whole or for some section of it. Thus the well-known "National Trust" preserves beautiful places for the public enjoyment, and there are many trusts for educational and religious purposes.

The only other type of civil obligation (it is not thought of as a wrong) that the beginner need hear about is the quasi-contractual obligation. Suppose that I pay you £5, mistakenly thinking that I owe it to you: I can generally recover it back[22] in quasi-contract. You have not agreed to pay it back, and so are not liable to me in contract; but in justice you ought to pay it back and so the law treats you as if (*quasi*) you had contracted to repay it. There are various other heads of quasi-contract besides the particular example just given, such as the obligation to repay money paid on a consideration that has failed.

THE TITLES OF CASES

It is helpful to know certain rules for the naming of cases. Trials on indictment are in the name of the Queen (as representing the State); thus a criminal case is generally called *Reg.* v. whomever it is—*Reg.* being short for *Regina* (pronounced "Rejyna"), and v. being short for *versus.* When there is a king on the throne, *Rex* is used instead of *Reg. Rex* and *Regina* both conveniently abbreviate to *R.,* which saves having to remember which is which.

---

[20] The O.E.D. gives the pronunciation "sestwee," but this is not common among lawyers. Winfield told me that Maitland's pronunciation was the one I have given, and that is good enough authority for anyone.
[21] See Sweet in 26 L.Q.R. 196.
[22] "Recover back" is not, in legal usage, pleonastic; *i.e.* the word "back" is not superfluous. You "recover" damages, a sum of money that you never had before. You "recover back" a certain sum of money corresponding to one that you did have at some time in the past.

Thus *Rex* v. *Sikes* or *Reg.* v. *Sikes* may both be written *R.* v. *Sikes*. Some textbooks on criminal law even print simply *Sikes*. This last is a convenient usage for the student of criminal law.

In some types of criminal case the title of the case will not contain *Rex* or *Reg.* before the "v.," but will contain the name of a private person. This happens when the case is tried summarily before magistrates (*i.e.* justices of the peace); here the name of the actual prosecutor (*e.g.* a policeman) appears instead of the nominal prosecutor, the Queen. Again, when an appeal is taken to the House of Lords, the name of an official prosecutor, usually the Director of Public Prosecutions, is substituted for the word *Reg.*[23] (It may be mentioned that the Director of Public Prosecutions acts as a kind of solicitor to the Crown in the more important criminal cases). Conscious of the confusion this causes, the editor of the Law Reports decided in 1961 to compromise: the title was given in its official form at the beginning of the case, but was printed at the head of each succeeding page as it was in the court below. For example, *Reg.* v. *Bhagwan* in the Court of Appeal (Criminal Division) is called *Director of Public Prosecutions* v. *Bhagwan* at the beginning of the report in the House of Lords,[24] but then *Reg.* v. *Bhagwan* again at the top of each succeeding page.

In 1974 an attempt to simplify was made officially: it was decreed, by a Practice Direction, that appeals to the House of Lords should henceforth carry the same title as at first instance.[25] Unfortunately, the legal profession has not yet accustomed itself to the new practice, and even the Law Reports backslide. So the case that started as *Reg.* v. *Lynch* in Northern Ireland is reported in the House of Lords as *D.P.P. for Northern Ireland* v. *Lynch* [1975] A.C. 653, and anyone who looks in the index to that volume for *Reg.* v. *Lynch* (which is the proper title) will look in vain. Moreover, the All England Reports steadily ignore these efforts at simplification, which in any case have not been extended to appeals other than to the House of Lords.

Civil cases will usually be cited by the names of the parties, thus:

---

[23] Occasionally the prosecutor may be a Government Department, as in *Board of Trade* v. *Owen* [1957] A.C. 602.

[24] [1972] A.C. 60.

[25] Practice Direction [1974] 1 W.L.R. 305.

Rylands v. *Fletcher*. If the Queen (as representing the Government) is a party she is, in civil cases, usually called "The Queen," and similarly with the King, thus: *British Coal Corporation* v. *The King*; but *R.* may also be used.

The party who appeals is called the *appellant*; the other is the *respondent*. In order to make life more difficult for us all, the name of the appellant is put first when an appeal is taken to the Divisional Court, even though he was the defendant in the court below; this means that the names may become reversed. Nattrass, an inspector of weights and measures, instituted a summary prosecution entitled *Nattrass* v. *Tesco Supermarkets Ltd.*; on appeal by the defendant company to the Divisional Court this became *Tesco Supermarkets Ltd.* v. *Nattrass,* and the title stayed the same on further appeal by Tesco to the House of Lords.[26] If the above-mentioned Practice Direction is followed, the title should now be changed back to what it was at first instance when it gets to the Lords, which will produce a different title from that in the High Court even though it was the prosecution that initiated both appeals. What we need, of course, is an edict saying that the titles of cases shall never change.

There are peculiar conventions in pronouncing the names of cases. (1) A criminal case, such as *R.* v. *Sikes,* can be referred to informally as "R. v. Sikes" (Pronounced as written), or "Rex" (or, "Regina") "v. Sikes" (again pronounced as written). In court, however, the proper method is to call it "The King" (or, "The Queen") "against Sikes." (2) In civil cases the "v." coupling the names of the parties is pronounced "and," both in court and out of it. Thus *Smith* v. *Hughes* is always pronounced (but never written) "Smith and Hughes," and similarly *British Coal Corporation* v. *The King* (which was a civil proceeding against the Crown) is pronounced with an "and." Lawyers thus write one thing and say another.

In some cases, as where a will is being interpreted, the name of the case is *"In re"* (in the matter of) somebody or something; for instance, *In re Smith.* It is permissible to shorten this to *Re Smith.* (*Re* is pronounced "ree"). Certain applications to the courts are labelled *"Ex parte"*: *Ex p. Smith* means "on the application of Smith." In probate cases (that is, cases concerned with the proof

[26] [1972] A.C. 153.

of a will) the title *In Bonis* (*i.e.* in the Goods of) *Smith* may be met with, and in Admiralty cases the name of a ship (*e.g. The Satanita*). Other possible ways of naming cases need not be considered here, but, in order to prevent the student from being puzzled, one oddity may be mentioned. The House of Lords is often the final court of appeal for Scotland (and Northern Ireland) as well as England, and a Scots case that goes to the House of Lords may become important in English as well as Scots law. Two such important cases are *McAlister* (or *Donoghue*) v. *Stevenson*[27] and *Hay* (or *Bourhill*) v. *Young*.[28] The oddity is the alternative name in brackets, for which the explanation is as follows. In Scotland a married woman, though she takes her husband's name, does not cease for legal purposes to go also by her maiden name. When she figures in litigation, her maiden name is placed first, and her married name is given as an alternative afterwards. Nevertheless, the correct mode of citation, when brevity is desired, is by the married name.[29] The two cases above may, for brevity, be cited as *Donoghue* v. *Stevenson* and *Bourhill* v. *Young,* but not *McAlister* v. *Stevenson* or *Hay* v. *Young.*

PLEADINGS

This chapter must not be concluded without a word about pleadings, which are the part of procedure that the student of substantive law most needs to know. Pleadings are not, as might be supposed, pathetic speeches before judge and jury; they are dry statements on paper of the bare facts on which each party to a civil case relies. They come after the service of the writ, which commences the action, and they are exchanged between the parties before the trial in order to reveal the apple of discord to the parties themselves and to the court. In technical language their function is said to be to settle the "issues" between the parties.

The first pleading[30] is the plaintiff's *Statement of Claim*

---

[27] [1932] A.C. 562.

[28] [1943] A.C. 92.

[29] See Lord Macmillan in 49 L.Q.R. 1; 61 L.Q.R. 109.

[30] The above statement is concerned with the Queen's Bench and Chancery Divisions. In divorce cases proceedings are commenced by a petition, and the defence is called an "answer."

(formerly called, in common law matters, a Declaration[31]). It may recite, for example, that the plaintiff was on the blank day of blank proceeding on foot down High Street when the defendant so negligently drove his car that he ran him down, thereby causing him personal injury and damage to his property. There will be particulars of negligence (driving too fast, on the wrong side of the road, without keeping a proper lookout, without giving warning of his approach, and so on—these particulars have become almost common form in such cases), and particulars of the injury and damage (the latter called "special damage" to distinguish it from the "general damage" that can be presumed to flow from the injury and so does not have to be specially pleaded).

Then comes the defendant's *Defence*. The defence may embody a number of defences, perhaps inconsistent with each other,[32] but they will all be found to belong to one or other of three types:

(1) A *traverse,* that is, a contradiction of some fact stated by the plaintiff. Using the language of Touchstone in *As You Like It,* we may call it the countercheck quarrelsome.

---

[31] Any part of a declaration that in itself, if it stood alone, would have constituted a ground for action, was called a *count*. The word *count* is still used to signify the several parts of an indictment, each charging a distinct offence.

Proceedings in Chancery formerly had a terminology of their own. Underhill's description of them was as follows: "A suit in Chancery used to be commenced by a document called 'a Bill in Chancery' ... an enormous screed ... setting out in great detail the story of the suitor's wrongs. . . . The next step was to turn this Bill into 'interrogatories' to be answered by the defendants on oath. . . . This was called 'scraping the Defendant's conscience,' and he was obliged to answer on oath in the utmost detail, and if he failed to do so further interrogatories were administered until sufficient admissions were obtained to make out a prima facie case. . . . This practice of interrogatories was usually delegated by junior counsel (equity draftsmen) to their clerks, and at times the rough drafts were somewhat comic. [Thus:] 'Did not the defendant fall down on her knees or on one and which of them and implore the plaintiff with tears in her eyes or in one and which of them to advance the said sum of £—— to her husband?' " Underhill, *Change and Decay,* 77–78.

[32] Hence the tale in *Punch* of the K.C.'s son who was charged by the Head with having broken the schoolroom window: "In the first place, sir, the schoolroom has no window; in the second place, the schoolroom window is not broken; in the third place, if it is broken, I did not do it; in the fourth place it was an accident." All these defences, except the last, are traverses; the last is a confession and (one hopes) avoidance.

(2) A *confession and avoidance,* that is, an admission (confession) of the facts stated by the plaintiff, but an allegation of other facts that destroy (avoid) their legal effect, in whole or in part. "True, I did agree to buy a tame lion from you, but I was a minor at the time and the lion was not a thing reasonably necessary for my station in life." "True, I negligently ran you down, but you were guilty of contributory negligence." This may be described as the retort courteous.

(3) An *objection in point of law.* This again admits the plaintiff's facts, but objects that in law they disclose no cause of action. "True, I gave you certain advice which was wrong and on which you acted to your detriment; but I am not liable to you because in law I owed you no duty of care." It is not strictly necessary to plead an objection in point of law, for any point of law may be taken at the trial although not pleaded.

For the purpose of reading the older cases, it is desirable to know something of the old terminology and practice relating to the defence. The name "defence" for the defendant's pleading is modern. Formerly, if the defendant pleaded a traverse or a confession and avoidance, this was called a *plea*; and an objection in point of law was called a *demurrer* (law-French *demorer,* to wait or stay).[33] The demurrer was so called because the party who demurred did not proceed with his pleading but rested his case on the submission of law and awaited the judgment of the court thereon. In technical language a demurrer was not a pleading. When arguing the demurrer the parties were entitled to imagine any state of facts consistent with the declaration. Judgment was given by the full court sitting in banc, so that cases decided on demurrer settled the law in a peculiarly authoritative way. Nowadays, however, the decision on an objection in point of law, whether the objection be raised on the pleadings or not, is made by the single trial judge, either at a preliminary hearing which may succeed in disposing of the whole case or after the evidence on the issues of fact has been heard.

[33] The "u" in "demurrer" is short, as also in "demurrage" (the detention of a vessel by the charterer beyond the time agreed upon, or the payment made in compensation for such detention). In the verb "demur" (from which "demurrer" is derived), and in its other derivatives "demurrable" and "demurrage," the syllable "ur" is pronounced "er."

After the defence there may sometimes be a *Reply* (formerly called a *Replication*) from the plaintiff. This reply may take any of the three forms of the defence, traversing the facts in defence, confessing and avoiding them, or objecting in point of law.

The defence may also be accompanied by a *Counterclaim,* which will result in a *Defence to Counterclaim* from the plaintiff.

It is necessary to take care in drawing pleadings, because the judge may refuse to admit evidence on or to decide matters that have not been properly pleaded.[34] But the court always has power to allow an amendment of the pleadings, and, being rightly reluctant to visit the sins of the pleaders upon their clients, will now allow amendment wherever this occasions no injustice to the other side, provided that the party amending pays any costs occasioned by his mistake.[35] This power to allow amendment diminishes the importance of the pleadings; but it must be remembered that if counsel does not ask for an amendment judgment will be given on the pleadings as they stand. Some judges, even today, when they perceive a defect in the pleadings do not call counsel's attention to it (which they could do if they were so minded), but keep silence on the point until delivering judgment, by which time it is too late for counsel to ask for an amendment. This regrettable attitude, which may still be heard

---

[34] See *Waghorn* v. *Geo. Wimpey & Co. Ltd.* [1969] 1 W.L.R. 1764.

[35] The modern attitude towards amendments was wittily explained by Bowen L.J. in *Cropper* v. *Smith* (1884) 26 Ch.D. at 711: "There is one panacea which heals every sore in litigation, and that is costs. I have very seldom, if ever, been unfortunate enough to come across an instance where a person has made a mistake in his pleadings which has put the other side to such a disadvantage as that it cannot be cured by the application of that healing medicine." See, however, *Soar* v. *N.C.B.* [1965] 1 W.L.R. 886, from which it appears that the court may refuse to allow a plaintiff at the late stage of the trial to raise a new case after failure of the pleaded case. Why should not an amendment (with adjournment) be allowed even then? In the county court, it is specifically provided (by Order 9, r. 8) that the delivery of a defence does not prevent the defendant from relying on any other defence, but all the same I have known cases lost in the county court for failure to plead the defence ultimately relied on.

A judge who allows an amendment of a statement of claim may, at his discretion, allow the defendant costs of the action up to the date of the amendment, on the ground that the plaintiff's statement of claim before that time disclosed no cause of action on which he could have succeeded.

defended by many lawyers, springs from the English tradition that a lawsuit is a game of legal skill in which the judge is neutral. It must also be pointed out that an appeal court regards itself as hearing an appeal on the case presented to the lower court; it will generally refuse to decide a point that was not before the court below on the facts as pleaded.

FURTHER READING

Dr. R. M. Jackson's *Machinery of Justice in England* is the best general description of our courts and their working, but useful additional information is given in Radcliffe and Cross, *The English Legal System*, and Walker and Walker, *The English Legal System*.

CHAPTER 2

COMMON LAW AND EQUITY

"You are too easily surprised," said Mr. Towkington. "Many words have no legal meaning. Others have a legal meaning very unlike their ordinary meaning. For example, the word 'daffy-down-dilly.' It is a criminal libel to call a lawyer a daffy-down-dilly. Ha! Yes, I advise you never to do such a thing. No, I certainly advise you *never* to do it."

—Dorothy Sayers, *Unnatural Death,* Chap. 14.

Two technical terms of great importance that are likely to puzzle the novice are "common law" and "equity."

The law of England may be said to be composed of three great elements: common law, equity and legislation. The most important kind of legislation is the Act of Parliament (otherwise called a statute), though nowadays what is called delegated legislation, like the many government orders generally known as statutory instruments, has come to be of great importance as well. Even a layman is not likely to experience difficulty in understanding the meaning of legislation. Not so, however, with the other two terms, which need fuller discussion.

THE COMMON LAW

The phrase "the common law" seems a little bewildering at first, because it is always used to point a contrast and its precise meaning depends upon the contrast that is being pointed. An analogy may perhaps make this clearer. Take the word "layman." In the foregoing paragraph the word was used to mean a person who is not a lawyer. But when we speak of ecclesiastics and laymen, we mean by "laymen" non-ecclesiastics. When we speak of doctors and laymen, we mean by "laymen" non-doctors. Laymen, in short, are people who do not belong to the particular profession that we are speaking of. Again, take "aliens." In England if we speak of "aliens" we generally mean by that word people who are not citizens of our own country ("patrials"). But in France the French equivalent of the word would mean people who are not French citizens.

It is somewhat similar with "the common law." (1) Originally this meant the law that was not local law, that is, the law that was common to the whole of England. This may still be its meaning in a particular context, but it is not the usual meaning. More usually the phrase will signify (2) the law that is not the result of legislation, that is, the law created by the custom of the people and decisions of the judges. Within certain narrow limits, popular custom creates law, and so (within much wider limits) do the decisions of the courts, which we call precedents. When the phrase "the common law" is used in this sense it may include even local law (in the form of local custom), which in meaning (1) is not common law. Again (3) the phrase may mean the law that is not equity; in other words it may mean the law developed by the old courts of common law as distinct from the system (technically called "equity") developed by the old Court of Chancery. In this sense "the common law" may even include statutory modifications of the common law, though in the previous sense it does not.[1] Finally, (4) it may mean the law that is not foreign law—in other words, the law of England, or of other countries (such as America) that have adopted English law. In this sense it is contrasted with (say) Roman law or French law, and in this sense it includes the whole of English law—even local customs, legislation and equity. It will thus be seen that the precise shade of meaning in which this chameleon phrase is used depends upon the particular context, and upon the contrast that is being made. When I said in the second sentence of this chapter that our law is made up of common law, equity and legislation, I meant it in a mixture of senses (2) and (3), as the context itself showed.

EQUITY

The term "equity" is an illustration of Mr. Towkington's proposition that some words have a legal meaning very unlike their ordinary one. In ordinary language "equity" means natural justice; but the beginner must get that idea out of his head when dealing with the system that lawyers call equity. Originally, indeed, this system was inspired by ideas of natural justice, and that is why it acquired its name; but nowadays equity is no more

---

[1] Lawyers sometimes use the term to mean only the civil-law part of the common law in sense (3), to the exclusion of the criminal law.

(and no less) natural justice than the common law, and it is in fact nothing else than a particular branch of the law of England. Equity, therefore, is law. The student should not allow himself to be confused by the lawyer's habit of contrasting "law" and "equity," for in this context "law" is simply an abbreviation for the common law. Equity *is* law in the sense that it is part of the law of England; it is not law only in the sense that it is not part of the common law.

The student will learn quite early in his historical studies how equity came into being. He will learn how, in the Middle Ages, the courts of common law failed to give redress in certain types of case where redress was needed, and how the disappointed litigants petitioned the King, who was the "fountain of justice," for extraordinary relief; how the King, through his Chancellor, eventually set up a special court, the Court of Chancery, to deal with these petitions; and how the rules applied by the Court of Chancery hardened into law and became a regular part of the law of the land. The most important branch of equity is the law of trusts, but equitable remedies such as specific performance and injunction are also much used. The student will learn how, in case of "conflict or variance" between the rules of common law and the rules of equity, equity came to prevail. This was by means of what was called a common injunction. Suppose that A brought an action against B in one of the common law courts, and in the view of the Court of Chancery the action was inequitable. B's proper course was to apply to the Court of Chancery for an order, called a common injunction, directed to A and ordering him not to continue his action. If A defied the injunction the Court of Chancery would put him in prison for contempt of court. Equity thus worked "behind the scenes" of the common law action; the common law principles were theoretically left intact, but by means of this intricate mechanism they were superseded by equitable rules in all cases of "conflict or variance."[2] The result

[2] The common law courts, after a famous struggle in the seventeenth century, lay passive under this process; they did not help but they did not hinder. In some cases they even took account positively of equitable doctrines. See *Master* v. *Miller* (1791) 4 T.R. 320 at 341, 100 E.R. at 1053; *Legh* v. *Legh* (1799) 1 Bos. & Pul. 447, 126 E.R. 1002; *Bosanquet* v. *Wray* (1815) 6 Taunt. 597, 128 E.R. 1166. But such cases were exceptional.

justified the sarcasm of the critic who said that in England one court was set up to do injustice and another to stop it.

This system went on until 1875, when as a result of the Judicature Act 1873 the old courts of common law and the Court of Chancery were abolished, and in their place was established a single Supreme Court of Judicature, each branch of which had full power to administer both law and equity. Also, common injunctions were abolished and instead it was enacted that, in cases of "conflict or variance" between the rules of equity and the rules of common law, the rules of equity should prevail.

All this is simple to understand; what is not so easy to explain to a beginner is how the two systems, of law (*i.e.* the common law) and equity, remain distinct at the present day. Lawyers are familiar with the proposition that the Judicature Act, although it fused the administration of law and equity, did not fuse law and equity themselves. As one writer put it: "the two streams have met and now run in the same channel, but their waters do not mix." For the beginner this is a hard saying. "How," he may ask, "can one say that law and equity are still different, when they are administered by the same judges? I can understand (he may go on) that before the Judicature Act one had to know whether a particular rule was a rule of law or a rule of equity, because you had to be careful to proceed in the right court to get your rule enforced. But now courts do not matter. Why, then, should I bother to learn whether a particular rule is part of the system formerly called the common law or part of the system formerly called equity? Is anyone the worse lawyer for not knowing it?" The student cannot appreciate the full answer to this question until he has studied equity, but I think that a satisfactory preliminary answer can be given him at once. To start with it may be admitted that very often the student's impression is right, and it does not now matter whether a particular rule is law or equity. But sometimes it does matter. When one says that a particular rule of modern law (using that term, this time, in its wide sense) is a rule of "equity," one means that it has to be read in the light of the whole complex of rules developed by the Chancellors. These rules do not necessarily apply if the rule in question is a rule of the common law. To take an illustration of these rules developed by the Chancellors, one of them was (and is) to the effect that "he who comes to equity must come with clean hands." This rule will apply whenever the plaintiff is relying upon an equitable right, but not necessarily when he is relying on a common law right. In other words, to say that a particular right is an equitable right is shorthand for saying that all the subsidiary rules of equity apply to it, including (for instance) the rule that the plaintiff must not have soiled his hands. On the other hand, to say that a particular right is a common law right is shorthand for saying that it is to be interpreted in a common law atmosphere, leaving out of account such equitable rules as apply only to equitable rights. Thus when a modern textbook draws a distinction between law and equity, saying that at law the rule is so-and-so but in equity[3] it is such-and-such, the author is not indulging in idle verbiage nor yet in mere historical reminiscence. Although the rule is that when law and equity conflict, equity prevails, there is always the possibility that a litigant who relies on an equitable rule may for some reason find himself outside the limits of that equitable rule; and when this happens the contradictory common law rule, which may generally seem to be a dead letter, becomes very much alive.

The distinction between law and equity, as I have tried to explain it, was vividly brought home to me in a case that I listened to in my student days. It was an ejectment action brought by a landlord against his tenant, whom we will call Mr. Isaacson. The latter had what is known as an equitable lease of the premises, that is to say, nor a formal lease under seal, but an informal lease valid only in equity. For nearly all practical purposes these equitable leases are just as good as legal leases, and they are habitually relied on, even though they are void at law. This particular tenant, however, had broken the terms of his equitable lease, for shortly after receiving it he had assigned it to a company by the name of Saxon, Ltd., and there was a covenant in the lease not to assign. Mr. Isaacson somewhat disingenuously explained that he did not think this mattered, for the company was his own creation and "Saxon," he said, was none other than the latter part of his name! But Mr. Isaacson's real defence was that, although he might be liable in damages for having broken his covenant not to assign, that was not any reason for his being ejected altogether from the premises. Had the document been a legal lease this defence would have been a good one, for the lease did not contain a proviso for

[3] Note the prepositions—*at* law, but *in* equity.

re-entry on breach of covenant. But unfortunately for the tenant it was an equitable lease, and by breaking an important term of it he had soiled his hands *and therefore lost his lease*.[4] Consequently the action succeeded, much, I remember, to my surprise.

The above is not the only answer to the question: What is the present difference between law and equity? But it is, I believe, the only answer that can be given in general terms without having to state exceptions; and it is the answer that is most easily apprehended by the beginner.

COMMON LAW AND JUDICIAL DISCRETION

When the term "common law" is used in contrast to statutory law, it may mean either of two things, though they are closely related. It generally means the body of law produced by decided cases without the aid of legislation. Occasionally, however, the invocation of the common law refers not to previously existing law but to the power of the judges to create new law under the guise of interpreting it. Nearly all the common law in the first sense is created by the common law in the second sense, that is to say by the judges in the exercise of their discretion.

How much discretion a judge has to expand the law is a complex question. Part of the answer to it will appear in Chapter 6.

FURTHER READING

For a lively account of these and other matters read Fifoot, *English Law and its Background,* Chaps. 1 and 3. The whole book can be read with advantage and pleasure. Further information will be found in the standard legal histories.

---

[4] *Cp. Coatsworth* v. *Johnson* (1885) 55 L.J.Q.B. 220. But the statutory restrictions on re-entry apply: see Law of Property Act 1925, s. 146(5)(*a*). For a similar situation except that the illegality was by the landlord see *Warmington* v. *Miller* [1973] 2 W.L.R. 654, [1973] 2 All E.R. 372.

CHAPTER 3

THE MECHANISM OF SCHOLARSHIP

I hold him not discreet that will *sectari rivulos,* when he may *petere fontes.*

—Coke, Preface to 4th part of Reports.

HE who wants to become a lawyer, and not merely to pass law examinations (which is not at all the same thing), must learn to use legal materials. He must get to know the way about his law library, and must acquire the habit of first-hand work among what lawyers call the sources. The great campaigner for this among teachers of law was the man affectionately known to his own generation as "F.P.," and I make no apology for repeating his words, since I cannot better them.

"We no longer make and transcribe notes and extracts, with infinite manual labour, in a huge 'commonplace book,' as former generations were compelled to do by the dearth of printed works of reference. But, since the law is a living science, no facilities of publishing and printing can ever perfectly keep pace with it. A student who intends to be a lawyer cannot realise this too soon. There is no need for him to make voluminous notes (indeed there is a great deal of vain superstition about lecture notes); but those he does take and use ought to be made by him for himself, and always verified with the actual authorities at the first opportunity. Another man's notes may be better in themselves, but they will be worse for the learner. As for attempts to dispense with first-hand reading and digesting by printed summaries and other like devices, they are absolutely to be rejected. No man ever became a lawyer by putting his trust in such things; and if men can pass examinations by them so much the worse for the examinations."[1]

Some may think that put a trifle too exuberantly,[2] but in

---

[1] Pollock, *Oxford Lectures,* 104–105.

[2] I am not quite sure what Pollock meant by "printed summaries and other like devices," which are thus absolutely to be rejected. He could not have meant textbooks, because he himself wrote several. He did not mean case books, because after writing the above passage he went on to approve them. I suppose he was referring to what are commonly called cram books, and, so understood, any teacher would agree with him.

essentials the advice is sound. The great disadvantage of confining oneself to textbooks and lecture notes is that it means taking all one's law at second hand. The law of England is contained in statutes and judicial decisions; what the text writer thinks is not, in itself, law. He may have misinterpreted the authorities, and the reader who goes to them goes to the fountainhead. Besides familiarising himself with the law reports and statute book, the lawyer-to-be should get to know his way about the library as a whole, together with its apparatus of catalogues and books of reference. To quote Pollock again:

"Facility in such things may seem a small matter, but much toil may be wasted and much precious time lost for want of it. To the working lawyer these things are the very tools of his trade. He depends on them for that whole region of potential knowledge which must bear a large proportion to the actual."[3]

But this is preaching; and I do not want to preach, but only to give practical advice to those who wish to hear it. Let us therefore pass at once to:

THE LAY-OUT OF THE LAW LIBRARY

Near the entrance to the library there will probably be either a catalogue of the contents of the library or a card index. In fact there may be two such catalogues or indexes, one arranged alphabetically under authors and another arranged by general subjects. They are both open to the use of readers.

Each entry contains a number of figures or letters or a combination of the two. This is known as the class mark, and it should be accurately noted, for it enables the volume to be traced in the library. You should make a point of discovering the system adopted in your library, by wandering round the shelves—assuming, of course, that it is a library in which you are allowed access to the shelves, and that it is not so large a library as to make this task impracticable. Some classifications use what may be called a decimal system, even though no decimal point appears. For example, volumes next to each other on the shelf may be marked AF 1, AF 2, AF 22 and AF 7. If you imagine a decimal point before these numbers you will see that they are not out of order. The system enables the library staff to insert new subgroups without altering the main order.

[3] *Ibid.* 106.

One has to use common sense in consulting a catalogue. Suppose you want a book by a man called Bowen-Rowlands. You should first try "Bowen," but if it is not there try "Rowlands." Libraries vary in their treatment of these hyphenated names. Anonymous books are usually included in the author catalogues under their titles. Thus, *Every Man's Own Lawyer*, by A Barrister, will probably be in the author catalogue under "Every," though it may be under "Barrister" or "A Barrister" or "Anonymous." Periodicals may be in the author catalogue either under their titles or grouped under the general heading of "Periodicals."

Near the catalogues or card indexes there will probably be works of reference, like dictionaries and bibliographies.

The law reports, statutes and periodicals will probably be found in special sections of the library. Usually, too, there will be special sections devoted to such subjects as Roman law, international law, jurisprudence and legal history. Most of the rest of the library will be taken up with English law textbooks. These may be arranged alphabetically under authors, starting (say) with *Abbott on Merchant Ships* and ending with (say) *Zouche on Partnership Accounts*. Or they may be classified by subject, but arranged alphabetically under authors within each subject. Where there is no subject arrangement, and it is desired to find books relating to a particular subject, it will usually be necessary to consult the subject catalogue in the library, or else one of the works mentioned later (p. 154).

We shall now look more closely at the law reports, statutes and periodicals.

LAW REPORTS

Law reports are reports of the more important cases decided by the superior courts. Not all cases are reported: only those of legal interest. The reports may be divided very roughly into the old and the new. The old run from the time of Henry VIII to 1865, and the new since that date. Before Henry VIII's time there were the Year Books, which will be described in the next chapter.

Pre-1865 reports were produced chiefly by private reporters under their own names. Altogether there were some hundreds of different series, though many of them ran only for a short time. Most, but not all, have been reprinted in a series known as the

English Reports (abbreviated E.R.). A chart supplied with the English Reports indicates the volume of the English Reports in which a particular volume of the old reports is to be found reprinted: the chart will either be found hanging in the library, or be found in a slim volume at the end of the series of English Reports. For instance, if your reference is to 1 B. & Ad. 289 (which means volume one of Barnewall and Adolphus's Reports at page 289), the chart will tell you that the corresponding volume of the English Reports reprint is volume 109. As you take down the volume from the shelf, notice the names in gilt letters at the bottom of the spine. These will tell you the order in which the old reports are reprinted in the particular volume. Volume 109 bears the legend: Barnewall & Cresswell 9–10; Barnewall & Adolphus 1–2. This indicates that 1 B. & Ad. will probably be found just beyond the middle of the book. Open the book, and you will find your page reference in heavy type at the top centre of the open pages (top outside corner in the first twenty volumes). If something goes wrong and your case eludes you, try the index at the end of the volume; failing that, Vols. 177–178 contain a complete index of all cases in the reprint.

A warning may be given that the chart just referred to is not quite complete, because it indexes each of the old reports under one title only, whereas in fact many of the old reports were known under various titles or under various abbreviations of the title. The much fuller chart in *Where to Look for your Law* will, therefore, often be found useful. The latter chart should be turned to if the former fails; it will indicate definitely whether or not the report that is being sought is to be found reprinted in the English Reports. For research purposes, the additional chart published in 7 Cambridge Law Journal 261 may be found useful. Alternatively, as said already, the index volumes can be used.

These old reports were of uneven quality, at least in the period before 1757, and need to be handled with some care. Of the worst of them many stories are told. In *Slater* v. *May* (1704)[4] a case was cited from 4 Modern, then a comparatively recent volume of reports. Upon search of the roll (that is, the official record of the case) it was found that the report in 4 Modern had omitted a material fact. Upon this Holt C.J. burst out: "See the

[4] 2 Ld.Raym. 1071, 92 E.R. 210.

inconveniences of these scambling reports, they will make us to appear to posterity for a parcel of blockheads." When another of the early reporters, Barnardiston, was cited before Lord Lyndhurst, the latter exclaimed: "Barnardiston, Mr. Preston! I fear that is a book of no great authority; I recollect, in my younger days, it was said of Barnardiston, that he was accustomed to slumber over his notebook, and wags in the rear took the opportunity of scribbling nonsense in it."[5] Reporters even of the nineteenth century did not always escape judicial condemnation. The one who got most kicks of all was Espinasse who reported Nisi Prius cases between 1793 and 1807. Pollock C.B. said of him that he heard only half of what went on in court and reported *the other half*.[6] And Maule J., when a case in Espinasse was referred to, said with some emphasis that he did not care for Espinasse "or any other ass."[7] Denman C.J.'s response when a case from Espinasse was cited was:

"I am tempted to remark, for the benefit of the profession, that Espinasse's Reports, in days nearer their own time, when their want of accuracy was better known than it is now, were never quoted without doubt and hesitation; and a special reason was often given as an apology for citing that particular case. Now they are often cited as if counsel thought them of equal authority with Lord Coke's Reports."[8]

[5] Wallace, *The Reporters*, 424.
[6] Anon., *A Lawyer's Notebook*, 43; (1938) 54 L.Q.R. 368.
[7] Biron, *Without Prejudice*, 88.
[8] *Small* v. *Nairne* (1849) 13 Q.B. 840 at 844, 116 E.R. 1484 at 1486. Some further comments may be added from A. J. Ashton's *As I Went on my Way*, 27–28: "More decorous, though not more learned, judges than Maule always insisted that the fifth Espinasse must not be cited, and would hardly admit even the earlier volumes. Lowndes, who reported on the Northern Circuit, would barely be tolerated. It is in his rare and amusing volume that the head note is to be found, 'Carlisle. Possession of trousers in Scotland evidence of larceny in England.' It was not desirable to quote the Modern Reports if you could find Lord Mansfield in any other report. Carrington and Payne depended a good deal on the number of the volume. The later it was, the less it was attended to. It would seem that Carrington, like Espinasse, went down the hill, and I have myself heard a judge refuse to hear Carrington and Kirwan cited. These reports follow Carrington and Payne in date; and the judge said he didn't believe the reporter could at that date be trusted. This was a bold commercial judge, now dead. Of Price's Reports in the Exchequer it used to be said that you could find in them anything you wanted, if you looked long enough. He was the Beavan of the common law reporters. I once looked a long time and thought I

I relate these tales only to put the student on his guard when dealing with some of the old reports, not to discountenance their use altogether. It sometimes happens that even poor maligned Espinasse is the only reporter to give us an important case— *Wilkinson* v. *Coverdale,*[9] which the student may perhaps come across in tort or in contract, is an example—and, as Denman, C.J. indicated, he and others of like stamp are not altogether unusable, though usable only with caution. Also, this sort of condemnation does not apply by any means to all the old reports, many of which are of outstanding quality.

If the student wishes to know more about these old reporters he may read Pollock's chapter in his *First Book of Jurisprudence,* 6th ed., 292 *et seq.,* or Veeder's article in (1901) 15 Harvard Law Review 1, 109, partly reprinted in 2 *Select Essays in Anglo-American Legal History,* 123, or C. G. Moran's *The Heralds of the Law* (1948). Detailed monographs are Wallace, *The Reporters,* and Fox, *Handbook of English Law Reports.*

In 1865 there commenced the semi-official "Law Reports" (with capital letters) published by the Incorporated Council of Law Reporting. At present they are published in three series, one for each Division of the High Court. They are:

---

found something in Price which seemed authority worth citing in a case in which Sir Horace Davey led me. At two or three consultations running, I brought this case forward after the second leader had finished, and Sir Horace always let me read the passage to him and murmured, 'Yes, that seems some authority.' I should point out to my American friends that Sir Horace did not mean what they mean by these words. But I never got him to take the book into his hands until he was arguing in court. He suddenly swerved round and said, 'Give me that case of yours,' and began turning the pages with a listless and indifferent hand—for he was very tired—and glancing at them in a lack-lustre way, said, 'Then there is a case, my Lord, in the fourth Price'—looking at the number on the back of the volume—'which decides a number of interesting matters, including, I see,' pausing at a particular page, 'the ownership of a pond in Hertfordshire, and there is somewhere,' turning a few more pages, 'something that seems to bear on this matter. But, however,' ceasing to turn any more pages from sheer inanition, 'I don't think I'll cite it,' handing the book back to me with a smile." (The author is mistaken as to Lowndes—the report of the case referred to is in 1 Lewin 113, 168 E.R. 980—and it was a horse, not a pair of trousers.)

[9] (1793) 1 Esp. 75, 170 E.R. 284.

the Queen's Bench Division (cited *e.g.* as [1975] 2 Q.B. 600,
   meaning the second volume for the year 1975 at p. 600);
the Chancery Division (cited *e.g.* as [1975] 1 Ch. 800);
the Family Division (cited *e.g.* as [1975] Fam. 200).

These three series contain judgments at first instance in the
three Divisions, and they also contain the judgments on appeal to
the Court of Appeal. If a further appeal is taken from the Court of
Appeal to the House of Lords, the decision of the Lords will be
reported in a separate series called the Appeal Cases (cited *e.g.* as
[1975] A.C. 100). The Appeal Cases also contain cases in the
Judicial Committee of the Privy Council.

Originally there were eleven series—roughly speaking, one for
each of the superior courts. After the Law Reports had been
running for ten years, the Judicature Act 1873 came into force,
and this (since it altered the superior courts) brought about
changes in the names of the series and reduced the eleven series to
six. Another change occurred in 1881, when the Exchequer and
Common Pleas Divisions of the High Court were incorporated in
the Queen's Bench Division, with the result that the corresponding reports were likewise incorporated, reducing the series to four.
A change in the mode of citation was made in 1890, when instead
of quoting the volumes by number the practice was started of
referring to them exclusively by the year. In 1972 the series called
Probate (abbreviated P., and containing cases in the Probate,
Divorce and Admiralty Division) was replaced by a series called
Family (containing cases in the new Family division). All these
changes are shown in the table on p. 34.

Take down any volume of the Law Reports and look at the
beginning of a case. At the head are what are called the
catchwords, indicating briefly what the case is about. They enable
the reader to make sure that the case is relevant to the point he is
concerned with. Then comes the headnote, which is again not part
of the report but simply a summary written by the reporter.
Occasionally inaccurate, it is nevertheless useful as a guide to the
judgments. Occasionally the leading judgment is delivered by the
senior member of the court when he is *dissenting*; if the student
reads it without having consulted the headnote, he will for quite a
time labour under a misapprehension as to what was decided.
Obviously it is better to read the judgments of the majority first,
though dissenting judgments may be valuable because they may

TABLE OF THE LAW REPORTS

The mode of citation is given in brackets. In the first, second and third columns, dots (...) are put where the number of the volume would appear in the citation. In the fourth column square brackets ([ ]) are put where the year would appear in the citation.

1866–1875	1875–1880	1881–1890	1891–present
House of Lords, English and Irish Appeals (L.R. ... H.L.)			
House of Lords, Scotch and Divorce Appeals (L.R. ... H.L.Sc. or L.R. ... H.L.Sc. and Div.)	Appeal Cases (...App.Cas.)	Appeal Cases (...App.Cas.)	Appeal Cases ([ ]) A.C.)
Privy Council Appeals (L.R. ... P.C.)			
Chancery Appeal Cases (L.R. ... Ch. or Ch. App.)	Chancery Division (...Ch.D.)	Chancery Division (...Ch.D.)	Chancery Division ([ ] Ch.)
Equity Cases (L.R. ... Eq.)			
Crown Cases Reserved (L.R. ... C.C., or, ... C.C.R.)	Queen's Bench Division (...Q.B.D.)		
Queen's Bench Cases* (L.R. ... Q.B.)		Queen's Bench Division (...Q.B.D.)	Queen's (or King's) Bench Division ([ ]Q.B. or K.B.)†
Common Pleas Cases (L.R. ... C.P.)	Common Pleas Division (...C.P.D.)		
Exchequer Cases‡ (L.R. ... Ex.)	Exchequer Division (...Ex.D.)		
Admiralty and Ecclesiastical Cases (L.R. ... A. & E.)	Probate Division (...P.D.)	Probate Division (...P.D.)	Probate Division ([ ]P.) Since 1972 Family Division ([ ]Fam.)
Probate and Divorce Cases (L.R. ... P. & D.)			

* Note that there is also a series called Queen's Bench Reports in the old reports (113–118 E.R.).
† After 1907 this includes cases in the Court of Criminal Appeal, later the Court of Appeal, in place of the previous Court for Crown Cases Reserved.
‡ Note that there is also a series called Exchequer Reports in the old reports (154–156 E.R.).

find favour in a higher court if the point is carried further.

Generally the headnote states the short facts of the case. If they appear to be adequately summarised, it is to my mind quite permissible in ordinary cases to skip the facts as stated in detail by the judge, and to come forthwith to the part of his judgment that deals with the law. Except as above it is unwise to rely on the headnote. At the very least, one of the (majority) judgments should be read, in whole or in part. It is also very improving to read the argument for the side that lost, or a dissenting judgment if there is one, in order to appreciate that there were two sides to the question, as there always are in cases that get into the law reports.

The Incorporated Council of Law Reporting also publishes a weekly series known as the Weekly Law Reports (W.L.R.), which in 1953 replaced the earlier Weekly Notes (W.N.). The W.L.R. are bound in three volumes, the first containing cases that are not afterwards included in the Law Reports, and the second and third those cases that are expected to be superseded by the version in the Law Reports. (Sometimes, as it turns out, they are not included in the Law Reports after all.)

In addition to the Law Reports various privately owned series are still current. The most important is the All England Law Reports (All E.R.). The Times Law Reports (T.L.R.) ceased at the end of 1952. The Law Times Reports (L.T.) became merged with the All England Law Reports at the beginning of 1948, and the Law Journal Reports (before 1947 cited as L.J.Ch., L.J.K.B., etc) likewise became merged with the All England Law Reports in 1950. Distinguish the Law Times Reports from the Law Times newspaper. Note also that many volumes of the Law Journal Reports have different page-runs for the different courts. Thus (1865) 34 L.J.C.P. 1 is not the first page of the bound volume but is in the middle of the volume. The All E.R. Reprint includes selected cases from the Law Times Reports and other earlier reports.

The student of criminal law should seek out in his library two series of reports of particular interest to him: Cox's Criminal Cases (Cox), and the Criminal Appeal Reports (C.A.R. or Cr.App.R.). Then there are the Justice of the Peace Reports (J.P.). Before volume 96, these are usually bound at the end of the Justice of the Peace newspaper (abbreviated J.P.N.: note the independent pagination after volume 67); from that volume onwards they are separate. Brief reports of cases are also given in the Criminal Law Review (Crim.L.R.). Labour lawyers will need to consult the Industrial Cases Reports, the Industrial Tribunal Reports, and the Industrial Relations Law Reports.

An advantage of having the collateral reports in the library is that if the reader wants a volume of the Law Reports and finds that it is being used by someone else, it is often more convenient to turn up the case in one of the collateral series than to wait for the Law Reports version. For citation in court the Law Reports are preferred, because the judgments they print have been revised by the judges. The Law Reports have the further advantage that counsel's argument is summarised.

The following works may be consulted to find the other reports of a case when the report you seek is not on the shelf. The *Law Reports Index* is particularly useful because it now gives references to the Law Reports, Weekly Law Reports, All England Reports, Criminal Appeal Reports, and other series. The *All England Reports Consolidated Tables and Index* gives only the All England Reports. The *Current Law Case Citator 1947–1977* covers all reports for the period specified, and later cases will be found in the annual volumes. Failing all else, use the index volumes to the *English and Empire Digest*.

Indexes of legal abbreviations used in references to cases and lists of reports will be found in the *Manual of Legal Citations* published by the Institute of Advanced Legal Studies (1959); *Where to Look for your Law*; reprinted in Osborn's *Concise Law Dictionary* and *The Pocket Law Lexicon*; Sweet and Maxwell's *Law Finder* and *Guide to Law Reports and Statutes*; Jelf, *Where to Find Your Law*; Mozley and Whiteley's *Law Dictionary*; any volume of Halsbury's *Laws of England*; any volume of the *English and Empire Digest*; the *Encyclopaedia of the Laws of England,* 3rd ed., 1: xii; Mew's *Digest*, 2nd ed., 1: xix; Stroud's *Judicial Dictionary*, 3rd ed., 1: cxcvii; Farrer, *Introduction to Legal Method*, 220–223; and Hicks, *Materials and Methods of Legal Research*.

The current Scottish law reports known as Sessions Cases are divided into three series all bound into one volume for the year: House of Lords, Court of Justiciary, and Court of Session. They are cited as, for example, 1978 S.C. (H.L.) 100, 1978 S.C. (J.) 100 and 1978 S.C. 100; note that there are three different page-runs in each volume. See also [1958] Criminal Law Review 368.

Sometimes the reader's reference will contain two page references, thus "[1892] 1 Q.B. 273, 291" or "[1892] 1 Q.B. 273 at 291." Here the first page contains the beginning of the case and the second page the dictum to which the real reference is being made. I have known beginners spend many hours reading a case to which they were referred only for a single dictum in the middle of it. Generally speaking, if a case is quoted for a dictum there is no need to read the whole of the case.

The use of square and round brackets surrounding the dates of cases requires a word of explanation. Compare the two following references:

> *Stanley* v. *Powell* (1890) 60 L.J.Q.B. 52.
> *Stanley* v. *Powell* [1891] 1 Q.B. 86.

Why are the dates different, and why the two different sorts of brackets? To answer the second question first, the custom is to use square brackets where the date is an indispensable part of the reference to the case, round brackets where it is not. As to the first question, the judgment in the case was pronounced in 1890, which is therefore its true date. But some time elapses before the cases are reported in the Law Reports, and this case did not get in till 1891, which is the date in the second reference. Where cases are reported in the Law Reports it is customary to adopt the date of publication of the Law Reports version as the date of the case. The reader need not trouble to learn any of this; it is explained here simply to save bewilderment.

STATUTES

Statutes are cited in three ways: by the short title, which includes the calendar year (*e.g.* the Fatal Accidents Act 1846[10]), or by the regnal year or years and the chapter (*e.g.* 9 & 10 Vict. c. 93[11]), or by a compromise of the two (*e.g.* the Fatal Accidents Act 1846 (c. 93)). Two regnal years are given (as in the foregoing example) when the session of Parliament in which the statute was passed did not fall within a single regnal year. The chapter indicates the

[10] Acts passed before 1963 had a comma in the short title before the date; in 1962 a change was made and the comma was omitted. It seems sensible now to drop the comma in pre-1963 Acts as well.

[11] Pronounced as "the statute nine and ten Victoria, chapter 93," or "the ninth and tenth Victoria, chapter 93."

number of the statute—formerly, the number in the session. It will be seen that "9 & 10 Vict. c. 93" means an Act that received the royal assent in the session of Parliament beginning in the ninth year of Queen Victoria and concluding in her tenth year, being the ninety-third statute passed in that session. Since 1962, chapter numbers have referred to the calendar year.[12]

The most convenient place in which to turn up a statute that is still in force is in Halsbury's *Statutes of England*. A particularly useful feature is the "Destination Table," which will be found at the end of consolidating Acts and which enables the provisions of the Act to be traced back to earlier legislation. At the beginning of volume 27, the index volume, is an alphabetical table of statutes according to their short titles; from this table the position of the statute in the whole work can be quickly traced. If only the regnal year and chapter are known, it will be necessary to consult the consolidated table in the same volume. If the statute is later than about 1968 it will be found in the Continuation Volumes, which are all indexed in the latest Cumulative Supplement. This Supplement also notes amendments to the statutes and cases decided upon them since they were published. Suppose you wish to find the latest annotation to a statute printed in the Continuation Volumes of Halsbury, such as the Children Act 1975. This is printed in the volume for 1975 under the heading "Infants, Children and Young Persons." Therefore it will be found in the latest Cumulative Supplement under the same heading.

The official publication *Statutes in Force* will be even more convenient when the series is completed. It is arranged in encyclopaedic form, in loose-leaf binders, some statutes being reprinted with amendments from time to time. There is to be an annual Cumulative Supplement which follows the order of the main work. The statutes can be bought separately.

There is also an official edition of the statutes in yearly volumes (called either *Public General Statutes* or *Law Reports—Statutes*). Before 1952 the only alphabetical index was at the end of the

---

[12] They do things better in some other parts of the Commonwealth like the provinces of Canada, which issue current statutes without a number. At the end of the year the statutes are arranged alphabetically and only then given a number. United Kingdom Statute Law Committee, please copy.

volume. Until 1940 these volumes contained the statutes passed during a particular session. This has one tiresome consequence, that if one knows only the short title and calendar year, the statute may sometimes be in either of two volumes, and nothing but a process of trial and error can ascertain which. Since 1939 a very sensible change has been made; each volume contains the statutes passed during a single calendar year, and so the difficulty arises only for statutes passed before 1940.[13]

Statutes since 1947 are better consulted in the annual volumes of *Current Law Statutes Annotated*[14] than in the official edition. It is sometimes more convenient than Halsbury, which is apt to split a statute between different headings. Amendments etc. to statutes can be traced through two *Current Law Statute Citators,* one for 1947–1971, and one for 1971 onwards.

The student should buy or note the principal statutes relating to his subject, particularly those that have been passed since his textbook was published. These he can find by consulting the

---

[13] "Before leaving the topic of regnal-year citation, it may be worth while to repeat a warning of one of its seldom explained mysteries. There is risk of confusion where one Parliamentary session is completed within a single year and another is begun in that year. We may then have to distinguish two citations which look somewhat similar—*e.g.* '22 Vict. c. 20' and '22 & 23 Vict. c. 20'; these are two different statutes, the Evidence by Commissions Act 1859 and the Military Savings Bank Act 1859. On the other hand, where one session runs into two regnal years, one may discover duplicate forms of citation for one and the same statute. Take, for example, the Law of Property (Amendment) Act 1924. It received the royal assent long before the end of the first regnal year of the session and was then correctly cited as '15 Geo. 5, c. 5.' King George V had come to the throne on May 6, 1910. When this Act was passed in December 1924, the King's Printer could not gamble on the probability of the session surviving the Accession Day on the following May and thus running into its second regnal year. Actually, as we know now, the session did so survive and thus became the session 15 & 16 Geo. 5. The result is that we find the same Act referred to as '15 Geo. 5, c. 5' and '15 & 16 Geo. 5, c. 5.' The latter citation, containing the two regnal years, should supersede the former; the incomplete and early part of the session becomes merged in the final whole; Mr. Gladstone was 'Master William' once, but nobody so referred to him when the boy had become a man. It cannot be helped that official copies of the Act where it is described as '15 Geo. 5, c. 5' will be in existence." Sir C. T. Carr in (1940) 56 L.Q.R. at 460–461.

[14] These collections do not include Local and Personal Acts which are published separately.

volumes of *Current Law Year Book* and the numbers of *Current Law* published since his textbook, or by consulting the latest Cumulative Supplement to the *Statutes in Force* or to Halsbury's *Statutes of England,* under the title of his subject. Statutes can be ordered through any bookseller.

The student is not likely to have much to do with Statutory Instruments ("S.I."—formerly known as Statutory Rules and Orders—"S.R. & O."), though exceptionally he may have to consult them.[15] When referring to Statutory Instruments, instead of calling the particular provisions of the Instrument "section" and "subsection" as with statutes, one calls them "articles" or "rules" and "paragraphs" respectively.[16]

Some statutory instruments are made in order to give effect to EEC law. A substantial part of EEC law takes effect directly on individuals and affects private rights and duties; this is true for some provisions of the EEC treaty and for nearly all *regulations* made under the treaty. These regulations are expressly incorporated into our law by statutory instruments under the European Communities Act 1972; but if for any reason a statutory instrument fails to express part of a regulation that is

---

[15] Those in force at the end of 1948 are published in the official collection, supplemented by annual volumes. There is an *Index of Government Orders,* published in alternate years, and a cumulative annual *Table of Government Orders,* which is in turn supplemented by Annual, Monthly and Daily *Lists of Statutory Instruments.* Statutory Instruments made under particular sections of statutes are listed under the section in the front of the *Index of Government Orders,* and in the *Index to the Statutes in Force.* All these are official publications. For the lawyer, the most convenient source is often Halsbury's *Statutory Instruments,* with Service volume, which is arranged like an encyclopedia.

[16] The following is the complete table of citation drawn up by Parliamentary Counsel and approved by the Editor of the *Revised Statutes.* It is inserted here for reference only.

Instrument	First division	Second division	Third division
Statute	Section	Subsection	Paragraph
Bill	Clause	Subsection	Paragraph
Order in Council, or Order	Article	Paragraph	Sub-paragraph
Regulations	Regulation	Paragraph	Sub-paragraph
Rules	Rule	Paragraph	Sub-paragraph
Schedules	Paragraph	Sub-paragraph	(None)

directly applicable to citizens of the EEC, the regulation itself retains full effect. The organs of the EEC also produce *decisions* and *directives*, which do not generally affect our law directly, but again may be incorporated into statutory instruments.[17]

Legal periodicals contain articles of great importance for the lawyer and student.

Special mention must be made of the Law Quarterly Review (L.Q.R.), which is published quarterly, the Modern Law Review (M.L.R.), published every two months, and the Cambridge Law Journal (C.L.J.), published twice yearly; students may obtain them at greatly reduced rates. Current Legal Problems appears annually.

The legal weeklies (New Law Journal, Solicitors' Journal and Justice of the Peace) are published chiefly for practitioners; the best coverage is in the New Law Journal, which is available to students at half price (£4.50 including postage). The monthly Law Notes is intended for students and costs the same; one must say that the New Law Journal is the better buy. Specialist publications include Public Law, the Criminal Law Review, the Conveyancer, the Journal of Planning and Environment Law, Family Law, the Industrial Law Journal, and the International and Comparative Law Quarterly. Space does not allow mention of the numerous periodicals published overseas, or of various others published in the United Kingdom.

The Times newspaper is available to students at a reduced price. Particulars can be obtained from a newsagent, or from the Circulation Manager, *The Times,* New Printing House Square, Gray's Inn Rd., London WC1X 8EZ. The Weekly Law Reports, the Law Reports and the All England Reports also offer considerable reductions to student subscribers.

---

[17] A sketch of law-making in the EEC will be found in John Farrar, *Introduction to Legal Method* (London 1977). For a useful study of the principles on which EEC law is directly applicable in member States see Derrick Wyatt in 125 New Law Journal 458, 575, 669, 793. Other useful short treatments will be found in 140 Justice of the Peace 456, 470; 142 *ibid.* 113, 190. There are various specialised treatises.

I should not need to remind my readers not to deface library books, however urgently the text may seem to need correction, emphasis or comment. It is distracting to have to endure the handiwork of other readers.

CHAPTER 4

METHODS OF STUDY

Learning by study must be won;
'Twas ne'er entailed from son to son.

—Gay, *Fables*, II, ii.

TEXTBOOKS

How is my time better spent: sitting in the library reading cases in
the reports, or stewing over a textbook in my own room? This is a
question often put by beginners, and it is a hard one to answer.
One can, of course, answer it discreetly by saying: do both. But
then the question is: in what proportion? What is the relative
importance of the two modes of study?

Before answering this question let me remind the reader that
when studying law he has not one aim but two. His primary and
most important aim is to make himself a lawyer. His secondary
(but also very important) aim is to pass his law examinations with
credit.

Now to a large extent these two aims can be pursued by the
same means. For both purposes one must study cases, either in the
original law reports or in case books. It is through applying
oneself to cases that one gets to understand how legal problems
present themselves and how legal argument is conducted. That
understanding is important whether one's object is to solve
examination problems or to give sound opinions on points of
legal practice.

But there is one difference between preparation for practice and
preparation for examinations. For the practising lawyer, having a
large field of what Pollock calls potential knowledge is more
important than having a small amount of actual knowledge.
What the practitioner needs is a grasp of general legal principles,
a sound knowledge of practice and procedure, an ability to
argue, and a general knowledge of where to find the law he

wants. But it is not essential for him—though, of course, it is a great help—to carry much law in the mind.[1] To shine at examinations, on the other hand, one must not only know how to argue, and be able to display a first-hand knowledge of the sources; one must also be able to parrot a considerable number of rules and authorities. From the examination point of view there is a danger in discursive reading that is not accompanied by a considerable amount of learning by rote.

Teachers of law regret this, but they have not agreed upon effective counter-measures. It is true that the introduction of problems into examination papers has done something to redress the balance between intelligence and memory; but too much memorising is still required. Often it seems to smother constructive thought. Some examination scripts are positively shocking for the amount of word-perfect memorising that they display, coupled with lack of individuality. Copies of statutes are now allowed to be used in some law examinations. The result is not to lower the standard of the examination but to raise it, for it means that the examination can be made more starkly a test of intelligence and lawyerly ability. There is no reason why case books should not be permitted, or at least lists of names of cases. In the United States, some teachers allow their pupils to take in to the examination all material that they have prepared themselves.

But I must not vex my present readers with problems of educational reform. My reason for writing the above was merely to underline the importance, as matters now stand, of memory work. It is distressing when a student who has worked industriously and read widely fails to achieve his due place in the

---

[1] There is an old tale of a solicitor who won great renown for his deep knowledge of the law. His secret was this. He had had three copies of *Every Man's Own Lawyer* bound to resemble law reports and lettered respectively "3 Meeson and Welsby," "1 Term Reports" and "7 Manning and Granger." When a client propounded a legal question, the solicitor would ring for his clerk and say: "Bring me 3 Meeson and Welsby," or "1 Term Reports," or "7 Manning and Granger." When the volume came he would gravely look up the point and then say triumphantly: "Ah! here it is. I thought so. The very authority we wanted." The solicitor was not such a fraud as a layman hearing this story might think. At least he knew his way about that particular book better than his clients did.

examination merely because he has not committed a due proportion of his reading to memory.

There is another observation to be made about the learning of law through the medium of textbooks. It is an observation that everyone inured to learning has already made for himself, but it is, perhaps, worth putting on paper for the sake of those whose acquaintance with this discipline has hitherto been slight. It is this. The more often a book is read, the easier and quicker it is to read (which is obvious), and the more it repays the reading (which is, perhaps, not quite so obvious). When a book on an unfamiliar subject is read for the first time it is rather heavy going, and one seems not to remember very much of it. The second reading is both easier and more interesting, and more (but still not much) is remembered. Many people take their examination at this point. Had they had the perseverance to read through the book a third, fourth and fifth time, they would have found that each successive reading came more easily and that the residue left in the mind each time went up in geometrical progression.

While on the subject of memory work it is worth pointing out that learning by heart is best performed in short periods distributed over as long a time as possible. For instance, it is better to devote one hour a day to revision than six hours at a stretch once a week. By the same token, you can learn the same amount in less learning time by distributing your learning evenly over term and vacation than by crowding your learning into the term and leaving the vacations an academic blank. The greater the gaps you leave between your periods of learning, the less learning you have to do.[2]

Psychological studies have shown that what is involved is the "ageing" of learning. Learning can be increased in strength by sleep or a rest period. It seems, therefore, that more learning can be accomplished in, say, three hours, by taking a ten-minute rest period in the middle than by working continuously. Also, "overlearning" delays forgetting.[3] If, therefore, you read a chapter of a book at night, try to read it again first thing in the morning, even though you feel you know it.

[2] See the experiment described by Ian M. L. Hunter, *Memory* (Penguin Books, 1957), 58.
[3] Peter McKellar, *Experience and Behaviour* (Pelican Books, 1968) 137–138.

"It has been found," says a psychologist, "that when acts of reading and acts of recall alternate, *i.e.* when every reading is followed by an attempt to recall the items, the efficiency of learning and retention is enormously enhanced."[4] This means that learning is best done by reading a paragraph or page or similar convenient amount, and immediately reciting the gist of it: it has been found better to recite aloud than to perform the recall in the head. If you find that you cannot remember the passage properly, read it again and then try another recall. The longer the passage that you set yourself for recall the better; in other words, read as much at a time as you will be able to reproduce at the next recall. Tests have shown that when time is thus distributed between reading and recall, fifty per cent more is remembered than when the same time is spent merely in reading the passage over and over.[5]

Heavy footnotes to a book are sometimes distracting, and it is then a good plan to read the book through a first time without looking at the footnotes.

It is a mistake to spend valuable time in digesting a textbook on paper, unless the digest consists of little more than subject-headings and names of cases. Mere transcription from a book that one owns oneself is certainly folly. "Many readers I have found unalterably persuaded," wrote Dr. Johnson, "that nothing is certainly remembered but what is transcribed: and they have therefore passed weeks and months in transferring large quotations to a commonplace book. Yet, why any part of a book, which can be consulted at pleasure, should be copied I was never able to discover. The hand has no closer correspondence with the Memory than the eye. The act of writing itself distracts the thoughts, and what is twice read is commonly better remembered than what is transcribed."[6]

---

[4] C. A. Mace, *The Psychology of Study,* 2nd ed., 38. Those who find it difficult to settle down to University studies may find further help in T. H. Pear, *The Art of Study* (1930), Chaps. 6–8.

[5] Ian M. L. Hunter, *op. cit.* 54. Sir Cyril Burt, who also gave the above advice, added: "Exploit your strongest form of imagery; if you are a visualiser, invent mental pictures; if you hear things easily in your mind's ear, use rhythms, rhymes, and alliterations" (*The Listener,* December 7, 1950).

[6] *The Idler,* No. 74.

CASE BOOKS

Some teachers of law do not recommend the use of case books. In their view, the only way to become a proficient lawyer is to sit down in the library and read cases, not contenting oneself with the headnote or any other bowdlerised version of the case, but reading through the whole of the statement of facts and the whole of the judgments. Faced with such a counsel of perfection the student may well echo from the heart the words of Doderidge J., written when legal literature was but a fraction of its present bulk: *"Vita brevis est, ars longa,* our life is short and full of calamities, and learning is a long time in getting."[7] A teacher must consider, before he gives advice like the above, the amount of time actually available to a law student for his studies. Taking first those at the universities, their period of residence is only about six months in the year, and few work for more than eight months in the year altogether. In that time they have to cover four or five subjects. This means an average of between six and eight weeks for each subject. Into this alarmingly short space they must fit attendance at lectures, the reading of the textbook, wider reading in the library, and revision, as well as the manifold activities that very properly occupy the undergraduate outside his work. Those attending technical colleges or studying for professional exam- inations, particularly those engaged in office work during the day, will probably have less rather than more time than undergraduates.

It becomes obvious, then, that time must be husbanded. Granting that the student must read cases, it is to my mind a permissible economy of time to buy a good case book for each department of law that is being studied. Using a case book has two advantages for the learner. First, the case book saves him some of the trouble (beneficial, but time-consuming) of making his own notebook of cases. Secondly, it does something to eliminate immaterial facts, thus helping in the search (again beneficial, but again time-consuming) for the facts that are legally material.

It should be added that the use of case books by no means dispenses with the need for reading the original reports. For one

[7] *The English Lawyer* (1631), 38.

thing, many of the more important cases in the case book can profitably be read in full in the law reports, using the case book version only for revision. Also, there are bound to be many cases that the keen student will come across and want to read that are not in his case book: among them, cases decided since the case book went to print.

To the student of modest means the high price of law books is intimidating, but it is false economy to do without basic works. Many are now available at reasonable prices in paperback. Money can sometimes be saved by buying secondhand books, but the beginner who does this should be careful never to buy anything but a latest edition, except on his teacher's advice.

The following is a London firm specialising in secondhand and new law books. A postcard will bring a quotation.

Wildy & Sons, Ltd., Lincoln's Inn Archway, Carey Street, London, WC2A 2JD.

LECTURES AND CLASSES

In the Middle Ages lectures were necessary because of the shortage of books. Now that printing has been with us for some hundreds of years, is there any need to continue the lecture system?

This is a vexed question, and perhaps the only comprehensive answer is that it depends upon the particular lecturer and the particular lectures. But, speaking generally, lectures may be said to possess several merits as a means of instruction. They can quicken interest. To listen to a competent lecturer makes a welcome change from the reading of books. The lecturer, too, can help his audience by giving the "basis and essentials" of the subject, elucidating the broad principles and indicating what is matter of detail. He can dwell on the parts of the subject that in his experience cause special difficulties. Another point in his favour is that by varying his emphasis he can make himself more readily understood than can the toneless words of a book. Finally, the lecturer can bring textbooks up to date, and in a smallish class he can solve individual difficulties.

Some lecturers regard it as their sole function to stimulate and inspire; they do not particularly want notes to be taken. Certainly there is no greater waste of time than to sit through the average lecture making notes mechanically without thinking what they are about. Either concentrate on the lecture and rely upon your books for acquisition of facts, or form the habit of taking notes and at the same time of following the line of argument. It may set an edge upon your attention if you imagine that you are due to be tested in the subject immediately after the lecture. Another inestimable habit (though few cultivate it) is that of spending a part of each evening reading through all the notes taken in the day.

Some lecturers are blamed for saying too many valuable things in too short a time, making it difficult for the pens of their audiences to keep pace with them. To meet this, use abbreviations. The following are particularly useful:

H	husband	W	wife
L	landlord	T	tenant
M	master	S	servant
P	plaintiff	D	defendant
P	principal	A	agent
V	vendor	P	purchaser

In land law it is customary to refer to imaginary pieces of land as Blackacre, Whiteacre, etc. The conventional abbreviations for these are Bacre, Wacre, etc.

Some traditional abbreviations make use of the stroke, /. Apart from a/c, account, they all represent two words, the stroke being placed between the initial letters of each:

b/e	bill of exchange
b/l	bill of lading
b/n	bank note
b/s	bill of sale
h/p	hire purchase
p/n	promissory note

This method can, of course, be extended to other common legal phrases:

a/b	act of bankruptcy
a/t	abstract of title
A/P	Act of Parliament
b/f	bona fide
e/r	equity of redemption
l/a	letters of administration
n/i	negotiable instrument
n/k	next of kin

p/a	power of appointment
p/p	personal property, part performance
p/r	personal representative
r/p	real property
r/c	restrictive covenant
s/g	sale of goods
s/p	specific performance

Alternatively the initial letters may be separated by periods:

b.f.(p)	bona fide (purchaser)
c.q.t.	*cestui que trust* (c.q.tt., *cestuis que trust*)
p.f.	prima facie

Or they may even be joined up:

DHSS	Department of Health and Social Security

Another traditional method of abbreviation is to write the first pronounceable part of the word and then write the ending. Common examples of this method are *assn* for *association*, *dept* for *department* and *insce* for *insurance*.

If you fail to catch or understand a particular sentence, no lecturer minds being asked to repeat or amplify it. Some lecturers invite questions and argument; in that case see that you play your part.

It need hardly be added, after what has already been said about transcription, that the making of a fair copy of one's own lecture notes is a dismal waste of time.

Considerably more important than the average lecture is the discussion class, generally called a class, supervision or tutorial. And of discussion classes, the most beneficial are those in which the discussion is centred on legal problems. With regard to these classes my injunctions are limited to two: first, attend them, and secondly, prepare for them by attempting to work out the problems for yourself before the class. Half the value of the class is missed if you sit supinely back and let the instructor or the other members of the class do the problems for you. The larger the class, the less likely it is that you will be pressed to speak, and the more important it is that you should speak—in order to cultivate self-possession and to get used to the sound of your own voice in public.

Talking about your work, whether in class or with a friend, has the further very important advantage of helping the memory. To quote one of our psychologists again: "Some form of action or of expression would seem to be essential to unimpaired retention. It seems that good conversationalists and great talkers generally have good memories. It is over-simple to suppose that this is due to the fact that, having good memories, they are well supplied with topics of conversation. The reverse connection would seem to be involved. What is talked about is more firmly impressed upon the mind. Such men when they read a book immediately discuss it with a friend, thus unconsciously employing the potent principle of active repetition."[8]

Apart from this necessary conversation, form the habit of working a full morning, because this is the part of the day when you are freshest. Do not do minor chores in the morning. As for the rest of the day, you will wish to make your own choice between the afternoon and evening, but at either time you will find that alcohol is totally inconsistent with study.

In conclusion, a few words on a comparatively humble matter, that of materials. The use of bound lecture note-books is not to be recommended, because they are cumbrous and inelastic. If you use such notebooks and have three or four lectures to attend in a morning, this means a considerable weight and bulk to be carried about. Also, if you want to expand the lecturer's remarks with notes of your own you will find it difficult to do so within the confines of the notebook. On both counts the loose-leaf system is greatly preferable. The student who adopts this system needs to take with him to lectures only a single loose-leaf notebook, the day's work being transferred to larger specialised files in the evening. Notes taken down in this form can be rearranged and expanded at pleasure.

THE STUDY OF HISTORY

In my experience, there is not one student in a hundred who approaches the historical side of law in the best way. The usual course is simply to study a textbook. Textbooks are, of course, necessary; but they need to be supplemented by reference to the

[8] C. A. Mace, *op. cit.*, 40–41.

original sources. For instance, when you read about the Assize of
Clarendon or the Bill of Rights, the sensible thing to do is to find
these historical monuments and read them for yourself, just as
you would read an important case or statute bearing on modern
law. In this way the interest of history is vastly increased, and it
becomes much more easily remembered.

Where, then, are the sources to be found? A good source book
on constitutional history, which can also be used for the subject
known as the history of the legal system, is Stephenson and
Marcham's *Sources of English Constitutional History*. The major
part of private law is excellently covered by C. H. S. Fifoot's
History and Sources of the Common Law—Tort and Contract.

But the student who has access to a good library should not
confine himself to source books. For example, having read about
Glanvil, Bracton, Littleton, Coke and the rest, you should seek
out copies of their works in the library (those originally written in
law-French or Latin are available in translation) and browse
among them. In doing so, look for the characteristics that your
textbook has led you to expect. See, for example, how "Glanvil" is
written round the forms of writs, and how Bracton builds up his
treatise not only from writs but also from decided cases and
Roman law.

When you have a nodding acquaintance with the text writers,
try your hand at the Year Books. Start with the Selden Society
edition, which gives both the original law-French text and a
translation on the opposite page. The easiest cases to understand
are, usually, the actions of trespass. At the end of some cases is a
"Note from the Record." Study it, and see how the version of the
case in the record (*i.e.* the plea roll) differs from the Year Book
version. (Better still, for this purpose, look at the full transcription
from the record in an Ames Foundation edition of the Year
Books of Richard II.) Then glance at the two other editions of the
Year Books: (1) the black-letter editions, published chiefly during
the sixteenth and seventeenth centuries, and (2) the Rolls Series
edition, published chiefly during the second half of the nineteenth
century. Note how the Selden Society and Ames Foundation
editions, which both belong to the present century, have improved
on the Rolls Series edition. Finally, look at one of the early
reporters, like Dyer (73 E.R.) and compare him with the Year
Books.

A well-stocked library will contain much more of the raw material of history to interest you. Examine a printed copy of the Register of Writs, an Abridgement, a Book of Entries. Several volumes in the Selden Society series, besides the Year Books, make good discursive reading, and often they have useful introductions. (Maitland's introduction to the *Mirror of Justices* is acknowledged to be better than *Punch*). On the history of the legal profession, turn to the entertaining account in Fortescue's *De Laudibus Legum Angliae,* Chapters 47–51. (There are several translations of this work.) Again, in reading the history of some part of common law or equity, make a point of reading in the old reports the more important cases referred to in the textbook, such as for instance, *Slade's Case* (1601) 4 Co.Rep. 92b; the *Case de Libellis Famosis* (1605) 5 Co.Rep. 125a, and the *Earl of Oxford's Case* (1615) 1 Chan.Rep. 1. Legal history at second hand is often a dull thing: go back to the sources, and it springs to life.

Before the student comes to the study of constitutional and legal history it is very desirable for him to have some knowledge of English history in general. The ordinary Englishman is supposed to acquire this at school, but for the overseas student, and for everyone who want to brush up his school learning, Trevelyan's *History of England* may be strongly recommended.

I suppose that most English students have some recollection of the order and the dates of the kings and queens of England. They will find such knowledge necessary in the study not only of constitutional but of purely legal history, for regnal years are the foundation of legal chronology. Overseas students, and others whose historical knowledge is shaky, may possibly be glad of the following mnemonic rhyme, which was once learnt by little Victorian boys and girls; I set it out with the corresponding regnal years at the side:

First William the Norman,	1066–1087.
Then William his son;	1087–1100.
Henry, Stephen, and Henry,	1100–1135, 1135–1154, 1154–1189.
Then Richard and John;	1189–1199, 1199–1216.
Next Henry the third,	1216–1272.
Edwards, one, two and three,	1272–1307, 1307–1327, 1327–1377.
And again after Richard	1377–1399.

Three Henrys we see.	1399–1413, 1413–1422, 1422–1461.
Two Edwards, third Richard, If rightly I guess;	1461–1483, 1483, 1483–1485.
Two Henrys, sixth Edward,	1485–1509, 1509–1547, 1547–1553.
Queen Mary, Queen Bess,	1553–1558, 1558–1603.
Then Jamie the Scotchman,	1603–1625.
Then Charles whom they slew,	1625–1649.
Yet received after Cromwell	[1649–1660].
Another Charles too.	1649[9] (1660)–1685.
Next James the second Ascended the throne;	1685–1688.
Then Good William and Mary Together came on.	1689–1702.
Till, Anne, Georges four,	1702–1714, 1714–1727, 1727–1760, 1760–1820, 1820–1830.
And fourth William all past,	1830–1837.
God sent Queen Victoria: May she long be the last!	1837–1901.

A racier version, and I think one easier to remember, is:

> Willy, Willy, Harry, Ste,
> Harry, Dick, John, Harry 3;
> One, two, three Neds, Richard 2,
> Henry 4, 5, 6. Then who?
> Edward 4, 5, Dick the Bad,
> Harrys twain and Ned the Lad;
> Mary, Bessie, James the Vain,
> Charlie, Charlie, James again;
> Will and Mary, Anna Gloria,
> Georges four, Will, Victoria.

Perhaps it is time to add to the edifice.

> Edward, George, then Edward 8,
> George; now Bess is Head of State.

If the regnal years are not already known, and the task of learning them all seems too great, the student should at least notice the sovereigns whose reigns commenced at or shortly after the turn of each century. Knowledge of this combined with a knowledge of the order of the sovereigns, will place every sovereign in his proper century. The sovereigns just referred to are:

---

[9] Although Charles did not become king *de facto* until 1660, his regnal years were computed from the death of his father in 1649.

Henry I	...	...	...	...	1100
Henry III	...	...	...	...	1216
Edward II	...	...	...	...	1307
Henry V	...	...	...	...	1413
Henry VIII	...	...	...	...	1509
James I	...	...	...	...	1603
Anne .	...	...	...	...	1702
George IV	...	...	...	...	1820

Not only regnal years but dates in general are often a bugbear to students of history. The intelligent way to remember dates is to memorise a few key dates, and then to remember others by working backwards and forwards from these. For instance, Lord Mansfield became Chief Justice of the King's Bench in 1756, an easy date to remember and an important one. Suppose that it is desired to remember also that Blackstone delivered his first course of lectures on English law in 1753. By relating this in the mind to 1756, and noticing the difference in years (3), the one will become linked to the other, and both can be recalled together. In time the same date can be related to several other dates, so that all important dates become interlocked in the mind. This method of memorising helps to build up the sense of historical perspective, which is the only rational justification for remembering dates.

Two useful dictionaries that may be found in the library are *Dictionary of British History,* edited by S. H. Steinberg, and *The Dictionary of English History* by Low and Pulling.

CHAPTER 5

TECHNICAL TERMS

'Zounds! I was never so bethump'd with words.

—Shakespeare, *King John,* II, i.

DICTIONARIES

AT first the beginner will find himself rather lost among the many
technical terms used in a report, and will find some difficulty with
Latin and law-French phrases and maxims.[1] Many are the tales
that are recounted of these difficulties. There was the youth who
innocently asked whether the phrase *en ventre sa mère* meant the
same thing as *in loco parentis.* There was the examination
candidate who expressed the opinion that the whole of Lord
Atkin's speech in *Donoghue* v. *Stevenson* was *per incuriam.* To two
other candidates belongs the credit of suggesting that *fructus
naturales* means illegitimate children, and that *animus revertendi*
means the transmigration of souls. Weak latinity may also result
in ungrammatical constructions. Thus the word *"obiter"* in
"obiter dictum" (a judge's "saying by the way" or "passing
remark") is not a noun: one should not write, as another examinee

---

[1] The law-French phrases survive from the time when French, or rather
Anglo-Norman, was the language of the courts. See Pollock, *First Book
of Jurisprudence* (6th ed., 1929), 297–302; Holdsworth, *History of
English Law,* ii, 477–484; Theo. Mathew in 54 L.Q.R. 358.

Latin was formerly the language for official documents, like writs;
and sometimes survives in the names of writs. Also, maxims are usually
in Latin because they are derived from Roman law or because they were
invented by medieval jurists.

In 1730 Parliament passed an Act abolishing law-Latin in legal
proceedings. But it was found that technical terms like *nisi prius, quare
impedit, fieri facias* and *habeas corpus* were (as Blackstone put it) "not
capable of an English dress with any degree of seriousness," and so two
years later another Act was passed to allow such words to be continued
"in the same language as hath been commonly used."

once did, that a lawyer in reading cases needs to "hack his way through the *obiter* to reach the actual decisions."

A good law dictionary can assist in such troubles. Two are suitable for students: Mozley and Whiteley's *Law Dictionary* (9th ed. £3), and Osborn's *Concise Law Dictionary* (6th ed. £3.25). In the library, consult Earl Jowitt's *Dictionary of English Law*, which is founded upon earlier works by Wharton and Byrne.

Alternatively, a good English dictionary can afford considerable assistance on the meaning of individual English words, though not, of course, on Latin maxims. The cheapest short dictionary is the paperback Penguin (£1.50); the best is the *Concise Oxford Dictionary*, nicely bound at £7.50.

PRONUNCIATION

A few words may be said about pronunciation. Latin words and phrases are generally pronounced by lawyers in the same old barbaric way as they were in the Middle Ages,[2] that is to say, as if they were English. To those who have been taught the new style of pronunciation at school this occasions some difficulty. *C* and *g* are soft where they would be in English,[3] and the pronunciation of such syllables as *atio* in *ratio decidendi* is also anglicised. Long vowels are pronounced as in English (the sounds being those in the names of the vowels).[4] Moreover, whether the vowel is to be pronounced long or short depends more upon English rules than upon Roman ones. (1) In words of two syllables, the first vowel is

---

[2] There is a medieval tale of some nuns who needed extra help about the convent and who accordingly sent down to the village by word of mouth for *servitia*. The request was understood by the villagers as a request for *cervicia,* an ale-feast, and they acted accordingly. The anecdote shows that the "c" in *cervicia,* and probably also the "t" in *servitia,* were pronounced like "s."

[3] Hence R. H. Barham's lines in allusion to Sir C. Wren's epitaph in St. Paul's Cathedral:

And, talking of epitaphs, much I admire his,
"Circumspice, si monumentum requiris,"
Which an erudite verger translated to me,
"If you ask for his monument, Sir—come—spy—see!"

[4] But there are no immutable rules, any more than there are in the pronunciation of English. Thus *si* is pronounced "see" by old and new school alike, though to be consistent the old school should pronounce it "sy," as indeed it does in the word *nisi*.

pronounced long even though it was short in Latin. Examples are
bonus, onus, opus, genus ("jeenus"), *capias* ("caypias"), *mens rea*
("mens reeah"), *modus vivendi* ("mōdus vivendy"), nisi prius
("nysy[5] pryus"), *ratio decidendi* ("rayshyoh deesidendy"), *sine die*
("synee dyee"), and *vice versa* ("vysee"). This lends point to Mr.
Punch's translation of *pendente lite*[6] as "a chandelier." (2) In
words of three or more syllables derived from the Latin, vowels
are generally pronounced short before the penultimate syllable,
whether or not they were short in classical Latin. This is seen in the
ordinary English words codicil, general and genera, ominous and
operate. (Strictly, we should pronounce "economic" and
"devolution" in the same way with a short first vowel, but they
have become lengthened by usage.) It will be seen that the
preferable pronunciation of *obiter*, according to the rule, is with a
short *o*.

Law-French words are pronounced much as they were in the
Middle Ages; it is a solecism to utter them as if they were modern
French. The pronunciation is, indeed, much nearer to modern
English than it is to French. Thus the town crier quite correctly
said "Oy-ez," not "Oy-ay." The following are pronunciations of
legal terms deriving from medieval French.

attorn   } (-er)
attorney }

autrefois acquit   } (oterfoyz, with "acquit" and "convict"
autrefois convict }   pronounced as usual in English)

detinue (det-)

distress damage feasant (feezant)

emblements (embliments)

formedon ("e" pronounced indeterminately, as in "added")

feme sole[7] (femm)

---

[5] There is an anecdote of how Lord Hewart C.J. "put down" counsel
who applied for a rule *nisi* (pronouncing it "nysy," which was correct).
Lord Hewart listened in silence and then said: "The judgment of the
court will be short, like the first *i* in *nisi.*" In this he displayed both his
classical education and his ignorance of the rules of English
pronunciation. The lawyer's traditional pronunciation of "patent"
with a short *a* breaks the rule.

[6] "While the suit is pending."

[7] Another tale concerns counsel who departed from usage by
pronouncing this phrase "femmee sole." The judge pricked up his ears
and said, "What is that? I have heard of a camisole, but not of a femmee
sole."

feme covert (cuvert)
feoffment (feff-)
laches (laytshiz)
lien (lee-en or leen)
mesne (meen)
misfeasance ⎫
nonfeasance ⎭ (-feez-)
pur autre vie (pur ōter vee)
que (in the phrase "in the *que* estate" and in *cestui que trust*; pronounced
  kee)
seisin (-eez-)
semble—anglicised as written
Statutes of Jeofails (jefailz)[8]
venue (vĕnue, with accent on first syllable)
villein (villen)

In some instances lawyers still jealously retain the archaic
pronunciations of English words. The noun "record" is
pronounced like the verb, with the stress on the second syllable.[9]
The term for an insured person, "assured," has the last syllable
pronounced like "red" and stressed. In "cognisance," "re-
cognisance" and "cognisable" we refuse to "take cognisance of"
the intrusive "g" in speaking, though we do in writing. (The "g"
comes through latinising the law-French word conusance). In
these words the lawyer's pronunciation is different from the
layman's. Lastly, the "committee" of a person of unsound mind
was a single person to whom the care of such person was entrusted
by the court, the stress being on the last syllable. Committees are
no longer appointed.

LEGAL ABBREVIATIONS

Legal abbreviations are another frequent source of vexation to a

---

[8] So the O.E.D. Sutton, *Personal Actions,* 119, gives "jeefailz."
[9]   Condemn the fault, and not the actor of it?
    Why, every fault's condemn'd ere it be done.
    Mine were the very cipher of a function,
    To fine the faults whose fine stands in record,
    And let go by the actor.
    —Shakespeare, *Measure for Measure,* II, ii.
    Then turning to the Judge, he cry's, My Lord,
    (And thus runs o'er their Crimes upon record).
    —Edward Ward, *A Journey to H——, or a visit paid to the
    D——* (or, *The Infernal Vision*), Part I, Canto II (A.D.
    1700–1705).

beginner. The possession of a law dictionary is again a great help, but something may be said here of the more common abbreviations and short-cut terms seen in print.

First, as to the titles of judges.[10] "Smith J." means "Mr. Justice Smith" (or Mrs. Justice Smith, as the case may be), and when speaking of him in public he will be given that full title. Never say "Justice Smith" or (except for a circuit or county court judge) "Judge Smith"; these are Americanisms, to be shunned and avoided on this side of the Atlantic. The plural abbreviation is JJ.: "Smith and Byles JJ.," which is read out as "Mr. Justice Smith and Mr. Justice Byles." Similarly, the following letters placed after the names of the judges have the following meanings:

B.	=	Baron [of the Exchequer]. A member of the former Court of Exchequer—not to be confused with Barons who are peers. Plural BB. Title now obsolete.
C.B.	=	Chief Baron: the head of the former Court of Exchequer. Title now obsolete.
C.J. (or L.C.J.)	=	(Lord) Chief Justice. Head of the Q.B.D.
J.A.	=	Justice of Appeal. Title found between 1875 and 1877, and now obsolete.[11]
L.C.	=	Lord Chancellor. Head of the judicial system.
L.J.	=	Lord Justice. Member of the C.A. Plural L.JJ.: Lords Justices.
M.R.	=	Master of the Rolls. Member (and virtually head) of the C.A.
P.	=	President. Head of the Family Division (formerly Probate, Divorce and Admiralty Division).
V.-C.	=	Vice-Chancellor. In effect head of the Chancery Division.

Do not omit or abbreviate "Lord" before the name of a judge who is a Law Lord or other peer. Thus you will write "Lord Elwyn-Jones L.C." not "Elwyn-Jones L.C."; and similarly "Lord Widgery C.J." (or "Lord Widgery L.C.J."). These are read out as "Lord Elwyn-Jones, Lord Chancellor" and "Lord Widgery, Chief Justice" (or "Lord Chief Justice"). In the case of Chief Justices who were not peers, like Rufus Isaacs, the written designation is "Isaacs C.J." (or "L.C.J."), which is read out as "[Lord] Chief Justice Isaacs." Lords Justices are not peers as such,

[10] Sometimes called puisne (pronounced "pewny"—ew as in few) judges, meaning any judge of the High Court (or the older courts that it replaced) other than the chiefs.

[11] See 61 L.Q.R. 231.

so that, for example, "Buckley L.J." is read out as "Lord Justice Buckley." "Buckley and Roskill L.JJ." are "Lords Justices Buckley and Roskill." Lord Denning M.R. is "Lord Denning, Master of the Rolls." Where this last office is not held by a peer the former usage was that one had to remember the holder's Christian name when speaking of him, so "Pollock M.R." was "Sir Ernest Pollock, Master of the Rolls," and "Brett M.R." was "Sir Baliol Brett, Master of the Rolls."[12] But at the present day it would be acceptable to say "Pollock, Master of the Rolls," and so on. A living judge like Megarry V.-C. should certainly be referred to as "Sir Robert Megarry, Vice-Chancellor."

Certain abbreviations and shorthand expressions supply a convenient mechanism for referring to authorities. A librarian once showed me a request form filled in by a reader asking for a supposed book called *"Ibid."* Evidently the reader had seen this referred to many times in footnotes, and thought that it must be an extremely important book, written perhaps by an eminent Persian. Of course, *"ibid."* is short for *ibidem,* meaning "in the same place"; it is simply a way of repeating a reference previously given. Similarly, *op. cit.* means the book previously cited, and *loc. cit.* means the page previously cited in the book previously cited. *Passim* means "everywhere in the book." S.C. means "same case" (*i.e. ibid.* as applied to a reported case), and S.P. "same principle." Other compendious expressions are *per, semble, aliter* (or *secus*) and *contra. Per* generally means "statement by": thus *"per* Lord Wilberforce" following a quotation means that the remark quoted is that of Lord Wilberforce. *Per curiam* and *per incuriam* are not opposites. *Per curiam* means that the statement is by the whole court. *Per incuriam* means that a judge's remark was made by mistake. *Semble* is law-French for "it seems" or "it seems that" (when the authority for a proposition is weak or not completely satisfactory; usually it indicates an *obiter dictum*). *Aliter* and *secus* means "otherwise" and *contra* refers to an authority contradicting what one has first said. Thus one can write *"Semble* the phrase 'carcase or portion of a carcase' in this statute does not include a sausage—see *per* Tripe L.J., *obiter,* in *Sage* v. *Onions* (C.A.); *contra, Ham* v. *Eggs* (Div.Ct.); *aliter* if the sausage meat is not yet minced." This may not be an elegant style but it does represent an economy of effort, which to some minds has a beauty of its own.

[12] 79 L.Q.R. 190.

Chapter 6

CASE LAW TECHNIQUE

Mastering the lawless science of our law,
That codeless myriad of precedent,
That wilderness of single instances,
Through which a few, by wit or fortune led,
May beat a pathway out to wealth and fame.

—Tennyson, *Aylmer's Field.*

RATIO DECIDENDI AND OBITER DICTUM

ENGLISH courts make a habit of following their previous decisions within more or less well-defined limits. This is called the doctrine of precedent. The part of a case that is said to possess authority is the *ratio decidendi,* that is to say, the rule of law upon which the decision is founded. Finding the *ratio decidendi* of a case is an important part of the training of a lawyer. It is not a mechanical process but is an art that one gradually acquires through practice and study. One can, however, give a general description of the technique involved.

What the doctrine of precedent declares is that cases must be decided the same way when their material facts are the same. Obviously it does not require that *all* the facts should be the same. We know that in the flux of life all the facts of a case will never recur; but the legally material facts may recur and it is with these that the doctrine is concerned.

The *ratio decidendi* of a case can be defined as the material facts of the case plus the decision thereon.[1] The same learned writer who advanced this definition went on to suggest a helpful formula. Suppose that in a certain case facts A, B and C exist; and suppose that the court finds that facts B and C are material and fact A immaterial, and then reaches conclusion X (*e.g.* judgment for the plaintiff, or judgment for the defendant). Then the

---

[1] Goodhart, "Determining the *Ratio Decidendi* of a Case," *Essays in Jurisprudence and the Common Law* (1931) 1.

doctrine of precedent enables us to say that in any future case in which facts B and C exist, or in which facts A and B and C exist, the conclusion must be X. If in a future case facts A, B, C and D exist, and fact D is held to be material, the first case will not be a direct authority, though it may be of value as an analogy.

What facts are legally material? That depends on the particular case, but take as an illustration a "running down" action, that is to say, an action for injuries sustained through the defendant's negligent driving of a vehicle. The fact that the plaintiff had red hair and freckles, that his name was Smith, and that the accident happened on a Friday are immaterial, for the rule of law upon which the decision proceeds will apply equally to persons who do not possess these characteristics and to accidents that happen on other days. On the other hand, the fact that the defendant drove negligently, and the fact that in consequence he injured the plaintiff, are material, and a decision in the plaintiff's favour on such facts will be an authority for the proposition that a person is liable for causing damage through the negligent driving of a vehicle.

The foregoing is a general explanation of the phrase "the *ratio decidendi* of a case." To get a clearer idea of the way in which a *ratio decidendi* is extracted, let us take a decided case and study it in detail. I set out below the case of *Wilkinson* v. *Downton*,[2] where the plaintiff was awarded damages by a jury for nervous shock, and the trial judge then heard argument on the question whether the verdict could be upheld in law. The first part of the judgment, which is all that needs be considered here, runs as follows.

WRIGHT J. In this case the defendant, in the execution of what he seems to have regarded as a practical joke, represented to the plaintiff that he was charged by her husband with a message to her to the effect that her husband was smashed up in an accident, and was lying at The Elms at Leytonstone with both legs broken, and that she was to go at once in a cab with two pillows to fetch him home. All this was false. The effect of the statement on the plaintiff was a violent shock to her nervous system, producing vomiting and other more serious and permanent physical consequences at one time threatening her reason, and entailing weeks of suffering and incapacity to her as well as expense to her husband for medical attendance. These consequences were not in any way the result of previous ill-health or weakness of constitution; nor was there any evidence of predisposition to nervous shock or any other idiosyncrasy.

[2] [1897] 2 Q.B. 57.

In addition to these matters of substance there is a small claim for 1s. 10½d. for the cost of railway fares of persons sent by the plaintiff to Leytonstone in obedience to the pretended message. As to this 1s. 10½d. expended in railway fares on the faith of the defendant's statement, I think the case is clearly within the decision in *Pasley* v. *Freeman* (1798) 3 T.R. 51. The statement was a misrepresentation intended to be acted on to the damage of the plaintiff.

The real question is as to the £100, the greatest part of which is given as compensation for the female plaintiff's illness and suffering. It was argued for her that she is entitled to recover this as being damages caused by fraud, and therefore within the doctrine established by *Pasley* v. *Freeman* and *Langridge* v. *Levy* (1837) 2 M. & W. 519. I am not sure that this would not be an extension of that doctrine, the real ground of which appears to be that a person who makes a false statement intended to be acted on must make good the damage naturally resulting from its being acted on. Here there is no *injuria* of that kind. I think, however, that the verdict may be supported upon another ground. The defendant has, as I assume for the moment, wilfully done an act calculated to cause physical harm to the plaintiff—that is to say, to infringe her legal right to personal safety, and has in fact thereby caused physical harm to her. That proposition without more appears to me to state a good cause of action, there being no justification alleged for the act. This wilful *injuria* is in law malicious, although no malicious purpose to cause the harm which was caused nor any motive of spite is imputed to the defendant.

It remains to consider whether the assumptions involved in the proposition are made out. One question is whether the defendant's act was so plainly calculated to produce some effect of the kind which was produced that an intention to produce it ought to be imputed to the defendant, regard being had to the fact that the effect was produced on a person proved to be in an ordinary state of health and mind. I think that it was. It is difficult to imagine that such a statement, made suddenly and with apparent seriousness, could fail to produce grave effects under the circumstances upon any but an exceptionally indifferent person, and therefore an intention to produce such an effect must be imputed, and it is no answer in law to say that more harm was done than was anticipated, for that is commonly the case with all wrongs.

The reader will notice that the judge does not cite any authority for his decision that the £100 is recoverable. The only authorities he cites are authorities on which he says he prefers not to rely. The reason is that at the date when the case was decided there was no English authority on the general question whether it was a tort intentionally to inflict bodily harm on another. There was, indeed, the very ancient tort of battery, which is committed when D hits or stabs or shoots P. But Downton committed no battery upon Mrs. Wilkinson; nor did he assault her by threatening a battery. Consequently, the case was one "of first impression," and the judge decided it merely on common-sense principles. It would be a grave reproach to a civilised system of law if it did not give a remedy on such facts.

Let us now see how the *ratio decidendi* is to be extracted. This is done by finding the material facts. The judge has already done much of the work for us, because he has omitted from his judgment many of the facts given in evidence that were obviously irrelevant to the legal issue—*e.g.* the address at which the plaintiff lived. But the judgment mentions the address at which the husband was supposed to be lying, which also is clearly irrelevant. As a first step in boiling it down we may say that the essential facts, and the pith of the judgment, were as follows:

> The defendant by way of what was meant to be a joke told the plaintiff that the latter's husband had been smashed up in an accident. The plaintiff, who had previously been of normal health, suffered a shock and serious illness. Wright J. held that the defendant was liable, not perhaps for the tort of deceit but because the defendant had wilfully done an act calculated to cause physical harm to the plaintiff, and had in fact caused such harm.

The above would represent the sort of note that an intelligent student would make of the case. How are we to frame the *ratio decidendi*? There are two main possibilities.

The first would be to take such of the detailed facts as may be deemed to be material, plus the decision on the facts. This would result in the following rule: that where the defendant has wilfully told the plaintiff a lie of a character that is likely (a clearer word than "calculated") to frighten and so cause physical harm to the plaintiff, and it has in fact caused such harm, the defendant is liable, in the absence of some ground of justification.

This *ratio* omits to specify the particular lie told by the defendant, because this was immaterial. What mattered was not the particular lie as to the plaintiff's husband's alleged injury, but the more general fact of lying. The particular lie told by the defendant was material only in the sense that it was the sort of lie that was likely to frighten and cause physical harm to the plaintiff.

But, it may be objected, such a *ratio* would be too narrow, because the learned judge evidently intended to lay down a wider rule. He did not confine his judgment to lies, but spoke only of wilfully doing an *act* which is calculated to and does cause physical harm; and this gives us the true *ratio*. It was immaterial that the particular form of mischief perpetrated by the defendant took the form of a verbal lie; it might have been some other act likely to cause harm, and the legal outcome would have been the same. This, indeed, is common sense. A person with Downton's juvenile sense of humour who dresses up as a ghost, or who puts a squib under somebody else's chair, would doubtless find himself in the same legal category as Downton.

Again, the learned judge did not speak of fright when he formulated the principle of his decision. He spoke of causing physical harm, which is much wider. On this principle, an outrageous *threat* causing suffering is a tort. In a subsequent case[3] which approved *Wilkinson* v. *Downton,* the defendant threatened to arrest and prosecute the plaintiff, a foreign servant-girl, if she did not give certain information; the defendant knew that any charge he brought against the girl would be quite unfounded, and the girl became ill with distress. It was held that she had a good cause of action. Another application of the principle occurs where the harm operates directly on the plaintiff's body, not indirectly through the mind—as where the defendant blackens a towel with which the plaintiff is about to wipe his face, or secretly adds poison to the plaintiff's drink. Although these situations have not been the subject of reported decisions, there is no doubt that they would fall under the principle of *Wilkinson* v. *Downton.*

The reader may now be feeling rather puzzled as to the meaning of *ratio decidendi.* We started off with a possible narrow *ratio decidendi* of the case, incorporating the fact of lying and the fact of fright. Then we passed to a wider *ratio,* which evidently accords with common sense as well as with the language of the judgment, in which the facts of lying and fright have disappeared. How can this be reconciled with our definition of *ratio decidendi* as the material facts plus the decision thereon? Were not the lie and the fright material facts in *Wilkinson* v. *Downton*? If there had been no lie and no fright, and no equivalent facts in their place, the plaintiff would not have won. What exactly do we mean by a "material fact"?

The answer is that we have not been using this expression in a consistent way, and it is necessary to restate the position in more exact language. What is really involved in finding the *ratio*

[3] *Janvier* v. *Sweeney* [1919] 2 K.B. 316.

decidendi of a case is a process of abstraction. Abstraction is the mental operation of picking out certain qualities and relations from the facts of experience. Imagine a baby in whose household there is a terrier called Caesar. The baby will be taught to call this dog "bow-wow," because "bow-wow" is easier to say than "Caesar." If he sees another dog he will guess or be told that this other dog is to be called "bow-wow" as well. This is an example of one of the baby's earliest feats of abstraction. Abstraction comes through the perception of similarities between individual facts, and all language and all thinking depend upon it.

The next point to be noticed is that this process of abstraction may be carried to progressively higher flights. The individual dog Caesar is, at a low level of abstraction, a terrier; at a higher level he is a dog; higher still, a mammal; and then an animal and a living thing. In the same way a man might say that he was born at the Piccaninny Nursing Home; in London; in England; in Europe. All these are "facts," but they are facts belonging to different levels of abstraction.

We are now in a better position to state the *ratio decidendi* of a case. The ascertainment of the *ratio decidendi* of a case depends upon a process of abstraction from the totality of facts that occurred in it. The higher the abstraction, the wider the *ratio decidendi*. Thus a rule that "it is a tort to tell a lie that is likely to and does cause fright and consequent physical harm" is a narrow rule, belonging to a low level of abstraction from the facts of the particular case in which it was laid down; leave out the reference to fright, and it becomes wider; replace "tell a lie" by "do any act with intent to affect the plaintiff in body or mind" and it becomes wider still. It is the last rule that is the *ratio decidendi* of *Wilkinson* v. *Downton*. We carry on the process of abstraction until all the particular facts have been eliminated except the fact of the doing of an act that is intended to affect the plaintiff adversely and is likely to cause physical harm, and the fact of the occurrence of such harm.

How do we know when to stop with our abstraction? The answer is: primarily by reading what the judge says in his judgment, but partly also by our knowledge of the law in general, and by our common sense and our feeling for what the law ought to be. It so happens that in the case we have been considering the learned judge formulates the rule fairly clearly, but sometimes the rule stated in the judgment incorporates facts which as a matter of common sense are not essential, and sometimes it goes to the opposite extreme of being too sweeping—as can be demonstrated either by the use of common sense or by referring to other decided cases. The finding of the *ratio decidendi* is not an automatic process; it calls for lawyerly skill and knowledge.

DISTINGUISHING

Certain general truths implicit in the foregoing discussion may now be stated more explicitly.

In the first place, a case may have not one but several *rationes decidendi,* of ascending degrees of generality. We have seen two or three possible *rationes* in *Wilkinson* v. *Downton*. The third was accepted not only because it was stated by the judge but also because it accorded with common sense and with other authorities. Sometimes a judge will lay down a rule that is narrower than is required by common sense, and a later court may then say that the rule ought to be read more widely, by abandoning some limitation unnecessarily expressed in it. Indeed, one such unnecessary limitation can be found in the judgment in *Wilkinson* v. *Downton*. The rule stated by Wright J. refers to a person who has "wilfully" done an act calculated to cause physical harm, and the primary meaning of a "wilful" act is one that is done with the intention of bringing about a particular consequence.[4] Downton did not, perhaps, intend to cause Mrs. Wilkinson a serious illness, but he did intend to frighten her, and that was sufficient. But, as a matter of common sense, the rule should extend also to one who is merely *reckless* as to the harm in question (and the word "wilful" is, indeed, capable of extending to recklessness). If Downton had made the lying statement to Mrs. Wilkinson in order to persuade her to accompany him for some secret end of his own, realising that the statement would be likely to frighten her but not desiring (and therefore not intending) the

---

[4] "Wilful act," or "doing an act wilfully," is a telescoped expression. In a sense, every act is wilful, or it is not an act but merely a spasm. In legal discussions, the notion of wilfulness or intention usually refers to the *consequences* of conduct; it is the consequence that is intended, or wilfully brought about, not the movement of the defendant's body that constitutes the act. Where mere movement is referred to, "intention" connotes knowledge of the circumstances.

fright itself, his liability should be just the same as for a tort of intention. This was the essential position in the case of the foreign servant-girl referred to before: what the defendant intended in that case was to put pressure upon the girl to make her talk; he must have foreseen the possibility of causing her great distress, but his mind was directed towards making her do what he wanted, not towards causing distress. In analysis, the case is one of recklessness as to the plaintiff's fright, not one of intention as to the fright; but the legal liability should be, and is, the same.[5]

One may argue that there is another unnecessary limitation contained in the judgment in *Wilkinson* v. *Downton*. The judge referred to the fact that the plaintiff had been in normal health, yet it is not only possible but probable that the decision would have been just the same even if her health had previously been poor—for the fact that the plaintiff is in poor health can be no excuse to a defendant who tells her a cruel lie that would be likely to cause her physical harm. The fact that the particular plaintiff had been in good health removed a complication that the judge might otherwise have had to consider, and for that reason he referred to it; but all the same a later court may, on mature consideration and when the question arises, decide that the limitation is unnecessary. Conversely, it sometimes happens that a judge will lay down a rule that is unnecessarily wide for the decision of the case before him; a later court may say that it is too wide, and needs to be cut down.

This point leads on to the second. The phrase "the *ratio decidendi* of a case" is slightly ambiguous. It may mean either (1)

---

[5] A word may here be added upon the meaning of the word "calculated," which Wright J. used in his judgment. Judges are fond of this word, but it is an unfortunate expression because it suggests a meaning which it is not intended to convey. Originally, "calculated to" bore its literal meaning of "intended to," but in time it came to mean merely "likely to," and it is in this sense that Wright J. uses it. What the learned judge means is that the defendant intended to give the plaintiff a fright (this was the "wilful act"), and what he did was likely ("calculated") to cause the injury it did, even though the defendant did not intend to cause the full degree of the injury that occurred. The judge's decision would not apply (1) if the defendant merely acted carelessly in passing on information which was not true (for then there would be no "wilful act"). or (2) if, although the defendant intentionally told a lie and intended to cause the plaintiff some slight perturbation, a reasonable man would not have foreseen that the plaintiff would be seriously upset (for then the lie would not be "calculated" to cause physical harm).

the rule that the judge who decided the case intended to lay down and apply to the facts, or (2) the rule that a later court concedes him to have had the power to lay down. The last sentence is rather clumsy, but what I mean is this. Courts do not accord to their predecessors an unlimited power of laying down wide rules. They are sometimes apt to say, in effect: "Oh yes, we know that in that case the learned judge purported to lay down such and such a rule; but that rule was unnecessarily wide for the decision of the case before him, because, you see, the rule makes no reference to fact A, which existed in the case, and which we regard as a material fact, and as a fact that ought to have been introduced into the *ratio decidendi*."[6] One circumstance that may induce a court to adopt this niggling attitude towards an earlier decision is the necessity of reconciling that decision with others. Or again, the court in the earlier case may have enunciated an unduly wide rule without considering all its possible consequences, some of which are unjust or inconvenient or otherwise objectionable. Yet another possibility is that the earlier decision is altogether unpalatable to the court in the later case, so that the latter court wishes to interpret it as narrowly as possible.

This process of cutting down the expressed *ratio decidendi* of a case is one kind of "distinguishing." It may be called "restrictive" distinguishing, to differentiate it from the other kind, genuine or non-restrictive distinguishing. Non-restrictive distinguishing occurs where a court accepts the expressed *ratio decidendi* of the earlier case, and does not seek to curtail it, but finds that the case before it does not fall within this *ratio decidendi* because of some material difference of fact. Restrictive distinguishing cuts down the expressed *ratio decidendi* of the earlier case by treating as material to the earlier decision some fact, present in the earlier case, which the earlier court regarded as immaterial.[7]

[6] A common form of statement is to say that the earlier judges "were speaking of, and their language must be understood by reference to, the particular facts which were brought before them in that case": 62 L.J.Ch. 126.

[7] Dr. Goodhart in the article cited above, p. 62, n. 1, says that (1) it is for the judge who decides the case, and for him alone, to determine what facts are material, and the judge may express his decision that facts are immaterial merely by leaving them out of the rule of law that he propounds. But on the other hand (2) the *ratio decidendi* of a case is not necessarily the rule of law stated by the judge, because that may be too

Wilkinson v. *Downton* has not been cut down, because the wide principle has commended itself to later judges.[8] If, however, a case ever arises in which Wright J.'s wide rule is thought to carry the law too far, the decision can be restrictively distinguished.

I have stressed this matter of distinguishing because it plays a most important part in legal argument. Suppose that you are conducting a case in court, and that the other side cites a case against you. You then have only two alternatives (that is, if you are not prepared to throw your hand in altogether). One is to submit that the case cited is wrongly decided, and so should not be followed. This is possible only if the case is not binding on the court. The other is to "distinguish" it, by suggesting that it contains or lacks some vital fact that is absent or present in your client's case. Sometimes you may have the sympathy of the judge in your effort to distinguish it, even though the distinction you suggest involves tampering with the expressed *ratio decidendi* of the precedent case and even though you have no authority for the suggested distinction. Your judge may be gravely dissatisfied with the case and yet, owing to our excessively strict doctrine of precedent, it may be impossible for him to overrule it. In such circumstances it is simply human nature that he will distinguish it if he can. He may, in extreme and unusual circumstances, be apt to seize on almost any factual difference between this previous case and the case before him in order to arrive at a different decision.[9] Some precedents are continually left on the shelf in this way, as a

---

wide. It seems to me that these two statements are contradictory, and the truth I take to be that the second is right and the first wrong. The rule stated by the judge may be "too wide" in the view of the later court, and that means that the judge has not an unlimited discretion to jettison facts as being immaterial. For Dr. Goodhart's reply to a controversy on this question, see 22 M.L.R. 117.

[8] The only English case in which *Wilkinson* v. *Downton* was directly relevant was *Janvier* v. *Sweeney*, p. 66, n. 3. But the validity of the principle is amply supported by American decisions.

[9] Perhaps Pollock C.B. had restrictive distinguishing in mind when, in a letter to his grandson, "F.P.," in 1868, he made the following remark: "Even Parke, Lord Wensleydale (the greatest legal pedant that I believe ever existed) did not always follow even the House of Lords; he did not overrule—oh no! μὴ γενοίτο but he did not *act upon* cases which were *nonsense* (as many are)." Hanworth's *Lord Chief Baron Pollock* (1929), 198.

wag observed, they become very "distinguished." The limit of the process is reached when a judge says that the precedent is an authority only "on its actual facts." For most practical purposes this is equivalent to announcing that it will never be followed. It is not suggested that this extreme form of distinguishing is a common occurrence, for generally judges defer to the decisions of their predecessors both in the letter and in the spirit, even though they dislike them. But restrictive distinguishing does happen, and the possibility of its happening makes it of great importance to the lawyer.

OBITER DICTA

In contrast with the *ratio decidendi* is the *obiter dictum*. The latter is a mere saying by the way, a chance remark, which is not binding upon future courts, though it may be respected according to the reputation of the judge, the eminence of the court, and the circumstances in which it came to be pronounced. An example would be a rule of law stated merely by way of analogy or illustration, or a suggested rule upon which the decision is not finally rested. The reason for not regarding an *obiter dictum* as binding is that it was probably made without a full consideration of the cases on the point, and that, if very broad in its terms, it was probably made without a full consideration of all the consequences that may follow from it; or the judge may not have expressed a concluded opinion.

An example of an *obiter dictum* occurs in *Wilkinson* v. *Downton* when the learned judge is considering the argument that the plaintiff is entitled to recover damages for the tort of deceit. At first sight this may seem a good argument, because the defendant could certainly be said in a popular sense to have deceived the plaintiff. But it is generally taken to be essential for the tort of deceit that the defendant should have intended the plaintiff to have acted on the statement, and that the plaintiff should have so acted to his detriment, for which detriment he now claims damages. Mrs. Wilkinson recovered 1s. 10½d. as damages for deceit, because this was a sum of money that she had spent in reliance on the defendant's deceitful statement. But the fact that she became ill was not an act of reliance upon the statement. It was a spontaneous reaction to the statement. Consequently, the learned judge preferred not to rest his judgment upon this ground. He did not positively pronounce against it, but his words seem to indicate that he thought that as the law now stands the claim could not properly be based on the tort of deceit. One may say, therefore, that there is a very tentative dictum against the plaintiff on this particular issue. But the point was not finally decided, and in any case was not made the ground of the decision, and so the observations made upon it were *obiter*.

There is another kind of *obiter dictum,* which perhaps is not, properly speaking, an *obiter dictum* at all, namely a *ratio decidendi* that in the view of a subsequent court is unnecessarily wide. It is not an *obiter dictum* in the primary meaning of that phrase, because it is constructed out of the facts of the case and the decision is rested upon it. But, as we have seen, later courts reserve the right to narrow it down, and in doing so they frequently attempt to justify themselves by declaring that the unnecessarily wide statement was *obiter*. The real justification for the practice of regarding what is really *ratio decidendi* as *obiter dictum* is the undesirability of hampering the growth of English law through the too extensive application of the doctrine of precedent.

It is frequently said that a ruling based upon hypothetical facts is *obiter*. This is often true. Thus if the judge says: "I decide for the defendant; but if the facts had been properly pleaded I should have found for the plaintiff," the latter part of the statement is *obiter*. But there is at least one exception. In the past, when the defendant pleaded an "objection in point of law" (the former "demurrer"), legal argument might take place on this before the trial, and for the purpose of the argument and the decision it was assumed that all the facts stated in the plaintiff's pleadings were true. A decision pronounced on such assumed facts is not an *obiter dictum*. However, the practice of arguing the law before adducing evidence is now virtually obsolete.

If a decision would otherwise be a binding authority, it does not lose that status merely because the point was not argued by counsel (this will be important only as a way of attacking a decision that is of merely persuasive authority). But what is called a decision *sub silentio* is not binding: that is to say, one in which the existence of the particular point was not perceived by the court, so that it was not discussed in the judgment.

HOW MUCH OF A CASE TO REMEMBER

A question that frequently vexes the beginner is: how many of the facts of a case should he remember, for the purpose of learning the law and for the purpose of making a good showing in the examination? Ought he to try to remember (1) all the facts stated in the report, or (2) a selection of those facts, or (3) only those facts that are incorporated in the statement of the *ratio decidendi*? Take again as an illustration the case of *Wilkinson* v. *Downton*. The three possibilities just referred to are exemplified by (1) the passage from the judgment on pp. 63–64, above, (2) the first attempt at condensation on p. 65, and (3) the statement of the *ratio decidendi* on p. 67.

The answer to the question is that both (2) and (3) should be remembered. (1) is obviously ruled out; it would be a waste of effort to remember every minor circumstance that may be stated in the report, such as the fact that Mr. Wilkinson was stated to be lying at The Elms at Leytonstone. On the other hand, (3) is as obviously included, for it is the pith and marrow of the law. About the necessity for remembering (2) the reader may be inclined to be argumentative. He may contend that he is learning to be a lawyer, not a chronicler of tragedies, and that if he learns the rules of law there is no need for him to burden his memory with the facts of cases that as a matter of history gave rise to those rules.

There are two answers to this objection, the first of interest to examination candidates only, and the second of wider interest.

The first answer is that examiners are suspicious creatures, and in particular they are suspicious of "footnote" knowledge. Suppose that in the examination your only reference to *Wilkinson* v. *Downton* is as follows: "A person is liable in tort if he causes physical injury by an act intended to affect the plaintiff adversely and likely to cause injury: *Wilkinson* v. *Downton*." The rule is correct and the name of the case is correct; and you may in fact have satisfied yourself that the rule is deducible from the case; but the examiner will not know it. For all he knows, you saw the rule in your textbook and the name of the case in a footnote. To dispel his suspicion, you must give some statement of the concrete facts.

The second answer is more important, but we need spend no further time over it because enough has really been said on it already. It is a mistake to suppose that every case has one and only one fixed and incontrovertible *ratio decidendi*. What exactly is the *ratio decidendi* of a case is often a matter for much argument. Also, the pick-lock art of distinguishing depends upon a critical examination of all the facts of the case that might by any possibility be regarded as material. If, therefore, there is any sort of doubt about the correctness of a decision, or about its limits, as many of the facts as can conceivably be looked upon as material should be remembered.

There are some cases, however, where nothing more than the simple *ratio decidendi* need be remembered, because apart from the facts stated in the *ratio decidendi* the case contains no facts except the trivialities of date, amount, etc. An illustration is *Byrne* v. *Van Tienhoven*.[10] The facts of this case were as follows:

October 1.—The defendants in Cardiff by letter offered to sell to the plaintiffs 1,000 boxes of Hensol Tinplates.
October 11.—The plaintiffs received this letter. The plaintiffs wired to defendants. "Accept thousand Hensols." But
October 8.—The defendants posted a letter revoking their offer, ending "and we must consider our offer to be cancelled from this date."
October 20.—The plaintiffs received second letter.

It was held that there was a good contract and that the defendants' revocation of their offer was ineffective.

The reason why the above facts are set out in a case book is to show the student how the legal question as to revocation of offers is likely to arise in practice. By digesting the facts in his own mind, and seeing how the problem arises out of them, the student is preparing himself to answer examination problems and to deal with cases in his legal practice. But this does not mean that he is expected to memorise any of the particular facts of *Byrne* v. *Van Tienhoven*. All the facts of this case are immaterial except the fact that the offerors attempted to revoke their offer by a letter that did not arrive until after the offerees had accepted; and the *ratio decidendi* is that such a revocation is ineffective. If this is grasped, all the rest of the facts can be forgotten.

DIVERGING OPINIONS

The establishment of the *ratio decidendi* is more complicated when

[10] (1880) 5 C.P.D. 344.

different members of a composite court express different opinions. The problem is particularly acute for the House of Lords, where all the members commonly express separate opinions, which may show great diversity. As a result, their Lordships not infrequently make the law more uncertain than it was before the appeal.

Where the opinions of different judges differ so greatly that there is no majority for any single view, all that can be done, to ascertain the *ratio decidendi,* is to add up the facts regarded as material by any group of judges whose votes constitute a majority, and to base the *ratio* on those facts. The result is to confine the *ratio* to its narrowest form. For example, if Lords L and M hold that the material facts are A and B, while Lords N and O hold that they are A, B and C, and Lord P dissents, the *ratio decidendi* must require the presence of A, B and C. It seems, however, that the confusion of opinion may be such that there cannot be said to be a *ratio decidendi.* This is so where, of the three majority Lords, Lord L holds that the material facts are A and B, Lord M holds that they are A and C, and Lord N holds that they are A and D, while Lords O and P dissent. It would be wholly artificial to say that the *ratio* requires the presence of A, B, C and D, since this is not the view of any one of the Lords.[10a]

Further complications can arise. The minority Lords, O and P. may agree with Lord L in thinking that if the facts were A and B the conclusion would be X, but they may hold that there is insufficient evidence that fact B existed, and for this reason conclude that the answer in this case is not X. So on the abstract point of law there is a majority of the House (L, O and P) in favour of L's view. Yet, strictly speaking, the expressions of opinion by O and P are *obiter.* All that can be said is that the joint opinion of L, O and P will carry great weight with lower courts, even though it is not binding.

THE NAMES OF CASES

Another question frequently asked by law students is as to remembering names of cases. The questioner realises, of course,

[10a] See Sir Rupert Cross in 93 Law Quarterly Review 378. He takes the view that the opinion of a majority of the majority can be controlling, even though it is a minority of the whole House (see at p. 381); *sed quaere.*

that he is expected to read cases and to quote them, where relevant, in his answers; but must he behave as though he were learning the telephone directory?

The first and most important reply to the question is this: *Never* refrain from referring to a case in the examination merely because you have forgotten its name. The name is the least important part of the case. Most important is the rule of law contained in the case; next important are the facts; even the name of the court that decided the case is of more legal value than the proper names of the parties. If the name of the case is imperfectly remembered the approximate name can be given, with a question mark in brackets; thus, *Derry* v. *Peek*[11] might be rendered as "*Perry* v. *Deek* (?)." Or the cases can be referred to by the name of the plaintiff if that only is remembered: *e.g.* "*Derry's* case." Or the name of only the defendant may be given—though in this case it desirable to make it plain that the name is that of the defendant: *e.g.* "in an action against one *Peek*," or "in ... v. *Peek*." Or the case can be identified by reference to some salient fact: *e.g.* "in the case concerning the tramway company's power to use steam." Even if both name and facts are forgotten, the student can at least indicate that there is authority for his proposition by saying: "In one case it was held that ..."

But although the name is the least important part of the case, it is not altogether without importance. For the immediate purpose of the examination a script in which cases are referred to by name has naturally a more "finished" appearance than one that merely refers to "cases" in the air. Moreover, in your professional life (if, indeed, you intend to make the law your profession), you will find that a memory of the names of leading cases will be of help. If you are turning up a point of law in a practitioner's book, and happen to remember a case bearing upon it, you will usually find that by tracing the case through the case index you will come upon that portion of law in the book more quickly than by any other method.

In order, then, to lay the foundation of a sound legal knowledge, it behoves the student to make some effort to remember the names of the outstanding cases. Many of these, the most important, will be acquired simply through pondering over and discussing the cases themselves. For the rest, the amount of

[11] (1889) 14 App.Cas. 337.

energy that he puts into the memorising of their names must be left to the individual. Certainly no more than a very small part of his time should be devoted to this task, and too much should not be attempted. Some students find it useful to compile a wall chart of cases (with an identificatory tag in brackets following the name), which they ruminate upon over their breakfast marmalade. Or a short recital of the cases can be recorded on tape. Another suggestion is to tabulate the cases on postcards, carrying a selection of them in the pocket and revising them from time to time at odd moments.

The precise date of a case need never be committed to memory, but if it is a very old case the century to which it belongs may be mentioned, for extreme old age sometimes weakens its authority. And it may be important to say that a case was decided before the passing of a particular statute.

THE HIERARCHY OF AUTHORITY

For my part I consider, as I have said already, that more important than the name of the case is the rank of the court in which it was decided. To mention the court that decided a case is a mark of awareness of the doctrine of precedent, with its hierarchy of authority. The rule is that every court binds lower courts[12] and that some courts bind even themselves. When the appellate court reverses or overrules a case in the court below, the case so reversed or overruled loses all authority. *Reversal* is when the same case is decided the other way on appeal; *overruling* is when a case in a

---

[12] *Broome* v. *Cassell & Co. Ltd.* [1972] A.C. 1027. But it seems that, exceptionally, the decision of the Crown Court in the exercise of its appellate jurisdiction will not be a binding precedent for magistrates' courts in other cases: see 140 Justice of the Peace Newspaper 242.

Whether a court is "lower" depends not only on whether an appeal lies from it to the other court but, additionally, on whether the latter court is inherently higher in rank. Thus a Divisional Court of the High Court exercising its appellate jurisdiction from magistrates regards itself as bound by decisions of the Court of Appeal even though the further appeal in these cases goes not to the Court of Appeal but direct to the House of Lords. See Sir Rupert Cross, *Precedent in English Law*, 3rd ed., 121. It is not clear whether a ruling on a point of law made by a judge sitting in the Crown Court with a jury is binding on magistrates' courts.

lower court is considered in a different case taken on appeal, and held to be wrongly decided.

In 1966 the House of Lords declared (reversing its previous practice) that it would not be bound by its own decisions.[13] The day after the declaration, Osbert Lancaster's cartoon in the *Daily Express* portrayed one Law Lord saying to another: "I say, Uptort, I can't get used to the fact that we can ever have been wrong." Their Lordships are still extremely disinclined to exercise their new-found freedom, but very occasionally they do so.[14]

The Court of Appeal generally binds itself, both on the civil and on the criminal sides. There has been a steady stream of criticism by writers of this "autolimitation" of the court, at any rate in civil cases, for when a decision of the Court of Appeal is plainly wrong, it seems absurd that the parties should be put to the expense of a further appeal to the House of Lords in order to get it set aside. When an appellant perceives that he cannot succeed in the Court of Appeal because a precedent stands in the way, he will save himself money if he can obtain leave to use the "leapfrogging" procedure before referred to, and go direct to the House of Lords.

In certain exceptional cases it is recognised that the Court of Appeal can refuse to follow one of its own previous decisions.[15] Although the precise scope of the exceptions is not fully agreed, it is generally thought that they are mainly as follows. (1) Where, by inadvertence or otherwise, the court arrives at inconsistent decisions, a later court must necessarily choose between them. It is not bound to follow either the earlier or the later.[16] (2) The court is bound to refuse to follow its earlier decision that has been overruled by the House of Lords or that cannot stand with a later

---

[13] *Practice Statement* [1966] 1 W.L.R. 1234.

[14] Cross, *op. cit.* n. 12 above, 134. In *R.* v. *National Ins Comr., ex p. Hudson* [1972] A.C. 944 their Lordships announced that they would not normally reconsider their own decisions on the construction of a statute. A Procedure Direction in [1971] 1 W.L.R. 534 requires advance warning to be given by a party to an appeal who wishes to ask the House to depart from its own precedent, presumably in order to enable the House to sit in extra strength. See M. D. A. Freeman in 121 New Law Journal 551.

[15] *Young* v. *Bristol Aeroplane Co. Ltd.* [1944] K.B. 718.

[16] But a lower court must follow the latest decision of the higher court: see *Broome* v. *Cassell & Co.* [1972] A.C. 1027, and Julius Stone in 35 M.L.R. 449.

decision of the House (*i.e.,* has been impliedly overruled). (3) It need not follow its own decision given *per incuriam* (by oversight), as where a relevant statute was not considered. Presumably another example would be where a relevant decision of the House of Lords was not considered. (4) A special rule applies to the Criminal Division of the Court of Appeal. The court can refuse to follow and in effect overrule its own prior decision rendered *against* the defendant in the precedent case (or the similar decision of the older courts that this court has superseded).[17] But the court does not always keep this point clearly in view, and sometimes remarks that it is bound by the precedent. The court is, indeed, supposed to be generally bound by its own decisions rendered *in favour* of the defendant; but here again it departs from the principle from time to time and changes its own mind in favour of the prosecution.

In addition to these four main exceptions, the court has shown a disposition to add to them whenever it feels a strong need to throw off the authority of its own precedent. So the court has held that it need not follow its own decision when it was inconsistent with a later pronouncement of the Privy Council,[18] or when it was the decision of a court of two relating to an interlocutory matter (a point of procedure arising before trial),[19] or when it laid down principles for the exercise of discretion in sentencing.[20]

For several years Lord Denning M.R. has spoken in the Court of Appeal (Civil Division) in favour of a general freedom from the court's own past decisions when they now appear to be clearly wrong. These expressions of opinion culminated in *Davis* v. *Johnson,*[21] where the court had to consider two of its own previous decisions restrictively interpreting a recent statute passed for the purpose of protecting a woman who was attacked by the man with whom she was living, whether or not she was married to him. The restrictive interpretations had been severely criticised in the Press, and the Court of Appeal, sitting as a court of five, was evidently anxious to disembarrass itself of them. A bare majority of the court decided that it was free to do so. Lord

[17] *R.* v. *Gould* [1968] 2 Q.B. 65.
[18] Cross, *op cit.*, 107 n. 2, 145.
[19] *Boys* v. *Chaplin* [1968] 2 Q.B. 1.
[20] *Newsome* [1970] 2 Q.B. 711.
[21] [1978] 2 W.L.R. 182, [1978] 1 All E.R. 841.

Denning gave his accustomed reason that the court was not bound by its own decisions. Sir George Baker, President of the Family Division, concurred in the result but assigned a narrower reason. "The court is not bound to follow a previous decision of its own if satisfied that that decision was clearly wrong and cannot stand in the face of the will and intention of Parliament expressed in simple language in a recent statute passed to remedy a serious mischief or abuse, and further adherence to the previous decision must lead to injustice in the particular case and unduly restrict the proper development of the law with injustice to others." Shaw L.J., the third member of the majority, tentatively drafted the exception in a much more limited way. "It would be in some such terms as that the principle of *stare decisis*[21a] should be relaxed where its application would have the effect of depriving actual and potential victims of violence of a vital protection which an Act of Parliament was plainly designed to afford to them, especially where, as in the context of domestic violence, that deprivation must inevitably give rise to an irremediable detriment to such victims and create in regard to them an injustice irreversible by a later decision of the House of Lords." These words are so tightly related to the facts of the case that Lord Diplock in the House of Lords racily but justly characterised them as creating a "one-off' exception, applicable to the facts of the instant case but probably not to any other. Judges who make up exceptions in this way are in effect throwing off the compulsive force of precedent, and it would be more convenient to say so. In form, however, the decision of the Court of Appeal merely adds one more exception to the general rule, though there was no agreement on its wording. On further appeal,[21b] all the Law Lords expressed the decided opinion that the Court of Appeal was bound by its own decisions, but two points should be noticed. First, their Lordships did not enter into the question whether the Court of Appeal could properly create fresh exceptions. Secondly, Lord Salmon said that Lord Denning's views could not prevail "until such time, if ever, as his colleagues in the Court of Appeal agree with those views." He thus recognised that the question whether the present practice of the Court of Appeal should continue is entirely a matter for

[21a] "Stand by the decided cases."
[21b] [1978] 2 W.L.R. 553, [1978] 1 All E.R. 1132.

that court, which is surely right. This is so for either of two reasons. One is that when the House of Lords is considering an appeal its function is to decide the case between the parties, not to consider whether the lower court was bound by precedent. Any pronouncement it makes on the latter point can be regarded as *obiter*. Alternatively, and preferably, the view may be taken that the rules of precedent stand outside the doctrine of precedent. To support the doctrine of precedent by reference to precedent would be to try to pull it up by its own bootstraps. *Stare decisis* is, in fact, merely the practice of the particular court, and a court can establish and change its own practice notwithstanding what it may have said in the past and notwithstanding what a higher court may say.

When counsel wishes to ask the Court of Appeal not to follow its own previous decision on one of these grounds, he may outline the point to the court, which may then arrange to sit with five or more members (the so-called "full court") instead of the usual three.[22]

Turning to Divisional Courts, their decisions are binding precedents for magistrates' courts in other cases. Also, Divisional Courts bind themselves,[23] except that they will presumably exercise the same freedom in criminal cases as the Court of Appeal. Presumably Divisional Courts bind judges and recorders when the latter hear appeals from magistrates' Courts because Divisional Courts are superior in the hierarchy—as was said before, a further appeal can be brought from the Crown Court to the Divisional Court.

However, the Divisional Court does not bind Crown Court judges who try cases with juries, because they do not form part of the same judicial hierarchy.[24] The Crown Court is a branch of the Supreme Court having equal status with the High Court,[25] and therefore with a Divisional Court of the High Court. It makes no difference that only one judge sits in the Crown Court while two or more sit in the Divisional Court.

---

[22] But this is not essential. For example, *Gould* (n. 17 *above*) was decided by a court of three, which declined to follow an earlier decision of the Court of Criminal Appeal rendered against the defendant.

[23] *Huddersfield Police Authority* v. *Watson* [1947] K.B. 842.

[24] *Colyer* [1974] Crim.L.R. 243.

[25] Courts Act 1971 s. 1.

Single judges of the High Court trying civil cases bind inferior courts (county courts, and magistrates' courts in their civil jurisdiction), but they do not absolutely bind other High Court judges. One such judge may, if he feels strongly enough, refuse to follow another judge, and the result will be a conflict of authority that will one day have to be settled by the Court of Appeal. In other words, a High Court judge cannot overrule one of his brethren, he can only "disapprove" his decision and "not follow" him. Refusal to follow is, however, rare.

Decisions of courts inferior to the High Court do not bind anybody, not even themselves.

In legal theory decisions of the Judicial Committee of the Privy Council do not bind English courts, nor even the Judicial Committee itself. But they have great "persuasive" authority.

My suggestion is that the student should try to remember when a case belongs to the House of Lords, the Court of Appeal (or its predecessors the Court of Exchequer Chamber, the Court of Appeal in Chancery, the Court for Crown Cases Reserved, and the Court of Criminal Appeal), or the Privy Council. Since he cannot remember everything, he can usually permit himself to forget the exact court that decided cases of authority inferior to these. Nothing is gained by trying to distinguish between the three common law courts (King's Bench, Common Pleas, Exchequer) before 1875, or the various branches of the High Court today. He should, however, remember whether a particular rule was established by the common law courts or by the Court of Chancery, *i.e.* whether it is a rule of common law or one of equity, for on that, important questions sometimes depend (see Chap. 2). Also, he should remember if a particular decision was simply that of a judge given by way of direction to a jury. Such decisions are of inferior authority, largely because in a jury trial questions of law are unlikely to have been fully debated. It is no longer usual to report these directions to a jury, though, as Pollock says, "many of the older ones have become good authority by subsequent approval, and some of them are the only definite reported authority for points of law now received as not only settled but elementary."[26] It may be added that directions to a jury have been more important in criminal than in civil law, because there used to

[26] *First Book of Jurisprudence*, 6th ed., 348. The old *nisi prius* cases are reprinted in Vols. 170–176 of the English Reports.

be no appeal from a jury verdict of not guilty, and thus if on a particular point of law judges were in the habit of directing the jury in the defendant's favour the appeal court may have had no opportunity to pronounce upon it. Since 1972 the Attorney-General may refer an acquittal for the opinion of the appellate courts, but this does not affect the particular defendant.[27]

American and overseas Commonwealth cases will sometimes be found cited in English legal treatises. Though not binding upon English courts, they have persuasive authority, particularly when English authority is lacking or unsatisfactory. Scottish decisions are generally in the same category, but they are accorded binding force on points common to Scots and English law.[28]

A word may also be said about international law. In studying this subject the student will be expected to know the more important decisions of international and municipal (*i.e.* national) tribunals. Always distinguish between the two, for the pronouncement of an international court is generally more authoritative for other international tribunals on a matter of international law than that of a merely national body. (But the decision of a municipal court may be more authoritative for other courts of the same State).

CIRCUMSTANCES AFFECTING THE WEIGHT OF A DECISION

The good lawyer will often make a mental note of some circumstances that go to increase or diminish the authority of a case. Among the circumstances adding to its authority are: the eminence of the particular judge or judges who decided it; the large number of judges who took part in it; and the fact that the judgment was a "reserved" one, *i.e.* not delivered on the spur of the moment. (This last is indicated in the report, at the end of the arguments of counsel, by the words *C. A. V., Curia advisari vult.*) Among the circumstances that detract from the authority of a case are: the presence of strong dissenting judgments; the fact that the majority do not agree in their reasoning but only in their result; the failure of counsel to cite an inconsistent case in argument; (in old cases) the low repute of the reporter; the

[27] Criminal Justice Act 1972 s. 36.
[28] See Bentil in 35 M.L.R. 537.

disapproval of the profession; and the fact that the case was taken on appeal and that the appeal went off on another point.[29]

These circumstances have no importance if the case is absolutely binding on the court before which it is cited and if it is incapable of being distinguished. But they are of great importance if the case is not absolutely binding, or if on the facts of the later case it is capable of being distinguished or extended at the pleasure of the court.

INTRODUCING CASES INTO AN ANSWER

Some textbooks state a proposition of law and follow it by a case in small type in a separate paragraph. Do not adopt this practice. It is a good teaching method, but you are not teaching the examiner the law: you are showing him that you can use authorities like a lawyer. Therefore, introduce cases into your answer in literary form.

Remember that the citation of cases is not an end in itself; it is a means to the establishing of legal principle. For this reason you should try to avoid making your written work look like a mere bundle of cases. As a matter of style, an essay that sets out the principle involved in the case before mentioning the case is preferable to one that merely blurts out one case after another without introduction. Here are two answers to the same examination question in constitutional law: both are made out of the same raw material, but observe how much more intelligible the second is than the first.

Q.—To what extent is Act of State a defence in respect of acts done on behalf of the British Government which would otherwise be torts?

---

[29] This last-mentioned event happened with Phillimore J.'s decision on the treaty point in *The Parlement Belge* (1879) 4 P.D. 429, which is known to students of constitutional and international law. It was reversed in the C.A. on a different ground: (1880) 5 P.D. 197. Nevertheless, Phillimore J.'s decision on the treaty point is universally approved—which shows that affirmation or reversal on a different ground, though it may prevent a decision from having binding authority, will not affect the usefulness of a decision that obviously accords with principle.

Answer 1.—"In *Buron* v. *Denman*[30] the defendant, a British naval commander, had set fire to Spanish slave barracoons[31] on the coast of Africa (not British soil), and his act was ratified by the Crown. It was held that the aggrieved Spaniard, being a foreigner, had no action in England, Act of State being a defence.

"In *Walker* v. *Baird*[32] the defendant, again a British naval officer, had trespassed upon the plaintiff's lobster fishery in Newfoundland. In doing so he acted under the orders of the Crown. The Privy Council held that Act of State was no defence, the reason evidently being that the plaintiff was a British subject and that the act was done on British soil. A similar conclusion was reached in *Nissan* v. *Attorney-General*,[33] where the plaintiff was a British subject and the act was done in the Republic of Cyprus.

"In *Johnstone* v. *Pedlar*[34] the plaintiff was an alien resident in England. His property was seized by the police with the ratification of the Crown. The House of Lords held that Act of State was no defence."

The foregoing answer sets out the authorities but it does not clearly extract the principles from them.

Answer 2.—"Act of State is a good defence where the tort was committed by a State servant against a foreigner outside British soil, and the act was authorised or ratified[35] by the Crown. In *Buron* v. *Denman* all these conditions were satisfied. The facts were that a British naval commander fired Spanish slave barracoons on the coast of Africa (not British soil), and his act was ratified by the Crown. The defence availed.

"The law has, however, been thrown into doubt by the decision of the House of Lords in *Nissan* v. *Attorney-General*.[36] According to Lord Wilberforce, Acts of State are confined to 'acts committed abroad in the conduct, under the prerogative, of foreign relations with other states.' It seems that not every act authorised by the Crown will fall under this definition. Could it even be applied to the act done in *Buron* v. *Denman*?

"Discordant views were expressed in *Nissan's* case on whether the defence availed in respect of a tort committed to a British subject on foreign soil. It seems that British subjects (or, at any rate, citizens of the

[30] (1848) 2 Ex. 167, 154 E.R. 450.
[31] Sheds.
[32] [1892] A.C. 491.
[33] [1970] A.C. 179.
[34] [1921] 2 A.C. 262.
[35] The difference between authorisation and ratification is that the first comes before the act, and the second after it.
[36] It has been said that this decision was "a disaster for students of the law. The decision of the House of Lords lacks any clear *ratio decidendi*.... Important questions of law were raised but left half-answered or unanswered, and points that once seemed clear were left shrouded in obscurity." S. A. de Smith, *Constitutional and Administrative Law*, 3rd ed., 133.

United Kingdom and colonies) are fully protected where the act is done on British soil: see *Walker* v. *Baird,* where the Privy Council held that Act of State did not excuse a trespass committed on a British subject's lobster fishery in Newfoundland.

"Equally the defence cannot be set up in respect of a tort committed against a person resident on British soil, even though that person is an alien: *Johnstone* v. *Pedlar,* H.L. (property of alien in England seized by the police with ratification of Crown; Act of State no defence)."

In writing down the name of a case it is a good habit to underline the proper names of the parties. It is because lawyers do this that the names of cases come out in italics in print. For the student the practice has two advantages. It helps him in revising, because it makes the names of the cases stand out to the eye; and it makes his examination-script easier for the examiner to read.

THE SUCCINCT WAY OF STATING CASES

A difficulty that is likely to press upon the better student in dealing with cases in the examination room is that of lack of time. If a single question demands the citation of (say) a dozen cases, how can these be adequately dealt with in the time allowed? The answer is as follows: If at all possible, each case should be dealt with fully, giving in due order the principle involved in the case, its name, its facts, (possibly) the argument of counsel, or the losing argument, (possibly) the court before which the case came, the decision, (possibly) the reasons for the decision, and the *obiter dicta* (if any). If time does not allow of this there is another method. This is to state the rule of law contained in the case, and then to put a full colon, followed by the name of the case, (possibly) the court that decided it, and (in brackets) some outstanding fact or facts. This method was used for *Johnstone* v. *Pedlar* in Answer 2 above. As another instance, the case of *Callow* v. *Tillstone,*[37] on participation in crime, could be stated as follows: "strict liability in crime does not extend to accessories, who are not liable unless they know the facts: *Callow* v. *Tillstone* (vet who certified unsound meat negligently not an accessory to its exposure for sale, since he did not know it was unsound)." An example from contract would be: "Where it is reasonable to accept by letter, acceptance dates from the posting: *Household*

[37] (1880) L.R. 6 Q.B.D. 79.

Fire Insurance Co. v. *Grant*,[38] C.A. (lost letter of allotment; held, contract to take shares was complete)." This shows in a minimum of words that the student knows the rule of law contained in the case and also could state the facts more fully if he had the time. But the method should not be used if a more orthodox presentation of the case is possible. Stating the facts and decision in the ordinary way occupies little more time and looks much better.

"MAY I CRITICISE?"

Some lawyers assert that no case in an appellate court can be said to be "wrongly decided." It is the law, until reversed or departed from. This is a mere matter of words. Obviously one can say that the case was badly decided, or poorly reasoned, or unfortunate in its outcome, or inconsistent with other cases. And why not say that it was wrongly decided, thereby expressing the hope that it will be overruled? Anyway, in university examinations you may always criticise decided cases, and statutes as well if you think it profitable. In professional examinations the primary object is to test your knowledge of the present law. But criticism is often relevant to deciding whether a case will be followed or not. An objectionable precedent may be distinguished, or not followed, or overruled.

Lawyers are much too prone to assume that what has been decided cannot be upset. It often happens that a plainly wrong decision is given at first instance or even by the Court of Appeal, which is followed unquestioningly for many years because counsel do not advise their clients to take the point further on appeal. When, eventually, some counsel is found who has the courage and acumen to take the point, the precedent is reversed.[39] Now that the House of Lords has decided that it can question its own previous decisions, there is hardly any decided point that cannot be reopened if the arguments against it are strong enough.

[38] (1879) 4 Ex.D. 216.

[39] *e.g. R.* v. *Gould* [1968] 2 Q.B. 65. In *R.* v. *Taylor* [1950] 2 K.B. 368 counsel had allowed his client to plead guilty on the strength of a decision in an earlier case notwithstanding that it was plainly erroneous. An appeal was taken against the sentence only, but, on being informed of the facts and of the earlier decision, the Court of Criminal Appeal was so surprised that it allowed the appeal to be converted into an appeal against conviction; it then allowed the appeal and overruled the precedent.

CHAPTER 7

THE INTERPRETATION OF STATUTES

The golden rule is that there are no golden rules.

—G. B. Shaw, *Man and Superman.*

FINDING THE MEANING OF WORDS

IN ordinary life, if someone says something that you do not understand, you ask him to explain himself more fully. This is impossible with the interpretation of statutes, because when Parliament has passed an Act the words of the Act are authoritative as words. It is only these words that have passed through the legal machinery of law-making, and individual Members of Parliament cannot be put into the witness-box to supplement or interpret what has been formally enacted. Hence the words of an Act carry a sort of disembodied or dehumanised meaning: not necessarily the meaning intended by any actual person in particular, but the meaning that is conventionally attached to such words.

The most important rules for the interpretation (otherwise called construction) of statutes are those suggested by common sense. The judge may look up the meaning of a word in a dictionary or technical work; but this ordinary meaning may be controlled by the particular context. As everyone knows who has translated from a foreign language, it is no excuse for a bad translation that the meaning chosen was found in the dictionary; for the document may be its own dictionary, showing an intention to use words in some special shade of meaning. This rule, requiring regard to be had to the context, is sometimes expressed in the Latin maxim *Noscitur a sociis,* which Henry Fielding translated: a word may be known by the company it keeps. One may look not only at the rest of the section in which the word appears, but at the statute as a whole, and even at earlier legislation dealing with the same subject-matter—for it is assumed that when Parliament passed an Act, it probably had the earlier legislation in mind, and probably intended to use words with the same meaning as before. Somewhat anomalously, reference may even be made to later statutes, provided that they are close in point of time.

A statute will often contain an interpretation section which assigns a special meaning to some of the words used in it. In addition, the Interpretation Act 1889 operates as a standing legal dictionary of some of the most important words used in Acts of Parliament. This Act declares, among other things, that the plural includes the singular, and the singular the plural, unless a contrary intention appears. Also, since 1889, if not before, "man" has embraced "woman."

INTERPRETATION IN THE LIGHT OF POLICY: "FRINGE MEANING"

When interpreting statutes the courts often announce that they are trying to discover "the intention of the legislature." In actual fact, if a court finds it hard to know whether a particular situation comes within the words of a statute or not, the probability is that the situation was not foreseen by the legislature, so that the Lords and Members of Parliament would be just as puzzled by it as the judges are. Here, the "intention of the legislature" is a fiction. What the court is really doing is guessing what the legislature *would* have said on the point *if* it had thought of it. The intention is not actual but hypothetical. There is, of course, a limit to what a court can do by way of filling out a statute, but to some extent this is possible.

An illustration is the familiar legal problem of "fringe meaning." The words we use, though they have a central core of meaning which is relatively fixed, have a fringe of uncertainty when applied to the infinitely variable facts of experience. For example, the general notion of a "building" is clear, but a judge may not find it easy to decide whether a temporary wooden hut, or a wall, or a tent, is a "building." In problems like this, the process of interpretation is indistinguishable from legislation: the judge is, whether he likes it or not, a legislator. For, if he decides that the wooden hut is a building, he is in effect adding an interpretation clause to the statute which gives "building" an extended application; whereas if he decides that the hut is not a building, he adds a clause to the statute which gives it a narrower meaning. The words of the statute, as they stand, do not give an answer to the question before the judge; and the question is therefore legislative rather than interpretative. This simple truth is rarely perceived or admitted: almost always the judge pretends to get his solution out of the words of the Act, though he may confess in so doing to be guided by its general policy. The rational approach would be to say candidly that the question, being legislative, must be settled with the help of the policy implicit in the Act.

This kind of "interpretation" may be legally and socially sound although it reaches results that would surprise the lexicographer. Thus it has actually been held that murder can be an "accident."[1] The word "accident" was being interpreted in the context of the Workmen's Compensation Act, and the result of the decision was that the widow of the deceased workman was entitled to compensation from the employer,[2] because the murder in question arose out of and in the course of the employment. The court admitted that it was giving an unusual meaning to the word, for a historian who described the end of Rizzio by saying that he met with a fatal accident in Holyrood Palace would fairly be charged with a misleading statement of fact. Similarly, Farwell L.J. remarked that one would not in ordinary parlance say that Desdemona died by accident, because "the horror of the crime dominates the imagination and compels the expression of the situation in terms related to the crime and the criminal alone." Yet, if one looks at the situation from the point of view of the victim, it is an accident, in the sense that it was not expected or intended by the victim himself. In preferring this wider meaning of the term "accident," which could not have been found in any dictionary, the court looked to the general purpose of the Act.

IMPLYING QUALIFICATIONS UPON STATUTES: THE "GOLDEN RULE"

Judges vary in the extent to which they are prepared to modify the words of an Act to arrive at a just and sensible result. Some judges

[1] *Nisbet* v. *Rayne & Burn* [1910] 2 K.B. 689.
[2] Now turned into an industrial injuries benefit as part of the national insurance scheme (Social Security Act 1975).

sometimes insist that a statute is to be applied literally, however absurd the consequences; it will be for Parliament to put the absurdity right. This is called the "literal rule" of interpretation. Others, more liberal in their approach, will modify the words to prevent absurdity; this is sometimes called the "golden rule."[3] The literal rule and the golden rule are not really two rules of law, for they are in flat opposition to each other. The one disregards absurdity, the other does not. They are, therefore, not fixed rules binding on the court, but rather modes of approach; and it depends on the temperament of the judge which is adopted in any particular case.[4]

At the present time the most forceful exponent of the liberal approach to statutory interpretation is Lord Denning. He said on one occasion:

"Whenever a statute comes up for consideration it must be remembered that it is not within human powers to foresee the manifold sets of facts which may arise, and, even if it were, it is not possible to provide for them in terms free from all ambiguity. The English language is not an instrument of mathematical precision. Our literature would be much the poorer if it were. This is where the draftsmen of Acts of Parliament have often been unfairly criticised. A judge, believing himself to be fettered by the supposed rule that he must look to the language and nothing else, laments that the draftsmen have not provided for this or that, or have been guilty of some or other ambiguity. It would certainly save the judges trouble if Acts of Parliament were drafted with divine prescience and perfect clarity. In the absence of it, when a defect appears a judge cannot simply fold his hands and blame the draftsman. He must set to work on the constructive task of finding the intention of Parliament.... Put into homely metaphor it is this: A judge should ask himself the question: If the makers of the Act had themselves come across this ruck in the texture of it, how would they have straightened it out? He must then do as they would have done. A judge must not alter the material of which it is woven, but he can and should iron out the creases."[5]

This opinion was expressed by Denning L.J., as he then was, in the Court of Appeal. The House of Lords, however, took

---

[3] *Mattison* v. *Hart* (1854) 14 C.B. at 385, 139 E.R. at 159. See particularly Sir R. Cross, *Statutory Interpretation* (London 1976) 81–88.

[4] Some commentators say that there is a single rule: that the task of the court is to find the meaning of the provision and that the absurdity of the literal meaning may lead to its rejection. The fact is, however, that some judges are ready to see a fatal absurdity in the literal meaning when others are not.

[5] *Seaford Court Estates Ltd.* v. *Asher* [1949] 2 K.B. at 498–499.

occasion to disapprove his views on interpretation, preferring what their Lordships regarded as a more literal approach.[6] At bottom the question is how one conceives the role of the judges and of Parliament. Are the judges mere automata to give effect to the literal words of statutes at their face value, leaving an active and all-wise legislature to rectify any injustices? Or have the judges a more creative part to play in securing the just result? Whatever the theory, the hard truth is that Parliament pays little attention to the working of the law, so that if injustice occurs, decades or centuries may pass before the position is remedied by statute. Also, the literal rule has the disadvantage of making statute law an arbitrary body of rules without underlying reason.

A judge's effort to avoid absurdity is generally limited to attaching an extended or restricted meaning to words, or implying extra words into the statute (or even ignoring words in the statute) in order to rectify a drafting mistake and prevent the statute having an operation clearly wider or narrower than that required by its purpose.[7] Occasionally, however, a judge may go further and restrict the statute by reference to a principle of justice. When the judges develop the common law they do so in the light of certain general principles of justice, and it seems obviously desirable that these principles should apply also to statutes, unless Parliament clearly intended to exclude them.

A striking example is *Re Sigsworth*.[8] Under legislation now contained in the Intestates' Estates Act 1952, a child has certain rights of succession on the death of the parent intestate. For the purpose of his decision in *Re Sigsworth,* the trial judge assumed it to have been proved that the deceased, Mary Ann Sigsworth, had been murdered by her son; and the question was whether the son was entitled to her estate as "issue" under the Act. The learned judge held not, for the reason that no one is entitled to profit from his own wrong. The decision was rendered somewhat easier by the fact that a similar conclusion had already been arrived at in the law of wills: a murderer cannot take under his victim's will. In *Re*

---

[6] *Magor and St. Mellons* v. *Newport Corporation* [1952] A.C. 189. For a corrective, see *per* Lord Reid in *Coutts & Co.* v. *I.R.C.* [1953] A.C. at 281. The most important recent pronouncement is in *Stock* v. *Frank Jones (Tipton) Ltd.* [1978] 1 W.L.R. 231.

[7] An illustration is given by Cross, *op. cit.* 59–60.

[8] [1935] Ch. 89.

Sigsworth, the judge extended this rule to the interpretation of the intestacy statute which made no mention of it. Even statutes may be read as subject to certain fundamental principles of justice which are to be discovered in the common law.

Incidentally, *Re Sigsworth* is enough to disprove the oft-repeated assertion that "where the words of an Act of Parliament are clear, there is no room for applying any principles of interpretation."[9] This proposition may have a useful application in limiting some of the more pedantic rules of interpretation. But it does not exclude the golden rule, which, as *Re Sigsworth* shows, may be used even where the words taken by themselves are clear.[10]

Sometimes the courts find the task of rectifying Parliament's wording to make it accord with common sense too difficult, and the statute has to be given its literal meaning even though it results in outrageous injustice.[11] And, of course, the notion of absurdity never justifies the court in making a political judgment disagreeing with the clear purpose of the legislation.

THE "MISCHIEF" RULE

The liberal approach to the construction of statutes is fortified by the "mischief" rule, otherwise known as the rule in *Heydon's* case.[12] This bids the judges to look at the common law before the Act, and the mischief in the common law that the statute was intended to remedy; the Act is then to be construed in such a way as to suppress the mischief and advance the remedy.

The practical utility of this rule depends to some extent upon the means that the courts are entitled to employ in order to ascertain what mischief the Act was intended to remedy. A true historical investigation would take account of press agitation, party conferences, Government pronouncements, debates in Parliament, and so on; but all these are ignored as the result of a rule excluding evidence of the political history of a statute. The

---

[9] *Per* Scott L.J. in *Croxford* v. *Universal Insce. Co.* [1936] 2 K.B. at 280.
[10] See the important abbreviations of the Law Commission and Scottish Law Commission, *The Interpretation of Statutes* (Law Com. No. 21) para. 31.
[11] As in the case instanced by Cross, *op. cit.* 75.
[12] (1584) 3 Co. Rep. at 7b, 76 E.R. at 638.

rule is justified by the burden that would be placed upon legal advisers and the uncertainty that would be introduced into the law if such historical materials had to be consulted.[13] In practice, therefore, the judge generally divines the object of a statute merely from perusal of its language, in the light of his knowledge of the previous law and general knowledge of social conditions.[14]

Many statutes are the result of recommendations made by Royal Commissions and departmental committees. Can the reports of these commissions and committees be looked at as an aid to construction? The rule as now settled is that they are inadmissible for the direct purpose of explaining the intention of Parliament, but admissible under the rule in *Heydon's* case to the extent that they show the mischief against which the Act was directed. It follows that these reports are always admissible, for *Heydon's* case applies to every statute: but the court is restricted in the use it can make of them. The indications are that eventually the restriction will be swept aside. It may be expected that the practice of referring to these reports will extend itself in the future, because they often supply the best commentary upon the wording of an Act.[15]

OTHER MODES OF RESTRICTING THE OPERATION OF STATUTES

Although the judge is supposed to adopt an impersonal attitude to statutes, he is but human and his decision will sometimes be coloured by whether he approves of the legislation or not. The judges approved the policy of the Statute of Treasons 1351, and they extended its scope to cover various "constructive treasons" as a matter of interpretation—disregarding the fact that part of the object of the statute was to clarify and limit the law, in the

---

[13] Although the reason is convincing, the rule sometimes has unhappy consequences. On one occasion, when a section was included in an Act for the avowed purpose of getting rid of a certain decision, a Divisional Court, not realizing this, followed the decision, whittling down the section by applying rules of interpretation, and saying that Parliament could not have intended to change the law. See Cretney in 119 New Law Journal 301.

[14] See *Davis* v. *Johnson* [1978] 2 W.L.R. 553.

[15] See the close vote on this subject in *Black-Clawson International Ltd.* v. *Papierwerke Waldhof-Aschaffenburg A.G.* [1975] A.C. 591, discussed by Cross, *op. cit.* 136 ff.

interest of political liberty. On the other hand the Statute of Frauds 1677 was found to work badly: designed to prevent fraud, it came to be used as an instrument of fraud. Hence the courts limited it somewhat by interpretation, and also by inventing the remarkable doctrine of part performance as an exception to the statute. These are both extreme examples, and generally judicial adaptation will work within narrower limits.

In the past the judges' attitude towards statutes has usually been restrictive. Pollock put this caustically when he said that the courts tend to interpret statutes "on the theory that Parliament generally changes the law for the worse and that the business of the judges is to keep the mischief of its interference within the narrowest possible bounds."[16] Since Pollock wrote the judges' outlook has changed; but the older attitude has marked the law deeply. In particular, many rules of interpretation have a distinctly restrictive effect. One of these is the *ejusdem generis* rule, according to which, when a series of particular words in a statute is followed by general words, the general words are confined by being read as of the same scope or genus as (*ejusdem generis* with) the particular words. An illustration is one of the Sunday laws (now repealed) which provided that "no tradesman, artificer, workman, labourer or other person whatsoever shall do or exercise any worldly labour, business, or work of their ordinary callings upon the Lord's Day or any part thereof (works of necessity or charity only excepted)." On any rational interpretation, the words "or other person whatsoever" would be taken to mean what they say; but the courts chose to confine them to persons who were of the same genus as tradesmen, artificers, workmen and labourers; consequently professional men, such as estate agents, were not covered.[17] The effect was to leave the general words with hardly anything to do. It was no accident that this restrictive interpretation was practised on an Act that was out of harmony with the prevailing mores. At the present day legislation is rarely drafted in this "etc." form; and, if it were, the courts would be much less inclined to interpret it restrictively. One might imagine some contexts in which general words were not intended to bear the full width of their literal meaning, and then the so-called *ejusdem generis* rule would properly be invoked; but

[16] *Essays in Jurisprudence and Ethics* (1882), p. 85.
[17] *Gregory* v. *Fearn* [1953] 1 W.L.R. 974.

it would not be used for the purpose of emasculating a modern statute. In short, the "rule" is not a rule at all, in the sense that its use is obligatory; and for modern legislation its application will probably be the exception rather than the rule.

In interpreting statutes, various presumptions may be applied, all of which are of a negative or restrictive character. Some embody traditional notions of justice, such as the rule that a statute is presumed not to be retrospective (except in procedural matters). Others reflect what was almost certainly the intention of Parliament, as that an Act applies only to the United Kingdom unless the contrary is expressed. The most controversial presumptions are those enshrining the values of a capitalist society—the presumption against interference with vested rights, the presumption against the taking of property without compensation, and the presumption against interference with contract. The last of these now has few followers; but the first two still retain vitality. So does the presumption against interference with personal liberty.

These few words are perhaps sufficient to enable the student to understand what is involved in the interpretation of statutes. A fuller account of the technical rules will be found in Sir Rupert Cross's *Statutory Interpretation*.

CHAPTER 8

WORKING OUT PROBLEMS

> I scarce think it is harder to resolve very difficult cases in law,
> than it is to direct a young gentleman what course he should take
> to enable himself so to do.
>
> —Sir Roger North, *On the Study of the Laws.*

[Since much of the value of this chapter must depend upon the concrete
illustrations it gives, I have been forced to assume the reader's knowledge
of a certain amount of elementary law. He should postpone reading it
until he has made a start with the study of a case-law subject like
Constitutional Law, Criminal Law, Contract or Tort.]

THE object of including problems in the examination paper is to
discover legal ability. But it is not easy even for an intelligent
candidate in the heat of the examination to show the calm
judgment that a problem requires. It is, therefore, most important
to train oneself in problem answering before the examination. In
doing so the student will not merely be preparing in the best
possible way for his examination: he will also be developing his
mind as a working instrument and preparing himself for legal
practice. The technique of solving academic problems is almost
the same as the technique of writing a legal opinion upon a
practical point. The chief difference is that in practical problems
the material facts often lie buried in a much larger mass of
immaterial detail, while the examination problem contains
comparatively little beyond the material facts.

If the student is studying under a tutor or supervisor an
adequate number of problems will be supplied to him. If not, he
will have to buy or otherwise get sight of copies of past
examination papers.

Perhaps the most important piece of advice with problems, as
with all examination questions, is to *read every word of the
problem*. Almost every word has been put in for a purpose and
needs to be commented upon. In the law of contract, for instance,

the word "orally" or "verbally" or "on the telephone," in describing the formation of a contract for the sale of land, will invite discussion of section 40 of the Law of Property Act 1925. Even if you are of opinion that a fact stated in the problem is immaterial, you should not (in general) pass it by in silence but should express your opinion that it is immaterial, and, if possible, give reasons. However, there is no need to deal in this way with an argument that, if raised, would not receive a moment's serious consideration from the court.

FACTS STATED IN THE PROBLEM ARE CONCLUSIVE

A common query on the part of the novice when he reads an examination problem is: "How could such facts ever be proved?" The teacher's answer is that the student must assume this proof. (Actually, it is surprising how facts often can be proved in practice that at first sight seem to be unprovable if the defendant is prepared to contradict them. But in any case the student is not concerned with this question.)

The student should not assume facts *contrary* to those stated in the problem for the purpose of giving the examiner a piece of information for which he did not ask. Also, there is generally no need to assume facts that go clean beyond those given in the problem: had the examiner wanted a discussion of such facts he would have inserted them himself. Here is an example of a problem in criminal law where the examiner clearly wanted to confine the facts to a narrow compass.

X and Y, discovering that Z intended to commit a burglary in A's house, arranged together to persuade him to steal therefrom certain articles for them. Have X, Y or Z committed an offence?

The fact that the question is thrown into the perfect tense shows beyond doubt that no other facts than those stated in the first sentence are to be assumed. The question is: have they *on those facts alone* committed an offence? An answer that assumes that X and Y have persuaded Z to steal, or that Z has stolen, will therefore miss the mark. The correct answer to the question is that X and Y are guilty of conspiring to incite (or, indeed, of conspiring to commit) a crime (though whether the indictment should charge the conspiracy of being a conspiracy to incite or commit burglary or as a conspiracy to defraud has become doubtful since the Criminal Law Act 1977[1]). Z is not guilty of anything on these facts; he will not become a party to the conspiracy until he agrees to steal.

OMITTED FACTS

Although supplementary facts should not, in general, be added to a problem, the case is different with what may be called omitted facts. One of the marks of a competent lawyer is his ability to know what gaps there are in the facts of his case. The solicitor, for example, when interviewing a client has to draw from him by questions many legally relevant facts that the client has not thought of disclosing. The barrister, too, may find that such facts are missing from his brief, and have to extract them from his instructing solicitor in conference. In order to test the candidate's perspicacity a problem may deliberately omit something that is important. Always look for such omissions and state how your answer will be affected by the presence or absence of the fact in question. Here is a simple illustration from the law of tort.

B is A's employee. Discuss A's liability for an accident caused by B's negligence in the following cases:
  (i) B, when driving A's van, picks up his friend C and gives him a lift to the station. An accident happens by B's negligence.
  (ii) [etc.]

Two vital facts are omitted from this casually stated problem. First, we are not told who was injured. We are to understand that owing to B's negligence an injury was sustained either by C or by some other user of the highway. But the answer may differ according as the person injured was C or some other user of the highway. This distinction should therefore be taken, and each of the two possibilities discussed separately.

Secondly, we are not told whether the station lay on or near B's proper route, or whether it was so much off the route that every yard he went was a yard away from his employment and not to it. This distinction, coupled with the previous one, yields four possible combinations of fact, each needing discussion.

---

[1] See my *Textbook of Criminal Law* (London 1978) Chap. 28 §4.

Another example of an economically worded problem, this time taken from criminal law:

A killed his baby thinking that it was a rabbit. Discuss A's criminal responsibility.

Here A's mistake is so extraordinary that we are justified in wondering whether he was not insane at the time of the deed, his insanity being an omitted fact. On the other hand we are not positively told that he was insane: he may have been shooting rabbits at dusk, and his baby may have crawled out of its cot into the garden. Or, more plausibly, A may have killed his baby in the course of a dream.[2] The answer, then, again falls into two parts: (i) on the assumption that A was insane, (ii) on the assumption that he was sane. However, it is not justifiable to discuss a problem from the angle of insanity if there is no indication of insanity in the facts of the problem.

One more example, again from criminal law:

A, a mountaineer, roped to his fellows, cut the rope in order to prevent them from dragging the leader of the party to death. Discuss.

Presumably A is being prosecuted for murder; but the question does not actually say that A's fellows were killed as a result of what he did. We must assume that they were killed, or at least injured, in order to create a legal problem. Presumably, too, A sets up the defence of necessity; we are not expressly told that there was no other way of saving the leader's life, but this is a fair inference from the question. Finally, the question tells us that A's object was to save the leader; it does not tell us whether his object was also to save himself. In other words it does not tell us whether he cut the rope above or below himself. If he cut it below himself his object was presumably to save himself as well as his leader. If he cut it above himself he presumably fell, and in that case his life was evidently saved by something approaching a miracle—at any rate, we know that he was saved because otherwise he would be beyond the jurisdiction and the question would have no legal interest. Perhaps this last doubt is irrelevant; it may not matter whether A's object was entirely altruistic or partially self-interested. But on the other hand it may, and so the point ought to be taken.

[2] As in *H.M. Advocate* v. *Fraser* (1878) 4 Couper 70.

Having thus discussed the interpretation of this problem, you would, of course, go on to consider the law relating to it.

If, as in the last illustration, you decide that a fact can be inferred from what is given, though not explicitly stated, it is wise to guard yourself by stating expressly that you assume the fact to exist. For the examiner may not agree that the fact is implied in the question; but he will not mind about this if he sees that your assumption is not the result of carelessness but is your considered interpretation of the question. If you are in any doubt whether a fact is implied you should "play safe" and take the problem each way, that is, first on the assumption that the fact exists and then on the assumption that it does not exist.

Even if all the relevant facts (in one sense of the word "facts") are stated, what is legally called a "question of fact" may still arise on the problem—*e.g.* a question whether the defendant has, on the facts, been negligent, or whether a lapse of time is "reasonable." In a real case these would be questions for the jury (if the case were tried with a jury), although the judge might withdraw the issue from the jury if satisfied that there was no evidence of negligence or unreasonableness. On such a problem, although you may venture an opinion as to the proper verdict on the point, and argue your opinion to the best of your ability, you should not, in the last resort, usurp the function of the jury (or of the judge when there is no jury). The most you should say is that on these facts there is evidence of negligence (or unreasonableness), and that a finding to that effect would clearly be right. If the point is at all doubtful, take the facts each way and state the legal result following on each possible finding. The following problem in the law of contract illustrates the importance of this.

A telegraphed an offer to sell his library to B for £1,000. B telegraphed in reply: "Will give £900. B." A day elapsed in which nothing further occurred. Then at 9 a.m. A handed to the post office a telegram to B: "You can have the library for £900. A." At exactly the same moment B handed to the post office a telegram to A: "Cancel my first telegram. I will take the library for £1,000. B." A received B's telegram at 9.30 a.m. B received A's telegram at 9.40 a.m. What contract, if any, exists?

Everything in this problem turns on the unobtrusive sentence: "A day elapsed...." The question is whether this was an unreasonable delay on the part of A in replying to B's counter-offer of £900. If it was unreasonable, the offer (*i.e.* B's counter-offer) has lapsed, and there is no contract. If it was not unreasonable, the offer was still alive when A handed in at the post office his telegram of acceptance, and the contract was therefore completed at that moment.[3] Now it is not possible to give a confident answer to the question whether the delay was unreasonable. The only rule of law is that an offer by telegram raises a presumption that a speedy reply is expected (*Quenerduaine* v. *Cole*[4]), and therefore the lapse of a whole day would normally be too long. But it is to be noticed that in our problem the telegraphing business was started not by B but by A. B may have sent his counter-offer by telegram simply out of politeness, and not because *he* was in any hurry. It is not certain, therefore, whether the rule in *Quenerduaine* v. *Cole* would apply, though on the whole I think it would, because I do not think that a court would speculate on the reasons that moved B to telegraph rather than write.

There is more to say about this problem, but the essence of it is this question of fact. (Although telegrams are now little used in business matters, the question could arise in connection with international cables.)

It may be added that where facts are given from which the negligence or unreasonableness (or absence of it) may be inferred, you should argue from these facts in much the same way as if you were addressing a jury. But, as I have said, your opinion on this should not (except in a completely unarguable case) deter you from taking the problem each way.

TWO POINTS OF TECHNIQUE

Some examiners conclude the statement of facts in a problem with the direction to discuss it: others adopt the mannerism of requesting you to advise one of the parties. This second form of question does not mean that you are expected to bias your answer in favour of the particular party; the legal advice you give in your answer will generally be the same whichever party you are supposed to be advising. However, there may be some practical advice to be given to the party you are supposed to be advising, and you should certainly comply with the examiner's direction as

---

[3] *Cowan* v. *O'Connor* (1888) 20 Q.B.D. 640. Distinguish the Telex case, *Entores Ltd.* v. *Miles Far East Corporation* [1955] 2 Q.B. 327.

[4] (1883) 32 W.R. 185.

far as you are able. By the way, do not use the second person in your answer—make the answer impersonal. thus you should say "X is liable," not "You are liable."

If the examiner has exercised his fancy by using fictitious names, like Tomkins, you are perfectly entitled to abbreviate them to the initial letter—unless, of course, two parties in the same problem have the same initial letter.

RULES AND AUTHORITIES

Next, a few remarks upon the giving of reasons and authorities for an opinion. A bald answer to a problem, even though correct, will not earn many (perhaps not any) marks, because the examiner cannot tell whether the student has knowledge or is just guessing. Reasons and authorities should, therefore, always be given. Pretend to yourself that the examiner will disagree with your point of view, and set yourself to win him over by argument.

One of the most important of a lawyer's accomplishments is the ability to resolve facts into their legal categories. The student should therefore take pains to argue in terms of legal rules and concepts. It is a common fault, particularly in criminal law, to give the impression that the answer is based wholly upon common sense and a few gleanings from the Sunday newspapers. The following illustration of a question and answer in criminal law may show this.

Q.—A fire-engine driven at full speed to a fire knocks down and kills somebody. Discuss the criminal responsibility of the driver.

Student's answer.—"If the driver has been careful he is not responsible. (1) It is a well-known custom that as soon as the siren of a fire-engine is heard, other vehicles should pull up at the side of the road, in order to afford free passage. It is therefore safe for a fire-engine driver to proceed at a higher speed than would be possible for other drivers. Further (2) it is reasonable for a fire-engine to proceed quickly to a fire, for life and property may be in danger. But I do not put much weight on this second ground, for great as may be the importance of putting out a fire, it is not sufficiently great to justify the driver in leaving a trail of destruction behind him."

Upon reading this answer the examiner may well comment: "A commendable effort by an intelligent student who has not read the textbook and knows no criminal law." The answer, to be complete, should have stated the crimes for which the driver may be prosecuted (manslaughter, causing death by reckless driving, or, in the magistrates' court, driving without due care and attention); it should have stated the requirements of each crime, so far as relevant; and it should have pointed out that the burden of proving these requirements beyond reasonable doubt lies on the prosecution. It should also have discussed the possible defence of necessity, referring to it expressly by that name, not vaguely as the last two sentences of the answer do. Put into this legal setting the answer would have been first-class.[5]

It is bad style to begin an answer to a problem by citing a string of cases. Begin by addressing yourself to the problem. If the law is clear, first state the law and *then* give the authorities for your statement. If the law is not clear, first pose the legal question and *then* set out the authorities bearing on it.

When citing cases, the mere giving of the name is of little use. What is wanted is not only the name but also a statement of the legal points involved in the decision, and perhaps also a consideration of its standing—*i.e.* whether it has been approved or criticised. This is so even though the case directly covers the problem. Still more is it so when the case is not on all fours with the problem. New points often occur in the law, and the lawyer in advising his client must, in effect, predict the probable decision of the court. So also in examinations: a problem is often set upon some point of law that is not covered exactly by authority. No candidate who fails to see this point can get a first class on that question. The late Dr. Coulton, in his autobiography, told a tale of a great mathematical teacher at Cambridge who met a candidate in the College court just after the Tripos. "That was a d—— good answer of yours, A, to the sixteenth question." Yes, sir, but it was a b—— good question, wasn't it?" In order to create this relationship of mutual esteem between yourself and your examiner, pay him the compliment of searching for the point of his problem. Ask yourself what is the point it raises that is not precisely covered by authority.

Failure to follow this common-sense rule is a frequent error of the tyro. Take again, for instance, the "mountaineering" problem already given (p. 101). Most raw beginners think that they have adequately solved this problem if they quote *R*. v. *Dudley and*

---

[5] The point may also be made that firemen are by statute exempt from speed limits.

Stephens[6] and declare that necessity is no defence. But if they paused to reflect, they would discover several differences between *R.* v. *Dudley and Stephens* and the facts of their problem. It cannot be asserted with confidence that every, or even any, of these distinctions would find favour with a judge, but at any rate they are possible distinctions which would certainly be made much of by an experienced counsel for the defence. They are as follows:

(1) In *Dudley and Stephens* there was a choice as to who was to die. It will be remembered that *Dudley and Stephens* was the case where three men and a cabin-boy were compelled to take to an open boat after the wreck of their yacht *Mignonette*. On the twentieth day after the wreck two of the men killed the boy for food; four days later they were rescued. The two men were convicted of murder. It may be said that these facts are materially different from those in our problem, for in our problem there seems to be no choice as to who is to die: it is simply (one supposes) a question of some or all. It is true that in *Dudley and Stephens* the jury found that the boy was in a much weaker condition than the others and was likely to have died before them. But the jury did not find that the boy might not have been revived had one of the others been killed to provide food for him. So long as the boy was alive and had a chance of survival he was as much entitled to retain that chance as the others; whereas in our problem it may be that the men who are cut away have no chance of survival at all.

(2) It is not certain on the facts of *Dudley and Stephens* that the two defendants would have died had they not killed the boy. All that the jury found was that had they not done so they would *probably* not have survived to be rescued. It may be that on the facts of our problem the death of the leader is certain, not merely probable, if the rope is not cut. But it must be admitted that this is not a very strong distinction, for in *Dudley and Stephens* the jury also found that "at the time of the act there was no sail in sight, nor any reasonable prospect of relief"; and it would seem that if the law recognises necessity as a defence it should proceed upon the facts as they appeared to the defendant at the time.

(3) In *Dudley and Stephens* the cabin-boy was not by his own conduct, voluntary or involuntary, bringing the others nearer to

[6] (1884) 14 Q.B.D. 273.

death. In our problem the men whom the defendant presumably sends to death are themselves dragging the leader to what will otherwise be his death. It is true that they cannot help it; but does that matter? If a lunatic attacks me, I am surely entitled to defend myself, even though he is not criminally responsible for his conduct. Also, I am entitled to defend another. Is not our problem a case of defending another?

Another illustration, this time from the law of contract, is as follows:

> A writes to B offering to sell him his horse Phineas for £100. B posts a letter accepting, but he misdirects it and in consequence it is a week late in being delivered to A. Meanwhile A has sold Phineas to C. Discuss.

The ordinary beginner answers this problem simply by quoting *Household Fire Insurance Co.* v. *Grant*,[7] or some other authority to the same effect, and saying that the contract is complete on the posting of the letter of acceptance. But the whole point of the question is whether *Grant's* case applies to a misdirected letter of acceptance. I cannot help thinking that the booby who so completely misses the point of the question is often actuated by some hidden (and mistaken) motive of self-preservation. He really scents the difficulty but thinks it too hard for discussion and so conveniently pretends that he has not seen it. If this ostrich only knew, he would gain more marks *by posing the legal difficulty,* even though he suggested no solution, than he ever could by blinking it completely. If, in addition to posing the difficulty, he could say that there is no authority in point and that *Grant's* case is distinguishable, and could also suggest some reasons why on these facts it ought to be distinguished, he would get a first class on that question instead of a very doubtful pass. In all legal problems, *have the courage to argue.*

If a case falls midway between two authorities, this may indicate that there is a fundamental conflict of principle between the two authorities, and that it is necessary to hold that one of them was wrongly decided. Alternatively, you may come to the conclusion that there is a real distinction between the authorities, and in this event the problem must be looked at from the point of view of general legal principle or public policy to decide whether it should be brought under the one head or the other. The situation

[7] (1879) 4 Ex.D. 216.

was characterised by Paley, an eighteenth-century divine, as the "competition of opposite analogies."[8]

To sum this up, when the problem is possibly distinguishable from the authority or authorities nearest in point, a careful analysis of the possible distinction or distinctions should always be given. This is particularly important if the authority in question has been doubted by judges or criticised by legal writers. It may be that the student does not feel competent to discuss the various distinctions, but even so the existence of the possible distinctions should be pointed out in the answer. Moreover, distinctions should be pointed out even though in the opinion of the student they are not material, if it could conceivably be argued that they are material: of course the student should express his own opinion that they are not material.

If there is a possibility of the authority in question being overruled, it is more important than ever to give its status in the judicial hierarchy, as well as stating any objections that have been urged against it.

When you have a number of cases to quote, it is generally best to quote the nearest authority first and to allot it the most space; the other cases can be brought more casually into the discussion, as you have time. When you have read a case in the reports or in a case book, do your best to convey this fact by referring to some apposite passage in the judgment or some other relevant detail of the report which will indicate that you have not merely relied on a textbook.

If you know that there is no case bearing directly upon the problem, say so. The fact that the problem is not covered by authority is in itself a valuable piece of information. If the authority for a proposition is a statute, say this also, even though you have forgotten the name of the statute.

DOUBT

Where the law is doubtful, a categorical statement that the rule is one way or the other will earn few, if any, marks. This is particularly important in answering problems. If the answer to the problem is doubtful, say so, and then suggest what the answer

[8] *Moral and Political Philosophy,* vi, VIII. The classical discussion of Paley's remarks is in Austin's *Jurisprudence,* 5th ed., ii, 632–633.

ought to be. It is a mistake to simulate confidence where you have no certain knowledge.

After discussing a "mooty" problem, try to avoid the weak conclusion that "A is perhaps liable." Your conclusion may be that if the facts are so-and-so, he is liable; if they are such and such, he is not. Or, if the court follows *Smith* v. *Jones,* then A will be liable, but if it follows *Robinson* v. *Edwards,* which is to be preferred for reasons previously given, then A will not be liable.

A point can often be scored by demonstrating that the law applicable to a problem may depend upon the court before which the case comes. For example, there are some decisions of the Court of Appeal, like that in *Musgrove* v. *Pandelis,*[9] that would probably be reluctantly followed by the Court of Appeal but would quite possibly be overruled by the House of Lords. Consequently, the "law" on the subject of *Musgrove* v. *Pandelis* (strict liability for petrol in the tank of a car) may depend upon the number of appeals that the client is prepared to take.

PROBLEMS ON STATUTES

A problem may be set on a statute as well as on a case. You must then recall the words of the statute as best you can, apply them to the problem and, as in all problems, look for the "catch." Here is an illustration from constitutional law:

Aikenhead J., a judge of the High Court, is convicted of driving under the influence of drink. Can he be dismissed from his judicial office, and if so by whom?

The attitude of students towards a problem like this varies. Some, though knowing the terms of the Act of Settlement, or of the similar statute now in force, steer clear of the problem because they are afraid of it. Others write down simply:

By the Act of Settlement 1701, "Judges' Commissions [shall] be made *quamdiu se bene gesserint,*[10] but upon the Address of both Houses of Parliament it may be lawful to remove them."[11] Aikenhead J. can be removed under this provision.

[9] [1919] 2 K.B. 43.
[10] "For as long as they behave themselves."
[11] See now Supreme Court of Judicature (Consolidation) Act 1925, ss. 12, 13.

This is not a bad answer and would win a pass. Had the candidate added that dismissal was actually effected by the Crown he might have risen to a second. To obtain a first class, one needs to do a little thinking. Aikenhead J. was appointed "during good behaviour." He has been convicted of crime, and we shall assume for the moment that he has not behaved himself within the meaning of these words. Clearly he can be dismissed if both Houses present an Address to that effect. But can he not, in this case, be dismissed even without an Address? What the examiner is evidently after is the correct interpretation of the words of the Act of Settlement, or rather of the Act now in force replacing the Act of Settlement. Do these words mean that judges can be dismissed by the Crown *only* upon an Address of both Houses (with a direction to the Houses that they are not to present an Address unless the judge has misbehaved himself)? Or do the words mean that judges can be dismissed by the Crown *either* if they have not behaved themselves (*e.g.* been convicted of crime) *or* on an Address of both Houses? In other words, are the Houses the sole judges of the correctness of the judges' behaviour, or not? The second interpretation can be arrived at by reading the provision in two parts: (1) judges' commissions are to be made for as long as they behave themselves, implying that if they misbehave they may be dismissed by the Crown; (2) they may be removed by the Crown on an Address of both Houses, even though they have not misbehaved themselves. The first interpretation can be arrived at by reading the provision as a whole (judges are appointed during good behaviour, and the two Houses are the sole judges of bad behaviour).

A good lawyer, who reads carefully, ponders meanings and is prepared to discuss difficulties, might be able to see this point in the problem even though he had read nothing upon it. When one studies the literature one finds that, surprising as it may seem, the weight of legal opinion is in favour of the second view; and it is not even clear what is the proper legal means that the Crown should use to establish misbehaviour before dismissing a judge.[12] A further question that arises (and that might be perceived on the face of this problem) is whether dismissal by the Crown can only be for misbehaviour in office or whether it can be for an offence

[12] Anson, *Law and Custom of the Constitution,* 4th ed. ii 234–235; Sir K. Roberts-Wray, *Commonwealth and Colonial Law* (London 1966) 486 ff.

not related to judicial office or affecting judicial ability. If the latter, can it be for any offence or only for a serious one, and is the offence in the problem sufficiently serious? In practice the Crown would now be unlikely to dismiss a judge without an Address, and it would be for the two Houses to decide whether the misbehaviour justified dismissal.

This example shows how it is possible to display the qualities of a good lawyer without knowing much law. Here is another problem in constitutional law to reinforce the point.

A statute is passed giving power to make Orders in Council for the public safety and defence of the realm. Would it be a valid objection to an Order made under this statute that it imposes a tax?

The type of answer to be expected from the Painful Plodder would be as follows:

"A statute similar in terms to that in the problem was DORA,[13] passed in the First World War. By Regulations under this statute the Food Controller was empowered to regulate dealings in any article. Under these powers the Food Controller ordered that no milk should be sold within certain counties except under licence. In *Att.-Gen.* v. *Wilts United Dairies*[14] the question arose whether the Food Controller was entitled to charge for the granting of a licence under this Order. It was held by the H.L. that he was not. This case was cited with approval by the Court of Appeal in *Congreve* v. *Home Office*.[15] The answer to the question is therefore 'Yes.'"

This answer exhibits a common defect; it cites a case without explaining the legal principle involved in it, *i.e.* the legal ground on which the case was decided. Plodder says that in *Att.-Gen* v. *Wilts U.D.* it was held that the Food Controller could not charge for the licence. This is true, but we need to know why. The facts of the case contained three elements: (1) DORA, giving power to make Regulations for the public safety and defence of the realm; (2) the "daughter" Regulations made under DORA, allowing the Food Controller to regulate dealings in any article; and (3) the Food Controller's Order ("granddaughter" of DORA) that no milk should be sold without licence, coupled with his grant of a licence on condition of receiving payment. Now the decision was that the money promised could not be recovered by the Crown for

[13] The Defence of the Realm Consolidation Act 1914.
[14] (1922) 91 L.J.K.B. 897.
[15] [1976] Q.B. 629.

the reason that (*a*) any prerogative power to tax had been taken away by the Bill of Rights 1689, and that (*b*) as for the statutory powers of DORA, the Regulations under which the Food Controller was acting did not on their wording enable him to impose a tax. The Regulations enabled him to regulate dealings in an article, but regulation of dealings is one thing, taxing another. Order (3) was therefore *ultra vires*[16] the Regulations (2). Had the candidate understood these reasons he would at once have seen that the decision in *Att.-Gen.* v. *Wilts U.D.* did not conclude the question he was asked. All that the case decided was that the Food Controller was acting outside the *Regulations* since the Regulations did not give the power to tax. The question whether a Regulation that expressly gave the power to tax would itself be *ultra vires* DORA was not decided.

Now here is the answer of a gentleman who may be called the Discerning Dilettante. He knows nothing about the Bill of Rights or the decision in *Att.-Gen.* v. *Wilts U.D.*, but he addresses himself to the question and uses his intelligence.

"It may be that the Order is *intra vires*[17] the statute. The statute gives power to make Orders for the public safety and defence of the realm: in other words for the waging of war. Obviously you cannot wage war without taxing. Money, it is said, makes the sinews of war.

"To this it may be objected that although it is necessary to tax in order to wage war, it is not necessary for the Executive to tax without a statute. Parliament is still in being; why not leave taxation to Parliament?

"I think that a valid reply to this objection would be that it is a political objection to the passing of a statute worded in this wide way, not a legal objection to the validity of the Order, if a statute worded so widely has been passed. If the objection were legally valid it could be used to defeat almost all Orders made under this statute, which would be absurd. Suppose that under this defence statute the Government makes an Order requisitioning land for anti-aircraft missile sites. It would obviously be no valid objection to such an Order that the Order is not necessary for public safety because Parliament could have passed it. The object of the defence statute is to delegate to the Executive what in peacetime would be the function of Parliament. Surely the question whether Parliament could have passed the particular legislation is logically irrelevant to the question whether the legislation is for the public safety and defence of the realm.

"At the same time I do not suppose that a court would take the view that I am here expressing. The English tradition that it is for Parliament to do the taxing is so deep-seated that the court would probably assert a legal

[16] *i.e.* "outside the powers" conferred by the enabling provision.
[17] "Within the powers [of]."

presumption, as a matter of statute interpretation, that powers of taxation are not included in a statutory delegation of power unless clear words are used, and that a general formula like that in the statute stated in the question is not sufficient."

Or, as Atkin L.J. (as he then was) put it in *Att.-Gen.* v. *Wilts U.D.* in the Court of Appeal, "in view of the historic struggle of the legislature to secure for itself the sole power to levy money upon the subject, its complete success in that struggle, the elaborate means adopted by the representative House to control the amount, the conditions and the purpose of the levy, the circumstances would be remarkable indeed which would induce the court to believe that the legislature had sacrificed all the well-known checks and precautions, and, not in express words, but merely by implication, had entrusted a Minister of the Crown with undefined and unlimited powers of imposing charges upon the subject for purposes connected with his department."[18]

In thus unfavourably contrasting Plodder's answer with Dilettante's, I am not, of course, suggesting that book work is useless. As I have already said, book knowledge should always be used to provide a starting-point. Dilettante's answer would have been better if he could have shown that the *Wilts* case, though apparently relevant, was not conclusive on the question. The point is that although book knowledge is in itself a good thing, it is useless and worse than useless if it deflects your attention from the question that you are being asked.

RELEVANCY

When answering a problem, never preface your answer with a general disquisition on the department of law relating to the problem. Start straight away to answer the problem. Problems are set chiefly to test your ability to *apply* the law you know, and the examiner will speedily tire of reading an account of the law that is not brought into direct relation to the problem. Where the problem contains several persons, say A and B as possible plaintiffs and C and D as possible defendants, the best course is to begin your answer by writing down the heading: *A* v. *C*. When you have dealt with this, write (say) *B* v. *C,* referring back to your

[18] (1921) 37 T.L.R. 884 at 886.

previous answer for any points that do not need to be repeated. Then you will deal with *A* v. *D* and *B* v. *D*.

The advice to plunge into the specific problem, on the model of counsel's opinion, applies even where the problem is divided into several parts, all of which are on the same general department of law. For instance, suppose that in criminal law a question consists of a chain of short problems on insanity numbered (i), (ii), (iii), etc. In my opinion it is not advisable to preface the answer with a discussion of *McNaughten's* case,[19] even though *McNaughten's* case is relevant to each of the numbered problems. The examiner is impatient to see you answering the problems, and he may even ignore altogether anything you write before writing down figure (i). You should therefore write the figure (i) at the very beginning of your answer, and begin to tackle problem (i). In the course of doing so you can, of course, set out and discuss *McNaughten's* case. When you come to (ii), (iii) and the rest, it will be easy enough to put a back reference, if necessary, to your previous discussion of the case.

Although a problem is not an invitation to launch out into a general disquisition on the department of law on which the problem is set, it is important in working out the problem to state all the rules of law that are really relevant to it. A frequent blemish upon an otherwise good answer is that the relevant rule of law is not expressly stated but is left to be implied from the candidate's conclusion. Much the better practice is first to state the rule of law and then to apply it to the facts. Do not write: "D is liable on the contract because he did not communicate his revocation of his offer." It is better style to write: "An uncommunicated revocation of an offer is ineffective. Here D's revocation did not come to the notice of the offeree, so the offeree's acceptance of the offer was valid, and D is liable on the contract." Here is another illustration of the point, from the law of tort.

Q.—A, finding B, a tramp, in his shed, locks the door in order to keep B there while he fetches the police. Can B sue A?

Student's answer.—"B can sue A for false imprisonment because no 'arrestable offence' has been committed by anyone."

The answer and the reason given are correct, but will not earn

[19] (1843) 10 Cl. & F. 200, 8 E.R. 718.

full marks because the full rule of law has not been stated. The proper answer is:

The general rule under the Criminal Law Act 1967[20] is that anyone can arrest on reasonable suspicion of an arrestable offence, save that where the arrest is by a private person (as here) he must show either (1) that he reasonably suspected the arrested person to be *in the act of committing* the offence, or (2) that he reasonably suspected this person of committing the offence *and the offence had in fact been committed by someone.* An arrestable offence is defined as one for which a person may by virtue of any statute be sentenced to imprisonment for at least five years, or an attempt to commit such an offence. Theft comes within the definition. The person making an arrest must ordinarily inform the person arrested of the act for which arrest is made: *Christie* v. *Leachinsky*[21] [facts]. Here there is no suspicion of any crime—much less of an arrestable offence; nor has any crime been committed. The only legal wrong committed before B's arrest is the tort of trespass. There is, therefore, no right to arrest, and B can sue A for false imprisonment. *Aliter,* if tramps had previously stolen from A and if A reasonably suspected B of such theft; though even then A should as soon as possible communicate the grounds of arrest. This answer does not consider various specific statutory powers of arrest, which are unlikely to affect the position.

The question just considered asked: "Can B sue A?" This formula, very common in law examinations, means "Can B sue A *successfully?"* Examinees sometimes answer it by saying: "B can sue A but he will fail." This displays the writer's common sense but also his lack of knowledge of legal phraseology. It is true that there is virtually no restriction upon the bringing of actions: for instance, I can at this moment sue the Prime Minister for assault—though I shall fail in the action. But when a lawyer asserts that A can sue B, what he means is that A can sue B successfully; if he meant his words to be taken literally, they would not have been worth the uttering.

For much the same reason, you should never write a sentence like: "B can argue that ... but the argument will fail," or "B has committed such-and-such a crime, but he has a good defence." The proper way to put the last sentence would be to say: "If B is charged with such-and-such a crime, he will have a good defence."

When a problem is based on a rule—*e.g.* the rule in *Derry* v. *Peek*[22] or *Rylands* v. *Fletcher*[23]—it is usually advisable to state

[20] Section 2(2), (3).
[21] [1947] A.C. 573.
[22] (1889) 14 App.Cas. 337.
[23] (1868) L.R. 3 H.L. 330.

the whole rule in a sentence or two, even though some parts of the rule are not material to the problem. No further details should be given of parts of the rule that are not material.

Where the problem turns on an exception to a rule (*e.g.* an exception to the rule in *Rylands* v. *Fletcher*), there is usually no need to state any exceptions other than the one that is relevant.

QUESTIONS DIVIDED INTO PARTS

Questions are frequently divided into two or more parts, and this division raises difficulties of its own for the inexpert candidate.

Sometimes the problem begins with a common opening part before branching out into its subdivisions. The following is an example:

A writes to B offering to sell him his horse Phineas for £100.

(i) B posts a letter accepting, but he misdirects it and in consequence it is a week late in being delivered to A. Meanwhile A has sold Phineas to C.

(ii) B, after posting a letter of acceptance to A, sends A a telegram cancelling "my letter now in the post." The telegram is delivered to A before B's letter.

Discuss.

It should be obvious that in this type of problem (i) and (ii) are alternative possibilities, to be dealt with separately; (ii) is not meant to follow upon and include the facts of (i). Yet I have known students to suppose that this is all a single problem, to be disposed of in a single breath.

Another mistake that one student made with this particular problem was to suppose that the opening sentence was itself a question, inviting a general disquisition on the legal nature of an offer. This, of course, is not so.

A different type of two-part problem is one in which the second part commences: "Would it make any difference to your answer if . . .?" This means that the second part of the question is the same as the first part, except for the variation expressly stated. An illustration is as follows:

(i) A is firing with an air gun in his garden at a target on a tree. The shot glances off the tree and hits A's gardener, B. Can B sue A?

(ii) Would your answer be different if the shot had been fired by A's son, C?

Most students assume that (ii) is a question as to the liability of

C. Clearly on its wording the question is the same as in (i), namely, as to the liability of A.

Sometimes a problem is so worded as to involve two successive questions, but the second question logically arises only if the first is answered in a certain way. Suppose that the student has answered the first question in the *other* way; is he now to answer the second? The answer is "Yes." For the purpose of answering the second part of the question he should state that he is assuming that he is wrong in his answer to the first. An example from the law of contract:

Pickwick, who manufactures cricket bats, affixed a signboard on the boundary of the field belonging to the Dingley Dell Cricket Club, stating that if any batsman hit the signboard with a batted ball during the course of a match Pickwick would pay him the sum of £5. Podder hit the board whilst batting in a match between Dingley Dell and Muggleton, and afterwards orally requested Pickwick to pay £5 to Mrs. Jingle, to whom Podder was indebted for board and lodging. Mrs. Jingle demands payment of the £5 from Pickwick but it is refused. Discuss the rights of the parties.

This problem involves two issues: (i) whether there is a contract between Pickwick and Podder, resulting in a debt owed by Pickwick to Podder; (ii) whether Podder has validly assigned the debt to Mrs. Jingle. Issue (i) turns on the difficult distinction between consideration and the performance of a condition precedent to a gratuitous promise,[24] or if you like on the equally difficult question of intent to contract. It may well happen that the student in considering this comes to the conclusion that there is no contract between Pickwick and Podder. If this view is correct, issue (ii) does not really arise. All the same, it should be dealt with. It may be that the examiner disagrees with the candidate in his answer to (i), and although that may not affect the candidate's marks on (i), the candidate will lose the marks on (ii) if he does not deal with it. Even if the examiner agrees with the candidate in his answer to (i), the examiner must have meant (ii) to be dealt with, or else he would not have troubled to put it in.

A fourth kind of two-part question consists of a bookwork question followed by a problem. The difficulty here is often that it is not clear whether the problem is meant to bear a relation to the

---

[24] See Salmond and Williams, *Contracts* (1945), 100 *et seq.*; Cheshire, Fifoot and Furmiston, *The Law of Contract,* 8th ed. 76–77.

book-work question or not. No universal rule can be stated, because examiners differ in their practice, but nearly always there is meant to be a connection, at least if the two parts of the question are not subdivided by numbers or letters. I am conscious that this may not sound very helpful advice. But some examinees fail to search for a connection between the book-work question and the rider, thus missing the point intended by the examiner, while other examinees, finding no connection between the two (in fact there being none), avoid the question altogether. The student must be left to steer his own course between this Scylla and Charybdis.

THE OVERLAPPING OF SUBJECTS

In a problem on criminal law, make no statement as to the law of tort, unless of course the question whether a crime has been committed involves a question of tort. Similarly, in a problem on tort make no statement as to the law of crime, unless again the existence of a tort depends on the law of crime.[25]

This mutual exclusiveness of subjects does not hold between tort and contract. Where a problem is set in a tort paper or in a contract paper involving both a possible tort and a possible breach of contract, both aspects of the matter should be discussed. This is because a tort and a breach of contract can be proceeded upon in the same action; the distinction between criminal and civil law is more deeply marked. The overlap between tort and contract should be looked for particularly in problems involving the negligent carriage of passengers by rail or sea, and the sale (or repair) of goods or houses that turn out not to be of merchantable quality or reasonably fit and that cause physical injury to the buyer (or owner).

In problems on tort and criminal law the student is expected to enumerate and discuss all the possible torts or crimes that may have been committed on the facts given in the problem, and also all the possible defences that may be raised. In this respect the answering of an examination question differs somewhat from the giving of an opinion in legal practice. A practitioner will not argue legal points unnecessarily. He will not, for example, argue the

[25] As in a problem of false imprisonment (above p. 114), or on the rule that the imputation of a crime punishable by imprisonment is actionable without proof of damage.

question whether there exists a tort of offensive invasion of privacy, if his client has a clear remedy in defamation. But an examiner will usually be disappointed if, in an appropriate problem, both points are not discussed. In other words, if a point is *relevant,* discuss it, even though it be not necessary.

THE ANSWERING OF PROBLEMS IN CRIMINAL LAW

Always consider all the possible crimes that have been committed, by all possible persons,[26] and all the possible defences open to them. By "possible" I mean "seemingly possible to an ignorant person." If you consider that such-and-such crime has not been committed, or that such-and-such defence is not available (though an ignorant person might think it is), do not pass it by in silence but state your opinion expressly. You should also give the reason for your opinion as shortly as the importance of the point seems to require. The reason for this advice is that quite possibly the question was set as a trap, and if you refrain from commenting upon the trap the examiner may think that you have avoided it by good luck rather than good management.

Never come to the defences until you have stated the crime for which the defendant is in your opinion being charged. Start with the responsibility of the perpetrator (principal), taking accessories afterwards.

If you think that the problem leaves open some question of fact, state the law according as the fact is present or absent.

If the outcome is clear you can say so—*e.g.* "D is guilty of murder." But if the application of law to fact is not clear, you need not state a definite opinion or even "submit" that the position is so-and-so. For example, the question may state that the defendant shot at a burglar when a bystander was standing dangerously close, and hit the bystander. It is not for you to say that the defendant foresaw the possibility of hitting the bystander: that is for the jury. Never assume that the defendant had a particular state of mind unless the question states that he had it. Instead, consider whether there is any evidence for the jury (sufficient to require the judge to leave the case to the jury); if there is, explain how the judge would direct the jury, and state whether

[26] Unless, of course, the problem specifically asks for the criminal responsibility of some only of the *dramatis personae.*

a verdict of guilty would be likely to be upheld or upset on appeal. It is at these points in a jury trial that the legal opinion is important: a lawyer is not *directly* concerned with the work of the jury.

Often the problem will be found to fall short of one of the major crimes. In such a case it will very frequently involve a lesser or lesser-known crime. The student should note these lesser or narrower crimes very carefully when they are mentioned in his book. Here is a short list of them.

An act that falls short of:	may be:

Manslaughter	Assault and battery (O.A.P.A. 1861, s. 47).
	Offences under Road Traffic Act 1972 as amended:
	  section 1, causing death by reckless driving;
	  section 2, reckless driving;
	  section 3, careless driving;
	  section 5, driving "under the influence."
	Excessive speed (Road Traffic Regulation Act 1967, s. 78A, inserted by Act of 1972, s. 203).

Murder	Abortion (O.A.P.A. 1861 s. 58). Child destruction (Act of 1929). Concealment of birth (O.A.P.A. 1861 s. 60). Infanticide (Act of 1938). Manslaughter (O.A.P.A. 1861 s. 5). Manslaughter on account of diminished responsibility (Homicide Act 1957 s. 2).
Attempted murder (O.A.P.A. 1861 s. 15)	Assault and battery. Wounding, etc., with intent (O.A.P.A. 1861 s. 18 as amended). Malicious poisoning resulting in danger to life, etc. (O.A.P.A. 1861 s. 23). Malicious wounding, etc. (O.A.P.A. 1861 s. 20). Occasioning actual bodily harm by an assault (O.A.P.A. 1861 s. 47). Malicious poisoning with intent to injure, etc. (O.A.P.A. 1861 s. 24). Robbery (Theft Act 1968 s. 8). Offence under Prevention of Crime Act 1953 or Firearms Act 1968.

An act that falls short of:	may be:
Attempted murder (O.A.P.A. 1861 s. 15)	Possessing an article with intent to commit an indictable offence against the person (O.A.P.A. 1861 s. 64, as amended by C.L.A. 1967 Sched. 2).
Criminal damage (Criminal Damage Act 1971)	Cruelty to animals (Protection of Animals Act 1911). Theft (Theft Act 1968). Using threat (Criminal Damage Act 1971 s. 2). Having custody of article with intent (*ibid.* s. 3).
Theft (Theft Act 1968 s. 1)	Taking articles on public display (Theft Act 1968 s. 11). Taking motor-vehicle or other conveyance (Theft Act 1968 s. 12). Obtaining property by deception (Theft Act 1968 s. 15). Obtaining pecuniary advantage by deception (Theft Act 1968 s. 16). False accounting (Theft Act 1968 s. 17). Corruption (Prevention of Corruption Act 1906 as amended). Being found on private premises for an unlawful purpose (Vagrancy Act 1824 s. 4). Loitering with intent (*ibid.*). Going equipped for stealing etc. (Theft Act 1968 s. 25).
Robbery (Theft Act 1968 s. 8)	Assault and battery: aggravated assaults; carrying weapons. Blackmail (Theft Act 1968 s. 21). Threatening letters (O.A.P.A. 1861 s. 16).
Obtaining property or pecuniary advantage by deception (Theft Act 1968 ss. 15, 16)	False accounting (Theft Act 1968 s. 17). Offences under Trade Descriptions Act 1968.
Forgery Coining (Coinage Offences Act 1936)	Theft, obtaining property by deception. False trade description (Trade Descriptions Act 1968 s. 1).

When several crimes appear to emerge from the facts of a problem, it is best to start your answer with the gravest crime that seems clearly to have been committed. For it would be absurd to open your answer by considering some summary offence of which the defendant is guilty, and then to wind up with the conclusion that he has also committed, say, murder! The murder should come first, and the summary offence as a rather casual postscript. If the defendant is clearly guilty of a crime like wounding with intent, and only doubtfully guilty of murder, it is sensible to start with the clear crime before coming to the doubtful one.

Problems in criminal law often start with an inchoate crime—conspiracy, attempt or incitement. Even though the problem shows that the full crime was consummated, the culprits may be convicted of attempt or incitement, so that it may be relevant to mention these crimes—though normally, of course, the indictment would be for the completed crime, not for a mere attempt or incitement. If you mention the possibility of a conspiracy charge, it would be wise to add that the addition of conspiracy counts when the crime is consummated must be specially justified. As for incitement, if the crime is actually committed the inciter becomes an accessory to it. In other words, the difference between (i) incitement and (ii) being a participant in a crime as one who has counselled or procured it is that in (i) the main crime has not been (or need not have been) committed by the person so incited, and in (ii) it has.

THE ANSWERING OF PROBLEMS IN TORT

As in criminal law, look for all the possible torts that may have been committed, and consider whether their essentials have been satisfied. Draw into your net all possible defendants, and then turn round and consider all the possible defences open to them on the facts given.

There are not so many "obscure" torts as there are obscure crimes, but a considerable overlap occurs between some of the leading torts. The following are the chief examples:

Nuisance.	Negligence.
Rylands v. *Fletcher*.	Contractual duty to use care.
Negligence.	
	Negligence.
	Breach of statutory duty.

Defamation.
Offensive invasion of privacy
   [— at present non-existent.]
Slander of title.
Malicious falsehood.

Conversion.
Trespass to goods.

In the tort of negligence, it is frequently necessary to consider the machinery as to proof of negligence—the burden of proof, functions of judge and jury, *res ipsa loquitur.* Questions of negligence, contributory negligence and remoteness of damage are frequently wrapped up together, and so are questions of contributory negligence and *volenti non fit injuria,* and of necessity and private defence.

If the problem appears to be a novel one, it may raise the theory of general liability in tort.

CHAPTER 9

ANSWERING BOOK-WORK QUESTIONS

> He that knows, and knows that he knows,
> is asleep–wake him.

> —Anon.

THIS chapter is chiefly concerned with the answering of questions other than problems, though some of the remarks apply also the answering of problems. Like the last chapter it is not meant for hasty consumption immediately before the examination. The wise student will at the outset of his course look at the examination papers for the past few years, and, whether compelled to or not, will write out the answers to some questions (even though only in brief note form) in order to gain practice in self-expression. Past examination papers will also show him the probable lay-out of the paper that he will be expected to answer, and the amount of time likely to be allowed on each question.

SUBDIVIDED QUESTIONS

If your question is expressly divided into several sub-questions, answer each sub-question separately; and if the sub-questions are numbered (i, ii, iii) or lettered (*a, b, c*) number or letter them in the same way in your answer. A question may be divided into parts even though numbers or letters are not used. For instance, the question—

Summarise the provisions of, and the changes introduced by, the Unfair Contract Terms Act 1977 Part I.

—invites an answer in two parts: (1) the provisions of the Act; (2) its impact on the previous law. It would be wise to write your answer under these two headings (though there would be no objection to applying the double answer to the Act section by section). Always model your answer to conform to the question: do not, for instance, on this particular question adopt the chronological order of (1) the pre-Act law, and (2) the Act. The reason is that if the examiner is reading your script quickly (and he may have hundreds of scripts to mark) he may be puzzled and annoyed by your departure from the order of his question. Besides, he may have set the question like that with the object of seeing whether your mind is sufficiently adaptable to vary the order of what you have learnt.

RELEVANCY

In answering a question you should, of course, give as much detail as you can within the limits of the question. It is sometimes possible to answer a question literally in a couple of sentences, but this will not always impress the examiner. The extreme example of this kind of answer is the story told by Mark Twain, in his *Life on the Mississippi,* of his piloting lesson.

"Presently Mr. Bixby turned on me and said: 'What is the name of the first point above New Orleans?'

"I was gratified to be able to answer promptly, and I did. I said I didn't know."

Not many candidates would attempt this frankness in the examination room, but they often do suppose that an accurate answer directed to the very words of the question is all that is required. This is frequently a mistake. For instance, in the law of contract the question, "What is the difference between void and voidable contracts?" can be accurately answered by saying that a void contract is an apparent contract that is in truth no contract at all, while a voidable contract is a contract that is capable of being avoided at the option of one party. This, though correct, would not score many marks. It is an accurate statement of the difference of *definition* between void and voidable contracts, but it says nothing of their different *effects.* The candidate should, therefore, add, as a minimum, a discussion of such cases as *Cundy* v. *Lindsay*[1] and *Lewis* v. *Averay*[2] in order to illustrate the effect of each kind of contract (or apparent contract) upon third-party rights. To put this advice generally, if you are asked to distinguish

[1] (1878) 3 App.Cas. 459.
[2] [1972] 1 Q.B. 198.

between two legal concepts or institutions, you should give not only the difference of definition but also the difference of legal effect.

It need hardly be added that the examiner *always* wants reasons and authorities for the answer, even though he does not expressly ask for them.

To say that a question should be answered fully is not to say that irrelevant matter should be introduced into the answer. Questions are often worded to cover only a fragment of a particular subject; in that case the examiner does *not* want the whole of it.

This question of relevancy is often the examinee's greatest headache. Often he has to interpret a badly worded question, with no hope of redress if his guess as to the examiner's meaning should turn out to be wrong. My advice is this. If the question is reasonably clear do not wander outside it. If there is a doubt as to its meaning, the question will usually have at least a central kernel of meaning that is relatively clear. Answer this to begin with. Then, as to the doubtful "shell" of the question, if you still have time to write on the question, you should expressly point out the doubt in your mind as to what you are being asked, and proceed to write on the doubtful part of the question for the rest of the allotted time. If, on the other hand, you have no time left for the doubtful part of the question, declare your doubt whether the question was intended to have any further scope, and leave it there. The fact that you have been able to spend your whole time on the core of the question is itself some indication that the question was not intended to have any wider scope.

For instance, suppose that a question in the law of contract is:

Discuss the maxim, *In pari delicto potior est conditio defendentis.*

Clearly this invites a discussion of the general rule preventing recovery of money paid or property transferred under an illegal contract, and this rule, with its exceptions and quasi-exceptions, should therefore be discussed first. The problem then arises: does the question cover also the general rule against suing for damages for breach of an illegal contract? However you decide this conundrum, you should state your decision in the answer. If you rule this second topic out of order, and the examiner wished it to be included, the examiner will at least see that you have had the point present in your mind, and will probably also be brought to see that he was at fault in his wording of the question. In any case, the proper limits of time for the question should not be exceeded.

If in doubt whether a particular matter is relevant, a good test is to ask yourself whether, if the examiner had wished you to discuss it, he would naturally have framed an extra question upon it.

Once the limits of the question are settled, do not canter beyond them. The examiner cannot give credit for irrelevancy, because that would be unfair to others who have answered only the question that they were asked. There is, however, a clever way in which matters otherwise irrelevant may be lightly introduced. This is by the method of comparison. For instance, if in constitutional law you are directed to write a note on the "kangeroo" (a method of curtailing discussion in the House of Commons), a discussion of the closure and guillotine (two other methods of curtailing discussion) would generally be out of order. But a comparison of the kangeroo with the closure and the guillotine would be admissible, and credit would be given for it.

Many students begin an answer with a prologue. Cut it out. In particular, do not start with the historical background if you are not asked for it, unless you have some special reason for doing this—and if so, state the reason. Sometimes the historical background makes the law more intelligible, or supports one interpretation of the law rather than another. But if you are asked the history of the action of *assumpsit,* do not begin with a paragraph on the medieval precursors of *assumpsit*—debt, detinue and account. If the questioner had wanted these he would have said so. If you are asked to discuss, say, *Nordenfelt's* case,[3] begin by setting out the facts and decision—do not start in the Middle Ages. Having stated the case you may legitimately put it into its historical setting in order to show what advance it made on the previous law; and you may also indicate the trend of development that it started. But all this depends on the time you have left after giving your attention to the centre of the question.

Students (particularly advanced students) are frequently vexed by doubts as to the amount of detail that they should put into their answer. The best advice is: aim at concentrating all your intelligence on the specific question, and bring in your knowledge

[3] [1894] A.C. 535.

only so far as it is relevant. If you show that you are a master of the *relevant* knowledge, the examiner will readily give you credit for knowing the rest of the subject. An example would be the question: " 'The jury is a historical anachronism.' Discuss." This is not an invitation to give the whole history of the jury system: the question is whether the jury *is* a historical anachronism. Are there any features of the modern jury that can be explained only as historical survivals, which are out of place in modern society, or has the jury been so adapted that it is a truly modern institution?

Again, should you assume that your examiner is an ignoramus and explain everything to him, or can you assume that he is a lawyer so that a hint is sufficient?

The answer lies somewhere between these two extremes. On the one hand, the examiner wants to be told *nothing* that is irrelevant to the question. On the other hand, he is suspicious of nutshell knowledge and footnote knowledge, and he wants as full an explanation of everything that *is* relevant as is possible in the time allowed. More specifically, the following rules may be laid down.

(a) If a legal concept is mentioned in the question, do not attempt a full explanation of it unless explanation is requested or necessitated by the question. For instance, on a question involving the law of wagers, there is generally no need to discuss what is a wager. Had the examiner wanted such a discussion he would have asked for it in a separate part of the question. On the other hand, a question in the form of a quotation with a request for discussion normally requires an explanation of everything in the quotation. Thus the question—

"The use of impeachment at law as a method of control of the Executive by the Commons has been replaced by the convention of ministerial responsibility to Parliament." Comment.

—demands a detailed explanation of impeachment as well as of the convention of ministerial responsibility and of the reasons why the second replaced the first.

(b) If the legal concept is not mentioned in the question but is first introduced by the candidate in his answer, it should be explained. Take, for instance, the question: "When will the right to avoid a voidable contract be lost?" It is not enough, in the course of answering this question, to mention that the right will be lost if *restitutio in integrum* ceases to be possible. You must not assume that the examiner knows what *restitutio in integrum* means. Tell him what it means, and when such *restitutio* ceases to be possible.

GETTING AT THE POINT

Before unmuzzling your wisdom on any question, ponder the question carefully. Very often the examiner will have worded it in a particular way in order to enable you to show a little originality of treatment. Take, for example, the following question in criminal law.

Discuss the decision in *R*. v. *Dudley and Stephens* from the standpoint of the purposes of criminal punishment.

This is not simply a question on the decision in *R*. v. *Dudley and Stephens*, as most students seem to think, nor even is it simply a question on the defence of necessity in general. It is a question, primarily, on the purposes of criminal punishment. You are requested to set out the different theories of the purposes of criminal punishment (general and particular deterrence, incapacitation, reformation, ethical retribution) and to consider whether any of these theories can be used to support the conviction in *R*. v. *Dudley and Stephens*.

Another "angle" question, this time from constitutional law:

What parallels may be drawn between royal prerogative and parliamentary privilege? Examine, in particular, the attitude of the court in questions concerning (a) their exercise, and (b) their extent.

I have marked hundreds of scripts in which the answer offered to this question was a formless mass of cases and propositions concerning prerogative and privilege. These candidates simply vomited over the page everything they knew upon the two topics; they made no attempt to bring their knowledge into relation with the question, and did not even divide off their answer by the (a) and (b) of the question. The following is a skeleton of the answer that an examiner wants. It should be within the competence of everyone of moderate ability who has worked properly and who directs his mind to what he is being asked.

Prerogative and privilege are somewhat similar in definition. Prerogative may be defined as the exceptional position of the king at common law. Privilege is the exceptional position of the two Houses of

Parliament and of their members at common law *and by statute*. There is, of course, a difference of content between prerogative and privilege.

Turning to (a) in the question, the traditional rule is that the court will *not* inquire into the *mode of user* of an undoubted prerogative or privilege. [Demonstration of this by decided or hypothetical cases.] Some recent developments suggest that the exercise, of the prerogative can sometimes be questioned. [Demonstration[4].]

As to (b), the rule is that the court *will* inquire into the *limits* of both prerogative and privilege. [Similar demonstration of this.]

Both prerogative and privilege are subject to statute. [Demonstration.]

Some more examples. Here is a question of the "with particular reference" type.

> Discuss the proposals for devolution of powers to Scotland and Wales, with particular reference to relations between the proposed Scottish and Welsh institutions and the Government and Parliament of the United Kingdom.

When answering this, address yourself to the second limb, not the first. The examiner does not want a discussion of the proposals in all their details, but wants only a discussion of the relations between the new institutions and the central Government and Parliament. Perhaps the question is not very happily worded, but it is a safe rule that if you are asked for a particular reference you can confine yourself to that.

> "The legal sovereignty of Parliament has not been affected by the European Communities Act." Discuss.

This does not invite a discussion of the basic principles of sovereignty; still less is it an invitation to write a general essay on Parliamentary sovereignty. It is a question on the consequences of the Act.

It may seem unnecessary to add: if given a choice, do not attempt to answer a question that you do not understand (unless, of course, your plight is such that there is no other you can do instead). This may seem obvious advice, but it is often ignored. The following, taken from a constitutional-law paper, is a good example of the "wrapped-up" question.

> "Much of the structure of the Constitution is now mere form; it is tolerated only because in practice its form is no indication of the way it functions."
> Comment.

[4] See H. W. R. Wade, *Administrative Law,* 4th ed. 335–336.

What does this question mean? If it conveys no clear meaning to you, avoid it. For if you attempt to answer it and miss the point, the examiner may not be able to give you any marks, because you will not have answered his question. Actually the question is on our old friends, the conventions of the constitution. It is an invitation to enumerate the conventions and to contrast them with the law. Once the meaning is penetrated, the writing of the answer is easy.

Often the answer to a fearsome-looking question can be divined by a little patient thought. Here is another specimen from constitutional law.

What is the constitutional importance of the power to dissolve Parliament?

Very probably you have never given a moment's thought to this question. But that does not mean that you must stand mute to it. Just ponder for a moment. Probably you know that, under the Parliament Act, Parliament lasts for five years unless sooner dissolved by the Crown, and that the Crown acts on the advice of the Government of the day. We are asked to state the constitutional importance of this power possessed by the Government. Very well: to find the importance of x, the obvious thing to do is to consider what would happen if x were not present. Let us consider what would happen if the power to dissolve did not exist. Clearly Parliament would last its full five years and the Government could not bring it to a premature end. One result would be that the Government could not time a general election to its own advantage, going to the country at the moment when it feels most popular; so Governments might change more often. More important would be the effect on private members. Suppose that within the five-year term the Government were defeated in the Commons on a topic so important that it regarded it as a matter of confidence in itself. As things are the Government has the choice of either (a) resigning or (b) advising a dissolution—*i.e.* going to the country. If there were no power to dissolve it could only resign, and a new Government would have to be formed from the ranks of the existing House of Commons. What would be the consequence of that? A moment's reflection will show that it would make private members more independent. Government back-benchers do not like elections; they prefer a quiet life. It is the fear of an election that at present prevents them in many instances from disobeying their party whip. If they knew for certain that a vote of censure could not result in a general election, but would simply bring about a reshuffle in the Government, their conduct would become more robust. Governments would have to give way more often to the opinions of back-benchers, and not force every measure through as a matter of confidence. But it might occasionally happen that, rather than give way, the Government might prefer to reconstruct itself as a Coalition Government with the support of some middle-of-the-road members of the Opposition. This might cause a fragmentation of the present essentially two-party system, though in time our electoral system would probably cause the re-emergence of two opposing parties.

If you happen to know that it is the Prime Minister personally who advises the Queen to dissolve Parliament, you will realise that this gives him the whip hand over other members of the Cabinet—who fear the cataclysm of an untimely election as much as back-benchers do. Without power to dissolve Parliament, the Prime Minister could only resign, probably to be replaced by a rival within his own party. So we should have more changes of leadership. Is it too imaginative to suppose that all these consequences would follow an abolition of the power to dissolve? If they would, we have demonstrated the importance of the power. It is the existence of the power that ensures the supremacy of the Cabinet and of the Prime Minister within the Cabinet. Whether they are *too* supreme is another question.

CRITICISM

When the question quotes a statement and asks for a discussion of it, do not be afraid to criticise the statement if you think it is open to criticism. As often as not the examiner will have disagreed with the statement himself; that is why he thought of setting it.

THE USE OF FORENSIC MANNERISMS

It was said in the last chapter that doubtful law should not be represented as if it were well established. Conversely, to state the law as doubtful when it is not doubtful will also be penalised in marks. Excessive caution is therefore as much to be avoided as excessive dogmatism. This may seem obvious, but I have known students repeatedly use the phrase "I respectfully submit" before some trite proposition or other, purely out of affectation. Even words like "seemingly" or "probably" are out of place if the law is clear.

Strictly, a submission ("I submit that ...") is an argument advanced in court. Counsel will use deferential language in court, particularly in respect of a decision that he submits was mistaken; the worse the error, the deeper will be the respect that he expresses for the judges he is criticising. He will venture to suggest, with the greatest possible respect to Mr. Justice Blank, that his Lordship perhaps did not intend his words to be understood in their widest acceptation. Or counsel may suggest, again with the very greatest respect, that a certain decision may perhaps be reconsidered if the point arises again before a court having power to overrule it; meanwhile, it can be distinguished on the facts before the present court.[5] Counsel will, in the time-honoured phrase, "wrap it up." Similarly, a court that feels impelled to depart from its predecessor's decision will do so not only "with the deepest respect" but "with great regret." These punctilios, which help to moderate tempers and maintain the dignity of the courts, are admirable; but legal writings need not be encumbered in this way.

Some writers express humility in a particularly strange way: when they wish to express an opinion but feel that the first person singular is too assertive, they use the plural ("we submit"). It is not proposed to discuss the aesthetics of this usage for the text writer[6]; all that I wish to say is that it should not be copied by the student, for in his mouth it sounds too grandiloquent. Naturally, one desires to suppress the personal element so far as possible, but if one has an opinion to express there is nothing to offend anybody in a straightforward "in my opinion." Alternatively, expressions like "it is thought that" or "there are good grounds

---

[5] In *Broome* v. *Cassell & Co.* [1972] A.C. 1027 a decision in the House of Lords was characterised by the Court of Appeal as being "unworkable" and as having been rendered *per incuriam*; on appeal, the House waxed indignant, but accepted that the Court of Appeal might properly have suggested that the precedent might be reconsidered by the House.

[6] But I cannot forbear to record the observation that the use of "we" should be confined to kings, editors and women in the family way.

for saying that" or "it follows from the authorities that" can be used.

THE ARRANGEMENT AND WORDING OF THE ANSWER

Try to make your answer attractive. Examiners are human beings, and they are easily bored. If a question is capable of being answered in a sentence, answer it immediately in that sentence and proceed to explanation afterwards. Within limits, it is permissible (and often desirable) to divide up the answer into numbered "points," with subheadings underlined. This both saves your time and enables the examiner to see without effort how you have treated the subject. But the process of subdivision should not be pushed too far. An answer that is excessively divided and subdivided gives an unpleasant impression that the candidate has simply learned a crambook or correspondence course by heart.

Lecturers and text writers often indulge in what R. L. Stevenson called "a little judicious levity." The student, who usually cannot distinguish between the judicious and the injudicious sorts, should avoid levity altogether. He should likewise shun all colloquialisms and colloquial abbreviations ("it's," "isn't," etc.). In short, the student should write his script upon the model of a counsel's opinion or judge's judgment, with gravity and decorum.

A few remarks may be made about citing authorities. Never quote the textbook for an established principle of law. A sentence like "Every simple contract needs consideration to support it, as Treitel points out," is infantile. Textbooks should be quoted only if they express an individual opinion, and the lecturer (*qua* lecturer) not at all. When quoting authors, if the author is dead he may be referred to by his surname only, but if he is still with us it is polite to give him a handle—Sir or Prof. or Dr. or Mr. As regards judges the customary J., etc., should be used irrespective of whether they are alive or dead.

If you cross out some words and subsequently wish to restore them, the accepted way of doing it is to put dots underneath the words so deleted and to write "*stet*"[7] in the margin.

The commonest grammatical error (if it is an error) is the split

---

[7] "Let it stand."

infinitive. Fowler divided the English-speaking world into (1) those who neither know nor care what a split infinitive is; (2) those who do not know, but care very much; (3) those who know and condemn; (4) those who know and approve; and (5) those who know and distinguish. Most examinees belong to the first class, most examiners to the third. Whatever the merits of the dispute, the safe course for the student, as for every writer who does not wish to risk offending the susceptibilities of his readers, is to avoid splitting infinitives. A split infinitive occurs when a word (usually an adverb) is placed between the word "to" and a following verb, as in "to really understand." On grammar and style in general, Fowler's *Dictionary of Modern English Usage* is an invaluable guide; a more recent competitor is Eric Partridge's *Usage and Abusage*. Other useful works are H. W. and F. G. Fowler's *The King's English,* and *Good English* by G. H. Vallins.

Lastly, a word on handwriting and orthography. Some people write atrociously. If you feel apprehensive on this, give a page of your notes to a friend and ask him to tell you which letters or words in your handwriting gave him difficulty in reading. Make a special effort to improve them.

Some people cannot spell and do not care about it. This may be all very well for those who have no ambitions that involve writing. But if you want to make a good impression on examiners, prospective employers or clients, good spelling is a necessity. Test yourself with the following passage, which contains misspelt words taken from examination scripts. Some of the words are correctly spelt, others incorrectly. Pick out the words that you think are misspelt and write your own version. Compare your effort with the key at the end of this chapter.

"The Homocide Act does not effect this problem, for the Act has not superceded the common law on the point. The question that ocurrs here is whether responsibility is deminished because there is a likelyhood that the provokation would have lead a reasonable man to loose his self-control and inflict this grievous harm. The correct answer in cases of this catagory is always difficult to gauge. An analagus case is *Brown,* where something like these facts occured. The acussed alledged that he could not forsee the harm he would do, and proceeded to argue that since he acted inavertently, he did not committ the offence. The prosecution tried to rebutt this defence by offering evidence of an admission by the accused. There was a legal arguement on this, and the confession was ajudged to be admissable. The defendent appealed, argueing that when he made his statement he had been mislead, but the judgment of the court was against him. On the principle question in the case, the concensus of the judges was that the authorities against the existance of the defence were irresistable, but perhaps this payed too little regard to the paralell rule for the priviledge of self-defence. I beleive it would be indefensable to assert that the court leant it's authority to the test of reasonableness. In any case, it is permissable to observe that one cannot regard the same problem as occuring here. As to the wife, she is now treated seperately from her husband, and her responsability is independant of his. Her ommission to help the victim definately does not mean that she abetts the crime, or is an accessary to it. In the absense of other facts, she is not guilty."

The rule for verbs ending in the sound -*er*, such as *offer, prefer, occur*, is to double the *r* for the -*ed* and -*ing* endings if the accent is on the -*er* syllable, but not otherwise. Thus *prefer, occur, transfer*, make *preferred, preferring, occurred, occurring, transferred, transferring*, but *offer* makes *offered, offering*.

The spelling of words derived from *appeal* is confusing. Whereas *appellant* and *appellate* have two *l*s, *appealed, appealing* are like *sealed, sealing, peeled, peeling*, and have only one.

The "seed" words are also troublesome. Some are spelt "cede," as in *accede, concede, precede, intercede, recede*. Others are spelt "ceed": *exceed, proceed, succeed*. So you must write *preceding, proceeding*; yet *procedure* is so spelt. *Supersede* is exceptional, being derived not from *cedere* but from *sedere*, and means to "sit upon"; remember this, and you will remember the spelling.

To express the sound *ee*, the rule is: *i* before *e*, except after *c*. So: *achieve, believe, grievous*; but *deceive, receive*.

The word *foresee* takes an *e* in the middle, but you can write either *forgo* or *forego*. *Judgment* is spelt correctly in the above test, but an alternative spelling is *judgement*. The rule generally followed in dictionaries is that mute *e* is dropped before suffixes beginning with a vowel (*e.g. deplorable, desirable, likable, movable, notably, ratable, sizable, unusable, milage, suing*), but not before suffixes beginning with a consonant (*statement*). Statutes do not altogether follow the former rule: "rateable value" is an established statutory spelling. Mute *e* is generally retained after soft *c* or *g* (*e.g. unenforceable, changeable*); so *judgement* should really be the preferred spelling.

The adjectives *dependent* and *independent* take an *e* in the final syllable, but the noun *dependant* (meaning one who is dependent on another for his bread and butter) takes an *a*. The difference of spelling in the endings of *appellant, respondent*, derives from Latin.

Note that *criteria, data* and *dicta* are plural words: the singulars are *criterion, datum* and *dictum*. Say "this dictum," not "this dicta." Treating *data* as singular (as people are coming to do) makes it difficult to speak clearly of "this particular datum" as opposed to "the rest of the data."

If the test has convinced you that you are weak on spelling, a useful remedial book is the *Pergamon Dictionary of Perfect Spelling*, by Christine Maxwell. This gives common misspellings with the correct form.

Key to spelling test. Homicide affect superseded occurs diminished likelihood provocation led lose grievous category ["gauge" is correct] analogous occurred accused alleged foresee ["proceeded" is correct] inadvertently commit rebut offering argument adjudged admissible defendant ["appealed" is correct] arguing misled principal consensus existence irresistible paid parallel privilege believe indefensible lent its permissible occurring separately responsibility independent omission definitely abets accessory absence.

CHAPTER 10

IN THE EXAMINATION ROOM

> Examinations are formidable even to the best prepared; for the greatest fool may ask more than the wisest man can answer.
>
> —C. C. Colton, *Lacon*.

BEFORE starting to write, read through the whole of the examination paper and jot down in the margin the names of plaintiffs in any relevant cases you remember, the dates of statutes and any other details that are likely to elude you when you come to write out the question. You thus give your memory two chances of recalling the elusive details. Also, if during the examination you think of any fresh authorities that you do not propose to incorporate at once in your script, make a similar note of them on your question paper. Some candidates leave the examination room complaining that at one stage they remembered a case, but later forgot to cite it. The practice above suggested should obviate this.

The most important general piece of advice on examinations is that every question in the paper that the student is expected to and can answer should be answered. He should not spend all his time on a few only of the questions. There is nothing more tedious for the teacher than to hear one of his best students saying, after the examination: "Oh, I did very well, but I only had time to answer half the paper." In nearly all examinations the scripts are not judged simply on the questions that the student has answered, where he has not answered all he was expected to answer. On the contrary, the total possible marks are divided equally among all the questions, and no answer can earn more than the appropriate marks for that question. The result is that a student may have answered half the paper in a manner worthy of a Law Lord, and yet obtain a third class because he has not answered the other half. Another point to be remembered in this connection is that an examiner is much more willing to give the first 50 per cent of marks on a question than the second 50 per cent, and full marks are practically never given. A candidate may, therefore, get 50 per cent on the whole paper if he answers all the questions moderately well, whereas he certainly will not get 50 per cent if he answers half the questions almost perfectly. For the good student, therefore, there is nothing more important in examination technique than dividing up his time as equally as may be between all the questions.

The same remark applies to questions containing two or more distinct parts. Here the examiner will probably have divided up the possible marks in his mind among the component parts, and an answer to one part, be it ever so brilliant, can earn only the appropriate total for that part. It is, therefore, most important to search for all the possible angles to a question, and this involves reading the question with meticulous care.

THE CHOICE OF QUESTIONS

All law examinations give a certain choice of questions.

Sometimes questions of enormous width are found in the paper. They are meant for the pass man. If a first class student attempts them, he will usually find that the answer required is so long that it will throw his whole script out of balance.

Where a choice is given between problems and book-work questions, there are two reasons why the better candidate should prefer the problems. First, they are usually shorter to answer, and so save time. Secondly, an examiner tends to be grudging in his marks for book-work questions, which he knows do not require much intelligence in the answering. A good answer to a problem, on the other hand, at once evokes his admiration.

There is, it is true, a certain danger in problems, for if the point of the problem is completely missed the result may be catastrophe. But a good student should be able to sense whether he is getting the point of the problem or not. If the problem to his eyes appears "pointless," he had better exercise his choice elsewhere in the paper.

Perhaps I should add a corrective to the foregoing paragraph. I said that if the point of a problem is completely missed the result may be catastrophe. This is true, but on the other hand it must be said that to give the wrong answer to a problem is not necessarily to miss the point of it. If the point is seen and well argued, the fact that the examiner does not agree with your conclusion will not seriously affect your marks. In legal matters there is always a certain room for difference of opinion, and even though there be positive authority against your view, the examiner is anxious not so much to test the details of your knowledge as to assess your ability to argue in a lawyer-like way. A safe course to adopt if in any doubt is to present the argument for both sides—to turn yourself successively into counsel for the plaintiff (prosecutor), counsel for the defendant, and finally the judge. If then the examiner disagrees with your judgment, it will hardly matter because you will have presented (even though you have also rejected) the argument for his point of view. Incidentally, you will have shown your ability to accept a brief on either side, or even to be promoted to the Bench.

THE PRESSURE OF TIME

Abbreviations of technical words and expressions should be used only very sparingly in an examination. If, however, you find that time has run short for the last answer, the best course is to reduce the answer to bare note form, using as many key headings as possible and abbreviating freely. You may head such an answer with the words: "(In note form)." This course should be adopted only in case of absolute necessity, and you should be able to plan out your time so that it is not necessary.

It is no use writing "unfinished" at the bottom of your answer. Some candidates send in meagre scripts in which every answer is carefully labelled "no time to finish." Let me assure them that the phrase has no mark-getting capacity whatever. There is all the difference between an *incomplete* answer labelled "no time to finish"—when marks can be given only for what is written down—and a *complete* though condensed answer labelled "in note form"—when the examiner may of his charity overlook defects of style, excessive abbreviation and lack of full detail.

The legitimate way to save time in an examination is normally not by extensive abbreviation but by omitting windy phrases, such as "first it is necessary to consider whether." Long before the examination the student should have practised and perfected a clear, incisive style in which every word is made to count.

SELF-CONTRADICTION

There is a story of a party of Americans who stood by the Porters' Lodge at King's College, Cambridge. One of them pointed north and said: "That's the chapel." They turned round and another pointed south. "No, that's the chapel." "No," said a third, pointing west, "that's the chapel." "Anyway," they said, as they turned to go, "we've seen the chapel." Many examination scripts are guided by the same philosophy. The candidate will start with one version of the law and then gradually veer round to a contradictory version—thus making sure that the right rule is there somewhere, even though he cannot pick it out. Perhaps he hopes by this means to get the best of both worlds; actually, of course, he gets the worst. If you find yourself changing your mind in the course of an answer, either cross out what you have written and start afresh, or, if there is no time for that, say frankly that you have changed your mind. You must show not only that you have seen the chapel, but that you can identify it.

CHAPTER 11

MOOTS AND MOCK TRIALS

"In my youth," said his father, "I took to the law,
And argued each case with my wife;
And the muscular strength which it gave to my jaw
Has lasted the rest of my life."

—Lewis Carroll, *Alice in Wonderland.*

MOOTS

MUCH stress is laid by educationalists on literacy and numeracy, but we hear little about the importance of being articulate. Footballers practise passing and shooting; pianists, singers and clowns also practise assiduously. Why is it supposed that speaking comes naturally and needs no effort or concentration? Fluency and clear enunciation are particularly important for the lawyer, when our forensic practice is largely oral.

Taking part in moots will help you in these respects, and also give you experience in the art of persuasion, and of putting a case succinctly and intelligibly. Moots are legal problems in the form of imaginary cases, which are argued by two student "counsel" (a leader and a junior) on each side, with a "bench" of three "judges" (or perhaps only one) representing the Court of Appeal. The arrangement of the moots is usually the responsibility of the students' law society,[1] though a law teacher or practising lawyer can usually be persuaded to set the moot and preside on the "bench." If no one else is arranging them, organise one yourself. Mooting not only gives you practice in court procedure but helps to develop the aplomb that every advocate should possess.

Counsel should notify opposing counsel of the main points and of all the authorities on which they rely. (To exchange authorities

---

[1] Moots are held by students' law societies in the universities and Inns of Court, by the Law Society (*i.e.* the official one) at its Hall in Chancery Lane, and by some provincial Law Societies.

before the hearing is a practice of the profession.) The Master of Moots or other organiser should also be informed of the authorities to be cited, in order that he may arrange for such reports or case books as are available to be brought to the court-room.

Since the moot is attended by an audience it is important to confine the proceedings to a reasonable length. Between half an hour and 40 minutes for each side (to be divided between leader and junior as they think fit) is enough time. The appellant has a right of reply, and it is therefore a good plan to "sandwich" the two counsel for the respondent (or Crown) between the two for the appellant. The order of speaking is then: leading counsel for the appellant; leading and junior counsel for the respondent; junior counsel for the appellant.

After counsel have concluded their arguments the presiding judge may invite members of the audience to express their opinions upon the legal problem as *amici curiae*. The members of the court then confer, and may deliver their judgments in turn. If there are two student members on the bench they may be asked to deliver their judgments before the senior member. (My own opinion is that the moot is most efficiently conducted if the senior member alone gives the judgment of the court.) After the judgment or judgments the opinion of the audience may, if desired, be tested by a vote.

Both counsel and judges follow the punctilios of court procedure and conduct, and a few words may be said on these. Counsel rise to their feet when addressing or being addressed by the court. If your opponent interrupts you with a lengthy submission, resume your seat while he is speaking. If you have occasion to refer to your colleague he is your "learned junior" or "learned leader," as the case may be, and your opponent is "my learned friend," or occasionally, informally, "my friend" (*not* "the opposition"!). "It has been argued on the other side that" is permissible.

Do not interrupt anyone, ever, if this can be avoided. If you must interrupt, do so as gently and courteously as possible.

Beginners sometimes get confused between the two polite ways of addressing a judge—"My Lord" and "Your Lordship." The difference is that "My Lord" is the mode of addressing a judge in the vocative case, while "Your Lordship" is the mode of referring to the judge in the course of a sentence, *i.e.* as a polite substitute for "you."[2] The formula for opening a case is: "May it please your Lordship(s), I am appearing with Mr. —— for the plaintiff (prosecution) (appellant), and my learned friends Mr. —— and Mr. —— are for the defendant (respondent) (Crown). The claim (charge) is . . ." Other counsel will begin by saying: "May it please your Lordship(s)." The formula for submitting to a ruling of the judge during the case is: "If your Lordship pleases." Female judges are addressed as "my Lady," "your Ladyship."[3]

In referring to the Queen as prosecutor in the course of a case one speaks not of "the Queen" but "the Crown."

The most common breach of etiquette committed by the enthusiastic beginner when arguing a moot case is the expression of a personal opinion on the merits of his case. Counsel may "submit" and "suggest" as strongly as he likes, and he may state propositions of law and fact, but he should not express his own belief or opinion. It is disrespectful to the Bench to say: "My Lords, in my opinion the law is so-and-so," still more to say: "My Lords, in my opinion this man is innocent." Questions of law and fact are for the court to decide, not counsel; counsel's function is simply to argue.

Begin your address to the court by stating quite briefly what you wish to show. Speak slowly and get as soon as possible to the core of your case. Your time is much more limited than it would be in a real case, and you cannot afford to waste it; on the other hand, it is no use gabbling what you have to say, for then it will not be understood. Establish eye contact with the judge, and do not read out your argument if you can possibly avoid it.

A frequent fault is to read out passages from textbooks as though they represented the last word on the law. Although textbooks and treatises are not taboo in court, they should be used

---

[2] As in Richard Bethell's famous piece of rudeness to the judge who, after hearing the argument, said he would reserve the point in order to turn it over in his mind—"May it please your Lordship to turn it over in what your Lordship is pleased to call your Lordship's mind?" (It is said that the nearest approach Bethell ever made to politeness was in his reply to a judge who corrected him: "Your Lordship is quite right, and I am quite wrong—as your Lordship usually is.")

[3] For the modes of address of circuit judges, deputy circuit judges, and recorders, see below, p. 171.

Moots   145

sparingly and cautiously. What the judge wants to hear are the
relevant cases (and, of course, statutes), not the views of writers. If
a writer is quoted, the case that he cites in support of his opinion
should be read out and referred to. Read slowly, with proper
periods and emphasis. You want what you read to sink into the
judges' minds.

There used to be a rule that a writer was not an "authority"
until he had gone the way of all flesh[4]. Whereas dead authors
could be cited in court without apology, living ones could be cited
only by the subterfuge of "adopting" what they said as part of
counsel's argument. Nowadays, however, living authors are cited
in the ordinary way. If you meet a judge who cavils at this, you can
usually pacify him by stating that you are not treating the writer as
an authority but are merely adopting the writer's words as part of
your argument. It is always desirable, at least in the superior
courts,[5] to refer the court to the cases cited by the writer for his
propositions.

If possible, the reports of cases cited should be produced at the
moot. If the reports are not available, case books should be used
for the cases contained in them. Case books should also be
available for the use of the bench. When citing cases the reference
should always be given; and it should be pronounced in full, not in
abbreviated form.[6] For instance, [1944] A.C. 200 is: "reported in
the Appeal Cases for 1944 at page two hundred"; and 2 B. & Ald.

---

[4] Hence when Salmond died it was said that he had at last beaten his
friendly opponent Pollock (who was then still with us); for Salmond
had become an authority.
   During Pollock's lifetime Lord Wright remarked in one of his
judgments:
   "The matter is very clearly stated in a work, fortunately not a work of
authority, but to which we are all as lawyers indebted, Sir Frederick
Pollock's *Law of Torts*" (*Nicholls* v. *Ely Beet Sugar Factory Ltd.* [1936]
Ch. at 349). The printer of the case in the Law Times Reports
misunderstood the subtle compliment and turned "fortunately" into
"unfortunately" (154 L.T. at 533).
[5] In magistrates' courts a treatise may be used as an authority in itself:
Boys v. *Blenkinsop* [1968] Crim.L.R. 513.
[6] There is an old tale of a junior who cited the Law Reports to Lord Esher
M.R. as "2 Q.B.D." "That is not the way you should address us," said
Lord Esher. The learned counsel protested that he merely meant to use
the brief and ordinary formula for the second volume of the Queen's
Bench Division Reports. "I might as well," retorted his Lordship "say
to you, 'U.B.D.'"

6 is: "in the second volume of Barnewall and Alderson's Reports
at page six." The facts of cases should be read, unless the case is
relied upon only for an *obiter dictum*. Usually it is sufficient to
read the headnote and the passage you want; but if the case is an
important part of your argument you would, in court, read what
you consider the essential facts in full. Refer to judges by their full
title (see pp. 60–61).

Citing cases, though usually a necessary part of the moot, tends
to take a long time and to be boring for the audience. Try,
therefore, to pick out the cases that are most apt for your
argument, and rely on them. In professional practice it is the duty
of the advocate to call the attention of the court to all decisions
that are in any way against the submissions he makes; but this
may not be possible in moot conditions. It is not a bad plan to
have a positive rule that not more than, say, six cases shall be cited
on each side. The object of a moot is to provide practice in
developing an argument, and while the reading out of decided
cases is often the necessary foundation of an argument, it should
not constitute the whole of it. Remember that your primary object
as an advocate is to persuade: the citing of cases is only a means to
this end.[7]

Just as you should not overload your argument with cases, you
should not load it with too many separate points of law. "Mooty"
as the case may be, it is unlikely that there are many *good* points to
be made for your side. All first-class advocates concentrate on
what they consider to be their good points; they do not run the

---

[7] The observation of Lord Greene on this matter is worth quoting. If one
compares, he says, the student arguing a moot case with the
experienced practising lawyer arguing in court, "it will be found (at
least that is my own experience) that the student builds up his argument
on authorities which he refers to in great profusion, whereas the
experienced advocate builds up his argument out of his instinct for legal
principle and only uses his authorities to substantiate his points or to
convince a judge who declines to accept a proposition unless it is
supported by authority. Some of the best legal arguments which I have
heard on points of difficulty and complication have been conducted
with surprising economy of reference to authority. And the reason is
that the advocate's instinct for law and its principles has enabled him to
present in an attractive and logical way an argument which convinces
by its own inherent strength and does not require at every point to be
propped up by references to authority": [1936] J.S.P.T.L. 12.

risk of alienating the judge's affections by producing obviously bad ones.

Consider the timing of your moot. Half an hour is the minimum for each side; so if the moot starts at 8.30 p.m., and if three judges each take ten minutes to give judgment, it is 10 p.m. even if not a minute has been lost—and this does not allow time for the presiding judge to invite the audience to comment before judgment is given. It would be much better to hold the moot, say, between 2 and 5 p.m. The presence of an audience is relatively unimportant. Far better have many moots with a small or even no audience than one moot with a large audience.

We cannot improve the beauty of our countenances, but almost all of us can, if we wish, add to the attractiveness of our speech. For all who have to speak regularly, money is well spent on lessons in elocution; but some blemishes can be cured by self-help. Many experienced speakers mar their conversations as well as their orations with a profusion of ums and ers which distract attention. Other bad habits are using "I mean" and "you know." The simplest way to cure these defects—which probably exist in your own speech, although you are unaware of them— is to tape-record your conversation with some other person on a serious subject in which you are both interested, and then listen to it critically. Probably you will be surprised at the imperfections in your own expression. Only by means of a tape-recorder can you hear yourself as others hear you. Try to eliminate all the "filled pauses" in your speech: moments of silence are far more impressive than meaningless noises.

Poor, slurred speech is another common defect. Good diction can be heard on radio and TV, so that no one who wishes to improve himself need lack exemplars; yet many people are content to mumble and fumble their words. If your speech suffers from this defect, your teachers will not tell you of it. They have not the time to teach elocution, and are perhaps afraid to embarrass you, and by criticising your speech to add to your shyness in discussion. (They may themselves have fallen victims to the cult of mediocrity in articulation, as though slovenly speech is a way of expressing radical views.) Lawyers, above almost all others, should be able to express themselves clearly and pleasantly. Are you opening your mouth? No one can speak clearly through half opened lips. Do you need to turn your volume control up? Quite a number of the people you speak to will be getting on in years and have lost their sharpness of hearing. Some people not only fail to speak up but talk with their hands wandering to cover their mouths.

Listen to that tape-recording again. Do you make distinct sounds for each of the vowels, or do you use pretty well one indeterminate noise for the whole lot? What I am aiming against is the indistinct mutter; it is not a question of local dialect, which is often charming. Your aim should be to speak as educated people you admire speak, clearly and without affectation. Record a good speaker on the radio, play back a sentence and then record your own utterance of the same sentence. Compare. Repeat the effort until you feel that your own speech is as clear as his—and, if possible, as musical! Do not be afraid to mouth your words. And speak deliberately, not fast.

SPEAKING IN PUBLIC

It is an excellent thing to take part in debates. Here are a few hints for speech-making of any kind.

Plan your speech under a number of points so that it has a definite structure. Write it out in full, reflect on it overnight and polish it the next day. Then summarise the main headings on a small card or cards about the size of a postcard. Include in the card any figures, quotations, names, key phrases or other material which you wish to state exactly. Read through your full speech several times, preferably aloud and preferably into a tape-recorder, but do not try to memorise it word for word. You will probably not succeed in being word-perfect, and there is danger in reciting a memorised speech either of appearing unnatural or of forgetting a complete section or even coming to a dead halt. If you play back a recording of the rehearsal, consider whether you spoke at the right pace, and particularly whether you made an impressive pause at the right moment.

When on your feet before the audience, have the outline card or cards in your hand and, with this aid, speak naturally in the way you have planned.

The commonest fault among inexperienced speakers (and even many experienced ones) is to speak too fast. All good advocates speak with great deliberation and force. Tell yourself before you begin that you are going to speak slowly, and keep reminding yourself to do so. Of course you must not be monotonous, and your matter should be good enough to stand deliberate presentation.

Stand up: don't sit on an upturned seat. Don't hide behind any furniture if you can help it, and don't fold your arms or fiddle with anything.[8] Look at the audience as you speak, and turn to different sections of it. You may use your hands to emphasise points—not in too exaggerated a way, but sufficiently to show that you are putting your whole being into it. If you make a joke, practise getting the timing right—and let the audience know that humour is about to enliven the proceedings by enjoying it yourself beforehand.

If you are nervous, console yourself with the thought that the initially nervous speaker often performs far better than the stolid chap with no nerves. And remember that the audience are on your side. They want to be engrossed by your speech; they want the occasion to be a success. They are not there to criticise you, unless you force the criticism on them.

Ask a friend to observe your performance and to report to you on it with ruthless candour. Ask him particularly whether you have any irritating mannerisms: scratching yourself, adjusting your tie, pulling your clothes, waving your arms unduly, or swaying hypnotically.

MOCK TRIALS

A mock trial differs from a moot in that it is a mock jury-trial, with jury and witnesses, not an argument on law. The proceedings may be somewhat humorous; witnesses may dress themselves up, and court and counsel wear robes (if procurable). The audience may consist of non-lawyers, who, of course, come simply to be entertained. Since the trial is unrehearsed, it requires a high standard of forensic ability on the part of the student "counsel"; and the proceedings should either be leavened by humour or present an intellectual problem of the "whodunit" type.

There are two ways in which the "case" may be got up. It may

---

[8] If you are sitting around a table in committee, on no account place your hand in front of your mouth when speaking. Don't even hold your chin!

have been enacted beforehand by the witnesses, so that they
testify to what they have actually witnessed; alternatively, the
organiser of the mock trial may simply have given to each witness
a statement of his evidence, which he is expected to remember.
The former method requires some effort, but it makes the case
more realistic when it comes to cross-examination, and it enables
the preliminary proceedings, including the interviewing of
witnesses and briefing of counsel, to be done by student
"solicitors." The actual trial is, of course, a valuable experience
for budding advocates who take part in it as counsel.

It is a good plan to set the scene of the case (*e.g.* the murder) in
some place known to the audience (*e.g.* the College or Law
School). Alternatively, the case can be modelled upon an actual
case in one of the Trials Series (below, p. 200). Try to depart from
your model trial just sufficiently to prevent counsel using the same
speeches and the same questions to witnesses. Keep the number of
witnesses down to five or six. See that the legal participants have
attended real trials in order to learn how things are done; the clerk
of the court in particular should know his job. If you are at all
doubtful about the success of the evening, do not advertise the
event outside your Law Society.

As another diversion from the serious business of moots, the
students' law society may like to try one evening the game of
"Alibi." The gathering divides into groups of four, each group
being composed of two prosecuting counsel and two defendants.
It is assumed that the two defendants have committed some crime
at a stated time—say between 10 and 11 p.m. last Wednesday—
and have set up an alibi. They go out of the room for not more
than ten minutes in order to prepare their story. They then return,
one at a time, for cross-examination by the prosecuting counsel.
Counsel's aim is to break down the alibi by asking unexpected
questions and so getting contradictory answers from the two
defendants. After the two cross-examinations, lasting perhaps ten
or fifteen minutes in all, the two counsel put their heads together
for a minute, and then one of them addresses the rest of the
gathering, who have acted as jury, and submits that the alibi has
been broken down because of this and that discrepancy. The jury
signify their verdict by a show of hands, the opinion of the
majority being taken.

A master of ceremonies is needed to dispatch successive pairs of defendants out of the room, in order to keep the game going continuously.

Would-be lawyers will find this game not at all a bad test of their powers of advocacy. No training for would-be defendants is intended.

A somewhat similar game is called "False Evidence." Three masked "defendants" are interrogated on their day-to-day lives by two counsel. One of these defendants has assumed a completely false name and occupation, and it is the jury's task to decide which. Each defendant must submit to counsel a week in advance a couple of hundred words summarising his life, and this enables counsel to prepare their questions. Each defendant calls a witness who has also submitted a statement with the facts of his or her life, particularly where that life crosses that of the defendant. In the case of the innocent parties they must have known each other for at least two years. The witness is not in court during the interrogation of the defendant, and counsel try to shake the evidence and establish discrepancies between the defendant and his witness. Each defendant and his witness are given a limited time—say fifteen minutes altogether—in the box. The judge sums up briefly to the jury, who consider and announce their verdict. The imposter then declares himself, and it is interesting to see if the judicial process has succeeded in ascertaining the truth of the matter. It may be mentioned that the written statements do not contain sufficiently specific information to enable counsel to identify who the person is. Two or three trials may be held on the same evening.

Yet another variant is "Third Degree." One member of the party is selected as the defendant: he is told the outline of an alibi defence and has to fill in the details impromptu under questioning. For example, he may be told that his alibi relates to a period between 2 and 5 p.m. last Thursday, when he left the refectory after lunch and took a train to a named neighbouring town and visited a friend in time for tea. The defendant on being told this alibi must immediately amplify it under questioning, and can be "gonged" for undue hesitation in answering or for any vagueness in answering (he must not say "I think so" or "That is probably what I would have done"). He can also be gonged for self-contradiction. The object of the rest of the company, who question him for fifteen minutes, is to establish a self-contradiction. Leading questions may be asked: for example, if the defendant says that he was not carrying a mackintosh, he can later be asked whether his host put his mackintosh on a peg in the hall or where else? If the defendant is gonged, or runs for the allotted time without mishap, another outline alibi can immediately be supplied to another volunteer defendant. A beauty of this game is that it can be played by two players only, and it may help you to bring out unsuspected ability as an implacable interrogator.

BIBLIOGRAPHY

For illustrations of moot cases, see *The Moot Book of Gray's Inn.*

Books on advocacy are referred to in Chap. 13 (p. 172). For the procedure at a mock trial, consult any book on criminal or civil procedure. "Counsel" should make themselves acquainted not only with this procedure but with the main rules of evidence—*e.g.* those relating to leading questions.

Chapter 12

LEGAL RESEARCH

> First there's the Bible
> And then the Koran,
> Odgers on Libel,
> Pope's Essay on Man.

> —Mostyn T. Piggott, *The Hundred Best Books*.

GEORGE III is reputed to have said that lawyers do not know much more law than other people, but they know better where to find it. This chapter is written to help the reader to a more intimate knowledge of his law library, and also to guide the first steps of the research worker.

Whatever you write, remember that one of the prime qualities of a lawyer is accuracy. All your quotations must be verbatim; all your citations must follow accepted forms; all your statutes must be checked to make sure that they have not been amended or repealed; and if there be any doubt, your cases must be checked to make sure that they have not been reversed, overruled, or questioned.

LOOKING UP PRACTICAL POINTS

The only type of legal research that most practising lawyers want to do is research into the law relating to a case that they have on hand. A convenient place in which to start looking is frequently Halsbury's *Laws of England*. First look up the main volume, and note the number of the paragraph printed in heavy type. Then turn up the current Supplement to find the most recent annotations. You cannot look up the Supplement directly.

Often Halsbury will give the answer without further trouble, but if further detail is needed it may be necessary to turn to a specialised treatise. The experienced practitioner carries in his head the names of the best works on the subjects with which he usually deals, and the sooner the student gets to know some of them the better. Consult Raistrick and Rees, *Lawyers' Law Books* (1977) with supplement. A useful selective bibliography is A. G. Chloros, *A Biographical Guide to the Law of the United Kingdom, the Channel Islands and the Isle of Man.* An American counterpart is *Law Books in Print,* ed. J. Myron Jacobstein and Meira G. Pimsleur, which covers books in English published throughout the world. Recent books can be found in the catalogues published by Butterworth and Sweet and Maxwell.

If the name of a case is roughly known but not its date or reference, it can be traced through the index volumes of the *English and Empire Digest,* the current edition of which deals with all cases up to 1952. Cases between 1952 and 1966 are covered in Continuation Volumes and Annual Supplements. The Table of Cases published in 1968 includes cases digested in Continuation Volumes A and B. If your case is not there, try the Table of Cases in Continuation Volume C, D etc. The most useful work of reference for recent cases is the *Current Law Consolidation,* 1947–1951, and the *Current Law Year Books* for 1952 and subsequent years. (The *Scottish Current Law Year Book* is the same as the English with the addition of Scottish cases). A separate volume called *Current Law Citator* indexes all the cases reported from 1947 to a recent date and all the cases, of whatever date, that have been judicially considered or affected by statute since 1947. A reference to the Case Citator shows immediately if a case has been digested, overruled, applied, considered, followed, referred to, or made the subject of an article in certain periodicals. The Consolidated Index to the All England Reports covers cases reported in that series since 1936. A Consolidated Index to the Law Reports and Weekly Law Reports has been published each year since 1953. If the case is before 1865 and is included in the English Reports, it can be found through the index volumes of the English Reports. If it is in the All England Law Reports Reprint of cases before 1935 it will be listed in the Index volume.

If the date of a modern case is known but not its name, the best place to look for it is in *Current Law.* It appears in monthly parts with cumulative Year Books and consolidation volumes, as explained above.

In consulting the indexes at the beginning of a volume of Law Reports, distinguish between the "Table of Cases Reported" and the "Cases Judicially Considered." The former alone indexes the cases reported in the volume. Between 1940 and 1949 the latter table was omitted. The "Table of Cases" in the Criminal Appeal Reports is a snare and delusion; the true table of cases is headed "Appellants and Applicants."

There are five ways of tracing whether a statute has been repealed or amended. (1) Turn up the statute in Halsbury's *Statutes,* and then check the same reference in the current Cumulative Supplement, which shows how it has been affected by later legislation; to bring this even more up to date, consult the current numbers of *Current Law.* (2) An alternative is to use the cumulative *Current Law Citator,* which is published annually; then bring it right up to date with *Current Law Statutes,* which is published, usually, in six or seven parts during the course of each year, containing the statutes passed in that year, with, in the Statute Citator, a table of the effect the statutes have on earlier legislation. These give only amendments and repeals since 1947 (the year when *Current Law* began), which is satisfactory if your main statute was passed after 1947, but otherwise not. (3) Yet another method is to use the official work called *Chronological Table of Statutes,* which is also published annually. This will show amendments and repeals up to the date of last publication; more recent changes are listed in an annual publication entitled *Annotations to the Acts.* (4) When the official *Statutes in Force* is further advanced in publication than it is at the time of writing, it will be the best method of establishing the current text of legislation. (5) A very convenient source for some statutes is the Local Government Library, which publishes statutes and statutory instruments on certain topics in loose-leaf form with annotations and indexes. The subjects covered are: Health and Safety at Work; Highways; Housing; Planning; Compulsory Purchase and Compensation; Public Health; and Road Traffic. There are also the *British Tax Encyclopedia,* the *Encyclopedia of Value Added Tax*; the *Industrial Relations Encyclopedia,* and the *Encyclopedia of European Community Law.* Criminal statutes can conveniently be consulted in Archbold or Stone.

It may be mentioned that the Statute Citator in *Current Law Statutes* includes statutory instruments issued under rule-making powers, cases decided on the construction of statutes, and legal literature dealing with statutes, as well as all statutes of any year that are affected by legislation during the years covered.

If a statutory instrument is wanted, it can generally best be looked up in Halsbury's *Statutory Instruments,* the service volume stating any changes that may have been made. However, Butterworths do not publish an annual volume of statutory instruments, so recent instruments are not included until they go into a re-issue of the encyclopedic volumes. Meanwhile, they must be consulted in the Stationery Office volumes. A useful *Table of Government Orders 1671–1976* (H.M.S.O.) indexes all order by subject-matter. When you know the statutory instrument or other order you are interested in, you can check its current standing (whether it has been repealed or replaced or is still in force) in the *Index of Government Orders*, which is arranged chronologically according to the numbers of the orders up to about 1972. For orders published since you must consult the monthly parts of the Statutory Instruments, which have indexes; there is no yearly noter-up.

If the question is one of common law, much assistance can be got from the *English and Empire Digest*. This digests practically every reported case, and is well arranged and well indexed. It also gives the subsequent history of the case—whether it has been approved, overruled, and so on. The Case Citator in the *Current Law Citator* similarly shows what has happened to every case in the period since 1947.

A valuable aid to the interpretation of legal expressions is *Words and Phrases Legally Defined*. This is a collection of words and phrases in statutes which have been interpreted by the judges, together with statutory definitions of terms and definitions advanced by legal writers. Another excellent work of the same type is Stroud's *Judicial Dictionary*.

Further information is given in Derek J. Way, *The Student's Guide to Law Libraries* (1967), and *Manual of Law Librarianship*, ed. Elizabeth M. Moys.

RESEARCH PROPER

The ordinary practitioner will not need to dig any deeper than this—apart, of course, from references to the statutes and law reports. I should, however, add a few words for the benefit of any student who wishes to research more deeply. For periodical literature, consult the *Index to Legal Periodicals* and *Index to Foreign Legal Periodicals,* published for the American Association of Law Libraries; there is also an *Index to Periodical Articles Relating to Law* which is supplementary to the *Index to Legal Periodicals.* A list of American and other periodicals in English libraries is published by the Institute of Advanced Legal Studies. See also W. A. Friend, *Anglo-American Legal Bibliographies* (1944).

The finding of an undated Command Paper may give trouble unless the following table is known. There are five series. From 1833 to 1869 they were numbered "1" to "4222." From 1870 to 1899 they were numbered "C.1" to "C.9550." From 1900 to 1918 they were numbered "Cd.1" to "Cd.9239." From 1919 to 1956 they were numbered "Cmd.1" to "Cmd.9889." The new series is numbered "Cmnd.1" consecutively.

There is a rather vexatious custom of referring to some reports of commissions and committees by the name of the chairman instead of by the proper title. A dictionary of these informal citations will be found in *Where to Look for Your Law,* which unfortunately has not been kept up to date.

Much useful work can be done by comparing legal development in the various common-law countries. Part II of the *Manual of Legal Citations,* referred to before, explains the mode of citation of Commonwealth material. Australian cases can be traced through the *Australian Digest,*[1] Canadian through the *Canadian Abridgement,* New Zealand through the *Abridgement of New Zealand Case Law.* There are various Irish Digests. The Institute of Advanced Legal Studies, 17 Russell Square, London, WC1B 5DR, publishes a Union List of Commonwealth legal literature in English libraries. See also Reynold Boult, *A Bibliography of Canadian Law* (1966), and Paul O'Higgins, *A Bibliography of Periodical Literature relating to Irish Law* (1966).

Turning to American material, the Middle Temple possesses an excellent collection of American reports, and a certain number of American textbooks. The libraries of the Inns of Court have a duplicated list showing which American reports are in which libraries. The Middle Temple has the American equivalent of Halsbury, the *Corpus Juris Secundum.* Copies of the American

---

[1] For Australian sources in general see Enid Campbell and Donald MacDougall, *Legal Research: Materials and Methods* (1967).

Restatement are fairly common. The Institute of Advanced Legal Studies, already mentioned, is also building up a library of American law. Useful guides to American law reports and digests are Hicks, *Materials and Methods of Legal Research* (2nd ed., 1942), and the work by Beardsley and Orman already cited. There are an *Annual Survey of American Law,* an *Annual Survey of Commonwealth Law,* and an *Annual Survey of South African Law.* Chambliss and Seidman have compiled a research bibliography called *Sociology of the Law* (1970); this is based largely on American materials.

The libraries mentioned above are, of course, private libraries, and non-members of the bodies to which they belong must obtain permission to use them. In addition the Libraries of the Commonwealth Relations Office, Downing Street, S.W.1, the Privy Council, Old County Hall, Spring Gardens, S.W.1, and the Colonial Office, Church House, Great Smith Street, S.W.1, possess some series of reports of other Commonwealth countries. Members of the public are permitted upon application to consult them.

Those reading French law may be helped by A. W. Dalrymple's *French-English Dictionary of Legal Words and Phrases* (2nd ed., 1948); there is also a companion English-French volume. Similar dictionaries for German have been compiled by Erdsiek, Dietl and Weil, and for Spanish by Louis A. Robb.

There is a *Directory of Law Libraries in the British Isles,* edited by Barbara Mangles (1977): those working in London may be helped by Irwin and Staveley, *The Libraries of London* (2nd ed., 1961).

If the reader's research carries him beyond familiar legal fields into a large general library, he will find E. J. Dingwall's *How to Use a Large Library* a useful guide. Much the most important of general works of reference is the *British Museum Subject Index,* which classifies books according to their subject-matter. Where a book is not in a library, the librarian may be willing to apply to the National Central Library for a copy on loan.

Three hints may be given on the preparation of the finished script. (1) Frequently the date of decision of a case is a year before the date by which it is cited in the Law Reports. It is customary to take the date of the volume of the Law Reports as the date of the case. (2) If the case is reported in the Law Reports it may be thought sufficient to cite only the Law Reports; but if it is not in the Law Reports all the main "collateral" reports should be cited in which the case appears. A list of references can be obtained from one of the Digests. (3) Useful advice on citations will be found in Part I of the *Manual of Legal Citations* published by the Institute of Advanced Legal Studies.

Those who are troubled by questions of style and grammar would be well advised to read *Complete Plain Words*, by Sir Ernest Gowers. A revised edition by Sir Bruce Fraser has been published by H.M.S.O. in elegant hardback at a very reasonable price.

CHAPTER 13

FROM LEARNING TO EARNING

No Wind makes for him that hath no intended port to sail unto.

—Montaigne.

MANY Arts graduates (and even Science graduates) now find it impossible to obtain a post that matches their training and ability, unless they are willing to teach. Law graduates are in a happier position, but the state of the market changes continually.

PRACTICE AT THE BAR

At the time of writing (1978) there are severe discouragements to new entrants for practice at the Bar. First, you will need (unless you are a "mature student") an approved degree (not necessarily a law degree, though that gives you the advantage of providing you with examination exemptions). Then you will have to pay fees, eat dinners and pass at least Part II of the Bar examinations. (If you have an approved degree but not in law, you will first need to study law for a year at the Polytechnic of Central London or the City University.) So far, it is only a matter of funds and conscientious work; and some financial assistance is available. After or shortly before taking your call, if you intend to practise, you will read in the chambers of a junior barrister. This is called pupillage, and arranging it may present a problem. But the end of pupillage is likely to be only the beginning of your real difficulty: "no room in the Inns." The practising barrister is a member of a set of chambers, who share expenses; one of these barristers, the head of chambers, appoints the clerk and secretaries and allocates seats (places) to new entrants.[1] Your pupil-master is unlikely to be

[1] By an ancient absurdity, the tenant of the (whole set of) chambers must be a member of the Inn to which the chambers belong. But form is one thing, reality another. The tenant need only be the nominal tenant, and neither the head of chambers nor any of the other members need be members of that Inn.

able to arrange for an offer of a seat (*i.e.* a room, or share of a room) to be made to you. The situation has arisen because of recent large recruitments to the Bar, and the natural reluctance of established practitioners to colonise new chambers. In London there is the traditional but constricting attachment of the Bar to the Temple and Lincoln's Inn. Consequently, there are over a hundred "floaters"—unhappy beginners who, having no local habitation, are gravely handicapped in building up a practice. They live in perpetual hope of persuading some head of chambers to take them in when a vacancy occurs; meanwhile, to confer with a client they can only occupy someone else's desk, by his good grace, when he is not using it. Women and non-whites are likely to experience particular difficulty.[2] You should think long and hard before deciding to join the unhappy throng.

The position in the provinces is better than in London. If you obtain pupillage in provincial chambers, and perform satisfactorily, you are likely to be offered a place. In London the position will improve slightly as new chambers are opened—by conversion from residences in the Temple, or in Gray's Inn, or outside the ancient purlieus of the law. But it is unlikely that this will keep pace with the flow of new entrants.

Then there is the question of finance. During the first six months of pupillage the fledgling barrister is not allowed to accept briefs. During the second six months he can, and may get a little work; but until at least a year after the end of pupillage he will probably have to live on his parents or spouse. In addition to his living there will be professional expenses, including rent of chambers, clerk's commission, secretarial assistance, travel etc. The sum remaining from his fees will be subject to further deductions for income tax, national insurance and national insurance self-employed tax. Fees take months or years to come in, and quite a proportion are never recovered. In specialist chambers the time that must elapse before making a living is longer.

---

[2] As to women, the Bow Group in evidence to the Royal Commission on Legal Services in 1977 said that many chambers limited the number of tenancies given to women, on the ground that women tend to have children and not to engage in full-time practice, and so cannot pay a full proportion of the rent. For the same reason they are not appreciated by the clerk, whose income depends directly on the income of members.

As to the volume of work available, crime is still a growth industry, and the constantly increasing complexity of many parts of the law inevitably creates a demand for skilled legal advice. The enlargement of the powers and pretensions of government gives administrative law great practical importance, while tax law creates continual problems for business and industry. However, legal work tends to rise and fall with the prosperity of the country: people avoid litigation in hard times. Owing to legal changes, young barristers can no longer earn easy money on undefended divorces, which are now done by solicitors. A good deal of personal injury litigation will disappear if State insurance is introduced as proposed by the Pearson Commission. The staple of common law practice is criminal legal aid, but fees are still paid mainly on 1971 guidelines, despite an increase of 126 per cent in the retail prices index. On the civil side, the Bar has lost by the gradual extension of county court jurisdiction (where solicitors have the right of audience); and the income limit for legal aid in civil cases has lagged well behind inflation, so that few people are now eligible for it. Also, inflation has adversely affected the fees allowable by taxing masters.

How does all this come out in actual figures? A survey of earnings in the tax year 1974–1975 made by the Bar for the purpose of its evidence to the Royal Commission on Legal Services showed that nearly half of the sample of barristers earned *less than* £5,000 before tax, even though the survey excluded the lowest earners. The average amount earned by juniors before tax was £5,600. Some, of course, did far better than this, but by the same token others did far worse. It seems likely that since then earnings have fallen relative to inflation. The Bar evidence just referred to came to the conclusion that there is now a surplus of barristers for the work available, a surplus that could become substantial if the rate of growth between 1971 and 1976 were to continue.

Having done my best to put you off the Bar, I must add that the public interest strongly requires that the profession should continue to attract a flow of top quality recruits. Great success at the Bar leads to a large income and the strong possibility of a judgeship. Many barristers who fail in practice, or who do not find it congenial, find employment in salaried posts, as will be explained later.

Let me assume that you would like to enter for practice at the Bar and are prepared to brave all difficulties. Have you the right qualities? For advocacy, obviously, the prime need is the ability to communicate by speech. Judges confess in private that there are counsel now practising whom they cannot understand. If you mumble or burble, give up all thought of advocacy. Not only must you be able to speak up loud and clear, but you should be able to put a case relevantly, neatly, succinctly, and generally in a way pleasing to the tribunal before which you are appearing. The last means that good manners are important.

Quickness of thought is a considerable asset. Cases on the common law side are usually won not through counsel's address to the court, which there is usually a little time to prepare in advance, but through the effective examination of witnesses. Now cross-examinations cannot be prepared, because you can never be quite sure what the other side's witnesses are going to say until they are actually in the box. A certain nimbleness of wit is therefore essential. Some people are very sound but can formulate opinions only after prolonged consideration. That type of mind is no use for advocacy.

A good barrister must also be able to assimilate facts quickly. He may have a brief with correspondence numbering two or three hundred letters delivered to him the night, or two nights, before the case begins, and all the facts must be mastered before he goes into court. The best advocates have had prodigious memories, enabling them to retain the details of one complicated case after another for presentation in court. Lord Alverstone recorded that when at the Bar he was able to read the sheets of correspondence almost as fast as he could turn them over, and he never required to read them twice. Hawkins, one of the most powerful leaders of the common law Bar in the nineteenth century, used to give the following advice. "Never examine or cross-examine from your brief. Know your brief and examine from your head." The student can best test and foster his powers of advocacy by making full use of his debating society.

A sound constitution is another requirement, as can be realised from the following passage from Gilchrist Alexander's *The Temple of the Nineties.* Anyone who has seen a busy barrister at work will bear out the truth of the picture.

"Few people realise under what pressure successful barristers live. . . .

The busy barrister is on the *qui vive* all the time. In court he has to be on the alert every moment and is watched by a highly trained expert on the other side who pounces upon his slightest mistake. Out of court he has to work far into the night, night after night, working hard and continuously at a mass of detail. He cannot, like the head of a big business, delegate to subordinates the actual carrying out of his work. His 'devils' prepare for him notes of his material, but once he has gone into court he has to take entire responsibility on his own shoulders."

The advocate needs a sound knowledge of the law, especially that of evidence and procedure. If evidence and procedure are among the subjects available to you at the University, you should either include them in your course or, at least, attend the lectures as an extra.

On the Chancery side the chief qualifications are, I think, patience and thoroughness. There is not such a great deal of advocacy to be done; much of the work is non-litigious (such as drafting documents and advising on title), and the cases that do get into court tend to turn upon technicalities of company law, property and wills, or upon questions of company finance, rather than upon controversial questions of fact. Also, a good deal of litigious work is disposed of not in open court but before a judge or master in chambers. To some types of mind work at the Chancery Bar appears dull and repellent, because it tends to lack human interest. On the other hand, existence is more placid than on the common law side.

It is hardly necessary to emphasise the necessity of probity for all members of the Bar. A barrister must have the confidence of the Bench. Any kind of sharp practice or dishonest dealing will infallibly ruin his career.

A sound lawyer who has found a seat in chambers can expect at least some work on the common law side. Even indifferent lawyers may be kept going by their clerk arranging for briefs to be passed to them from dud solicitors. This is, of course, a criticism of the system. Since even the neophyte practises on his own, there is no senior partner to keep an eye on him and to clamp down upon him if he is incompetent.

In Chancery chambers and specialist chambers (such as taxation, family law, local government law, town and country planning, rating, commercial law, shipping, restrictive practices, and patent), it is harder for the beginner to get a start and less likely that the incompetent can make any headway. There may be virtually no briefs for a year or more, and it will be longer still before the young barrister pays his way. However, his prospects then are better than in general practice. His life is likely to be less hectic, and his income distinctly greater. There is no official limit to the fees chargeable to clients who are not legally aided, so that when practitioners in a particular speciality are in short supply, their fees rise. For those who have an eye to practise eventually at the Parliamentary Bar[3] a scientific qualification is a help, and in patent work it is a necessity.

Apart from the fees he earns, a practising barrister is not feather-bedded in any way. There is no pension, no goodwill to sell, no partner to help earn your money if you are ill. Even if you succeed in building up a good practice as a junior your troubles will not be at an end, because at that point in your career you will have to decide whether to apply for silk. These expressions need a word of explanation. A "junior" means any barrister who has not taken silk; and some highly successful barristers (especially on the Chancery side) remain juniors all their lives. "Taking silk" means obtaining the right to wear a silk gown by becoming a Q.C. or (to use the language of lawyers) a leader. Whereas a junior does both advocacy and the preliminary paper work, a leader confines himself to advocacy (apart from the giving of oral and written opinions, an activity common to both grades).

The grant of silk is entirely in the discretion of a political officer, the Lord Chancellor; and the grounds on which he makes his selection are, as *The Times* wrote in an unusually critical vein, "shrouded in mystery." Many juniors who are qualified do not succeed in their application. No doubt, the Lord Chancellor weighs the needs of the various circuits and branches of law. But, whatever his good intentions, successful leaders are in such short supply, and consequently are able to charge such high fees, that the cost of fighting an important case in the High Court is a public scandal. One day the whole silk system may be reconsidered. Why should it not be left to individual members of the Bar to decide whether they wish to specialise in advocacy?

Anyway, the position now is that if you do not take silk at the

---

[3] Members of the Parliamentary Bar are concerned with the passage of private Bills through Parliament. Planning inquiries are now of greater importance than Parliamentary work, and practitioners (as at most of the specialised Bars) are doing very well.

right moment, it may mean that you have to continue working much too hard for your time of life; on the other hand some barristers who take silk repent it, for they find too late that their services in the more expensive class of advocacy are not in demand. Once you have taken silk there is no going back to a junior's practice. It seems a perverse arrangement to add this hazard to a profession that is already too full of risks for our comfortable age.

Should you be interested in the Bar as a career, do not go any further without reading Sir R. E. Megarry's *Lawyer and Litigant in England*, which gives a fair picture of the hazards and rewards of the profession at the date when it was written.

Assuming that you decide to take the plunge, you should if possible determine at the same time whether you are going to practise on the common law or on the Chancery side. For the latter you will probably join Lincoln's Inn, for the former one of the three other Inns. (This is the usual course, but there is nothing to prevent a member of any Inn from practising on either side of the profession.) As between the three common law Inns the choice does not really matter: you can quite well be a member of one Inn, become a pupil in chambers belonging to a second, and in due course attain a seat in chambers belonging to a third. It has already been explained that for the ordinary person who has no special connections it is easier to get started on the common law side. This is largely because on the common law side there is a great deal of small work, in county courts and the criminal courts; on the Chancery side there is no criminal work and all the civil work tends to be fairly important. The Chancery side is much more concentrated in London than the common law side, though some Chancery chambers have now been established in the provinces.

The Bar student must, according to the quaint custom, eat dinners at his Inn of Court as well as passing the Bar examinations before he can be called. In general the dinners must extend over two years, but there are certain exemptions, and in particular students who are exempted from Part I of the Bar examinations (as most are) can cut their dining period down to one year by double dining, *i.e.* by dining 24 times that year instead of the usual 12.

There is no need to enter further into the details of dinners, examinations and fees. The Consolidated Regulations of the Inns of Court, together with particulars of the scholarships and prizes available, can be had by applying to the Sub-Treasurer at the Inner Temple or to the Under-Treasurer at the other three Inns.[4] The total fees up to and including call (including the cost of dinners) are about £670, with another £130 for robe and wig.[5] Attendance at the Part II course at the Inns of Court School of Law, including the practical exercises, is compulsory for those who intend to practise in England and Wales. Many local authorities award grants to students reading at the Bar on the same basis as University awards.

A year's pupillage is (in general) compulsory for those who intend to practise in England and Wales. Certain limited exemptions are allowed. No fee is charged for pupillage, but there are no local authority grants for maintenance, which has the unfortunate result that students without adequate parental means may find it impossible to establish themselves at the Bar. The Inns of Court and Senate have modest funds for the purpose of alleviating hardship.

How does one find a barrister who will accept one as a pupil? Many barristers take a pupil on the recommendation of a friend at the Bar (particularly a former pupil), or a solicitor; and this is the best method of approach if you can work it. Oxford and Cambridge undergraduates receive the benefit of advice from special committees of old University men. Each Inn of Court has a Pupillage Committee which manages to fix up all comers eventually. Those who think that they may wish to practise in the North may avail themselves of advice kindly offered by Mr. Rhys Davies, 18 St. John Street, Manchester M3.

The difficulties of the student in arranging pupillage make it rather theoretical to give advice on the assumption that he can pick and choose. If you have the opportunity of an introduction to a particular barrister, find out as much about him as you can. There are two dangers to be avoided, if you can avoid them, in the choice of chambers: reading with someone who is too busy, who cannot spare the time to give you instruction, except possibly over a snack lunch, and reading with someone who has not enough

---

[4] See also Sweet and Maxwell's *Guide to a Career in the Law*, 7th ed. (paperback).
[5] The Bar Council acts as agent for the sale of second-hand (and therefore well-ripened) robes and wigs.

work to give you proper experience. The ideal person, if he can be found, is the young barrister in good practice who is rapidly rising and who may take you up with him. Someone, in other words, who is likely to take silk, but likely to take it at a time sufficiently far in the future to give you a chance of stepping into part of his practice as a junior. If your master is in general practice, he should not be above doing the humbler type of work (in the county court or before magistrates) with which you will have to start in your own practice.

You may make your pupillage contract for six months in each of two different chambers. You may, for example, spend six months in London and six months with a local barrister if your intention is to join the local Bar. Sir Harold Morris Q.C., recommended first six months' pupillage with a barrister who has a good criminal law practice and then 12 in a mixed practice. Some prefer to spend six months in Chancery chambers before turning to the common law side.

A pupil must do his level best to please his master (and the clerk) if he hopes to be invited to remain. He has the right, which he should exercise to the full, of reading his master's papers and accompanying him to court. He may be asked to take notes of the evidence. There is a temptation on both sides for the pupil to spend his time doing this, but it soon becomes rather profitless. The pupil spends his days far better drafting a pleading or writing an opinion and having his master criticise his work afterwards.

When listening to cases in court the student should do so not passively, like the spectator of a play, but with active thought, as though he were himself taking part; framing in his mind during the examination-in-chief the questions that he would put to the witness if the cross-examination fell to him. If possible, the cases he attends should be those cases in which he has contrived to read the papers beforehand: the educational value of hearing them is then much greater.

By the way, barristers usually talk about cases by identifying themselves with their lay client. "I am a girl who was assaulted," etc.

It need hardly be said that the Bar examinations should be got out of the way before pupillage commences, for you cannot do two things at once.

Pupillage in itself does not give experience in the art of

advocacy, and you should therefore play your full part in the forensic exercises provided in the Inns of Court School and in the moots held at your Inn of Court. If insufficent moots are organised, try to get a barrister to judge a private one for yourself and friends.

To go back a little, there is something to be said for spending six months to a year (no more is allowed) in a solicitor's office before pupillage. This would, indeed, be a useful way of spending one of your Long Vacations while you are at the University. It gives extra experience, and it gives an understanding of the solicitor's difficulties and requirements.

When pupillage is over the young barrister may join a local Bar instead of practising in London.[6] The Bar Council keeps a register of vacant places in chambers, both in London and in the provinces.

If the young barrister has any spare time in his early years he should use it to prolong his pupillage in fact if not in name. Perhaps his former master will allow him to continue to read his papers; or he may be permitted to read the papers of another in his own chambers with whom he is on friendly terms. There are many gaps in his legal knowledge that he now has an opportunity to make good, as he never will again. When his own practice begins he will find that his clerk has arranged conferences for him, and before the conference he will often know nothing of the questions that are likely to be put to him. If, for instance, he is on the common law side, the case that he is asked to consider may turn on the Landlord and Tenant Acts, the Rent Acts, the Consumer Protection Act, the Sale of Food Act, the Town and Country Planning Acts, the Arbitration Act, tax law, separation, bankruptcy, conflict of laws, carriage of goods, insurance, and many other topics which he may never have studied at the University or for his Bar examinations. He will not be expected, and will not need, to have every detail of all these subjects in his mind. But complete ignorance of their general structure will not raise him in the esteem of his professional clients.

---

[6] Local bars exist in Birmingham, Bradford, Brighton, Bristol, Cardiff, Chester, Colchester, Exeter, Hull, Leeds, Leicester, Liverpool, Manchester, Middlesbrough, Newcastle on Tyne, Norwich, Nottingham, Preston, Sheffield, Southampton, Stoke on Trent and Swansea.

On top of all this there is the possibility of "devilling" for fellow members of the Bar. This means giving them assistance in their cases, and even (with the client's consent) taking cases for them in court if owing to some clash of appointments they find themselves unable to appear. It is now obligatory to pay the devil a share of the fees (usually half) and the work therefore helps one's livelihood, as well as providing experience and (sometimes) bringing one to the notice of the professional client. But the possibilities of devilling must not be exaggerated. On the common law side only the busiest barristers have any devilling to give: they will themselves do all that they possibly can. On the Chancery side there is rather more, because of the amount of drafting work to be done. But drafting for a fellow-barrister, though desirable for experience, does not bring one into contact with the instructing solicitor, and so does not nurture one's own practice.

If you have a social conscience you can satisfy it handsomely by taking part in your local legal advice centre; and the same remark applies, of course, to solicitors. Some Bar students and pupil barristers offer their services in a Free Representation Unit for industrial tribunals. Other barristers (as well as solicitors) take salaried employment in a community law centre, providing legal services for poorer people. A waiver is needed to permit working for clients without referral by a solicitor.

When your own practice starts it is of the utmost importance to give your cases the most meticulous attention of which you are capable, and particularly, before going into court, to familiarise yourself with the various procedural contingencies. When you ask for damages on a continuing cause of action, do you know precisely the period for which you are claiming, so as to help the judge in framing his judgment? When you ask for costs, do you know the relevant Rule stating the power of the judge or master in this matter? It is quite wrong to expect to be prompted by the judge. In criminal matters you should know the sentencing powers of the court in case your client is convicted; not only may this help you in your plea in mitigation (if one is possible), but it is your duty to intervene if the judge by mistake exceeds his powers.[7] Take with you to court all the authorities that you may possibly require: leave them in the robing room if you think they will

[7] *R.* v. *Dearden* [1978] Crim.L.R. 287.

probably not be needed, but have them ready to back you up in case they are. Otherwise you may land your client in an unnecessary appeal.

Since most of the beginner's forensic work will be in county courts and magistrates' courts, he should make a special point of familiarising himself with the procedure and powers of these courts. The Association of Magisterial Officers, in their evidence to the Royal Commission on Legal Services, spoke of a "woeful lack of knowledge with regard to the rules and procedures of magistrates' courts" by both solicitors and barristers, who were equally poor.

A few remarks on addressing your colleagues and your betters. Every barrister is entitled and expected to address other practising barristers of whatever eminence by their surnames. High Court judges and circuit judges are addressed by barristers out of court as "Judge" (not "Judge Smith"), a Law Lord as "Lord Smith," and other judges as "Lord Chancellor," "Lord Chief Justice" (or "Lord Chief"), "Lord Justice," "Master of the Rolls," "President," "Common Sergeant," and "Recorder." These conventions are followed both in speech and in correspondence.[8] Members of the public, on the other hand, would speak to a judge as they would to any other knight or peer—Sir John, or Lord Smith. (All judges of the High Court and Court of Appeal are knights, if they are not peers.)

In court, address all judges from the High Court upwards (including both circuit judges and recorders when acting as High Court judges, and including also all judges sitting at the Old Bailey[9]) as "my Lord/Lady." Otherwise, circuit judges (and their deputies) and recorders and bankruptcy registrars are called "your Honour,"[10] Masters are called "Master," magistrates are called "Sir/Madam" (or "your Worship"), and all other judicial officers (like registrars) are called "Sir/Madam."

A lively book of advice which all young barristers should read is Henry Cecil's *Brief to Counsel* (2nd ed., 1972). Of the many

---

[8] On the envelope, write "His [or, of course, Her] Honour Judge Smith" (circuit judge), or "The Hon. Mr./Mrs Justice Smith" (High Court judge), "The Rt. Hon. Lord Justice Smith," or "The Rt. Hon. the Lord Smith of Casterbridge," as the case may be.

[9] Including also the honorary recorders of Liverpool and Manchester.

[10] See Practice Direction, [1978] Crim.L.R. 215.

biographies and autobiographies of barristers giving some information about life at the Bar perhaps the most informative is Sir Harold Morris's *The Barrister* (1930). The seamy side of the legal profession is revealed with gusto by John Parris, in his book *Under my Wig* (1961). This makes some grave charges against solicitors, but it may be questioned whether the author should not have brought them to the attention of the Law Society, instead of merely putting them into a book of reminiscence. Also on the critical side, see C. P. Harvey's frank and entertaining little book *The Advocate's Devil* (1958). On advocacy, see Leo Page, *First Steps in Advocacy* (1943); also: Hilbery, *Duty and Art in Advocacy* (1946); J. E. Singleton, *Conduct at the Bar* (1933); F. J. Wrottesley, *Letters to a Young Barrister* (1930) and *The Examination of Witnesses* (3rd ed. 1961); Parry, *The Seven Lamps of Advocacy* (1923); R. Harris, *Hints on Advocacy*: (18th ed. 1948); Lord Macmillan, *Law and Other Things* (1937), 200 *et seq.*; J. H. Munkman, *The Technique of Advocacy* (1951); Richard Du Cann, *The Art of the Advocate* (Pelican Books, 1964). Some notion of the nature and difficulty of cross-examination may be derived from E. W. Fordham's *Notable Cross-Examinations* (1950). On drafting, Piesse and Smith, *The Elements of Drafting* (3rd ed., 1965), is to be warmly commended. A useful general work is *The Young Lawyer* by Clay, Frankenburg and Baker (1955). For the rules of etiquette see W. W. Boulton, *Conduct and Etiquette at the Bar*. A copy of this is presented to everyone upon call.

THE BAR AS A STEPPING STONE

About 3,800 barristers practise in this country. A considerable number of others have used the Bar as a stepping stone or crutch leading them on to other things. There is, in fact, a glittering array of dignified and sometimes very lucrative offices open to members of the Bar. I shall proceed to describe some of them, prefacing the list only with the warning that for the more attractive of them there is, of course, considerable competition.

For the brilliantly successful or the politically fortunate there are the offices of Attorney-General and Solicitor-General and about 80 superior judgeships, the latter carrying very comfortable stipends, plus pensions. As consolation prizes there are many pensionable posts as circuit judges, recorders, chairmen of industrial tribunals, stipendiary magistrates, official referees, bankruptcy registrars, and industrial injuries commissioners and deputy commissioners. Among miscellaneous posts are certain Parliamentary and Court of Protection appointments, and offices as Registrar of Companies, Masters of the Queen's Bench Division, Clerk of the Crown Court, Registrars of the Family Division, and Registrars of the Court of Appeal (Criminal Division). A list of most of the offices referred to in this paragraph, and others, will be found in the *Law Society's Handbook*, and in Halsbury's *Laws of England*, 3rd ed., iii, 29–33. A barrister who applies for any office may reckon as part of his qualification period any time he has spent in practice or in employment as a solicitor.[11]

There is no more important, exciting and intellectually rewarding work for a lawyer than that of drafting legislation. The post of Parliamentary Counsel is open to both barristers and solicitors, and candidates of adequate intellectual quality are in short supply. My little book will have performed a useful function if it persuades one or two of the best of its readers to take up this career.[12]

For all these posts a certain amount of actual practice is essential. In addition, most Government Departments make appointments from professional lawyers, and here, although practical experience is an important qualification, it is not always regarded as essential. Barristers and solicitors are appointed in about equal proportions, and pupillage or articles can be waived for candidates with outstanding examination results. (Even when the head of the department is a barrister, he may be known as the department's solicitor.) A list of the Departments concerned will be found in the *Law Society's Handbook* and in Halsbury. No examination is required; vacancies are advertised in the legal weeklies (*Law Society's Guardian Gazette, New Law Journal, Solicitor's Journal*), and in *The Times*. Since it is hard to change departments once you are in, choose the department in which you think you will be able to settle down. You can write to the Establishment Officer of the department of your choice and ask

---

[11] Barristers (Qualification for Office) Act 1961.
[12] For the work of Parliamentary Counsel see Sir Granville Ram in (1951) 1 J.S.P.T.L. 422; Sir Noel Hutton in (1967) 64 Law Society's Gazette 293.

for an interview in expectation of the next vacancy. In this case you will probably join as temporary legal assistant with a view to establishment later. Alternatively, you may be immediately recruited as an established legal assistant (or senior legal assistant) through the Civil Service Commission, the address of which is Alencon Link, Basingstoke, Hants, RG21 1JB.

Those who have worked in the legal civil service report that it is much more interesting than appears at first sight. The work is not purely legal, and in no department is it narrowly specialist. There are opportunities for foreign travel, as adviser to international conferences etc., in several Departments, including the Diplomatic Service. The Board of Inland Revenue has many problems wholly unrelated to tax law. A barrister who left the Inland Revenue for practice at the Bar summed up his opinion of the service in the following words: "I enjoyed it, they enjoyed me, and I would always consider returning if the Bar did not prove satisfying."

Most legal civil service posts do not require advocacy at any level. By a discreditable rule of the Bar, a member who is in paid employment (apart from the Attorney-General and Solicitor-General) cannot appear in court in his professional capacity. However, civil servants may appear in magistrates' courts as prosecutors without violating this restrictive practice. The legal staff of Customs and Excise, for example, carry on prosecutions for smuggling in magistrates' courts, and brief counsel for the higher courts.

The above information concerns the professional class of the civil service. Other classes will be discussed later.

Many private concerns also employ a legal staff of barristers and solicitors. (It was recently calculated that barristers employed in companies, local government and the civil service are three times as numerous as their fellows in private practice.) Banks, for instance, have executor and trustee departments. The work involves the legal processes of obtaining probate of wills and the winding up of a deceased person's affairs so that the wishes expressed in those wills may be carried out. This entails such transactions as the settlement of business contracts, the purchase and sale of stocks and shares, house property and lands, and provision for beneficiaries under wills and other trust instruments. It may mean managing an estate worth several millions of pounds.

Appointment to these departments is not confined to those with professional qualifications or a knowledge of law; men and women not uncommonly read for the Bar or for an external University degree after appointment. But naturally a person who already has these qualifications starts with an advantage. It may be added that there seems to be no prejudice against women. Similar remarks apply to the legal departments of transport undertakings and big insurance companies, which deal principally with claims for damages, and the legal departments of large business firms and combines. All the big newspapers employ a legal staff to read proofs in order to minimise the risk of libel actions, and also to watch the interests of the newspaper generally. Salaries are substantial; a survey in 1974 found that the average remuneration of barristers in commerce and industry was £9,500. Many of these posts carry fringe benefits such as a company car, free medical insurance, and assistance with house purchase. Information is given in a booklet published by the Bar Association for Commerce, Finance and Industry entitled *Barristers in Business*: address to 63 Great Cumberland Place, Bryanston Square, London W1H 7LJ.

SOLICITORS

The life of a successful solicitor is not so exacting as that of his opposite number at the Bar: the solicitor has his clerks and junior partners, assistant solicitors and legal executives to do some of his work for him. He misses the *camaraderie* of the Bar and the exhilaration of forensic battle in the exalted courts. Nor does his work lead to the same fame as does great success at the Bar; but some solicitors are as affluent as their opposite numbers at the Bar, and they achieve their wealth in a more relaxed way. Moreover, it seems safe to say that there is better assurance of reasonable success in the solicitors' branch. Not all solicitors have large incomes: the 1976 Remuneration Survey (given in evidence by the Law Society to the Royal Commission on Legal Services) showed that half of those working in private practice earned less than £7,050. The median earnings of all principals were £8,630, but of sole practitioners were £5,750, and of principals doing only contentious work were a disappointing £4,100.

The type of work done by a solicitor is well known. On the

property side he investigates title to land, prepares contracts of sale, conveyances and wills, obtains probate of wills, and frequently acts as executor and trustee. He interviews clients, advises them generally on their legal position, and writes letters. He pilots company promoters through the legal technicalities of forming companies. On difficult questions he takes the opinion of counsel, and he also prepares briefs for counsel in legal proceedings in which counsel are employed.

As in the United States, English lawyers are now distinctively class-structured. A few very large and affluent City firms have adapted themselves to act as the agents and advisers of commerce and industry; they have modern offices with every aid and convenience, and the partners specialise intensively. These firms may even have overseas branches. Next come medium-sized firms with about ten partners, specialising in some particular field of commerce or industry such as shipping or insurance or property development, and other smaller but still highly-specialised firms, all of them mainly in London. The great majority of solicitors continue in their traditional ways, making their staple living from conveyancing, probate, advising middle-class clients in minor disputes and business affairs, and litigation—though some firms prefer not to do the last if they can help it.

The qualities required of a country-town solicitor appear clearly enough from the foregoing description of his work. He should be able to interview all types of client in order to ascertain what their problem is. He should have a knowledge of human nature, practical wisdom, and the ability to dictate a good letter. Naturally he needs a working knowledge of property and company law and the law of procedure; and the better his knowledge, the better he is at his job. It is a great mistake to suppose that a solicitor can get along without having mastered the legal topics with which he is called upon to deal. However, the finer points of such subjects as tort can with relative safety be left to repose in his books of reference.

The traditional argument for our bifurcated profession is that barristers are the professional advocates; but in fact solicitors conduct much the greater number of cases in the lesser courts—county courts and magistrates' courts. What I have written in relation to barristers as advocates applies equally to solicitors. The training provided for solicitors now lags behind that of the

Bar; it does not invariably include the instruction in advocacy, practical exercises and discussions of court cases now required for Bar students. If you find, as a solicitor, that your talents run to advocacy, and so wish to change over to the Bar, you can do so without too many formalities. One day we may see the artificial division of the profession reduced, so that everyone will begin as a solicitor and, after gaining experience, will be able to elect to specialise in advocacy with a minimum of upheaval.

The spate of new legislation imposes a great strain upon the smaller firm. One client will have a problem under some recent Act relating to divorce or maintenance; another will need advice on capital gains tax, or redundancy payments, or VAT, or company law, or agricultural tenancies, or rent control; another will be enraged by a refusal of planning permission, or the threat of a motorway through his garden. Each of these subjects involves a highly intricate body of law, and it is not to be expected that any one man or even three or four men can master them all. At present, many solicitors simply fail to give adequate advice, and this is not because of any immediate fault on their part but because they are operating in units that are too small.

The constantly increasing complexity of the law is one reason, but by no means the only reason, why many solicitors in small practices are now dissatisfied with their position. Over the years, the solicitor has slowly lost the prestige he formerly held as family counseller and preserver of the family property. Lawyers are criticised for being slow to adapt to demands for new legal services, particularly services to the poor (Although the charge has some basis, the lawyer is a professional, not a charity, so the failure to make proper provision is primarily a failure of government.) Again, many solicitors are incompetent, and leave important matters to unsupervised articled clerks or inadequately trained legal executives. The very work that solicitors are called to perform, which includes doing certain nasty things to people, cannot be expected to make them universally popular; so the profession can retain public respect only if it observes high ethical standards, which not all practitioners do. Many solicitors, in writing a letter for a client, will misrepresent the law, even though they are addressing themselves to a layman, and will lend themselves to various abuses and suppressions (not involving a breach of law) in order to obstruct a just claim. The Law Society takes no interest in these matters, or in the too frequent instances of gross negligence or dilatoriness by solicitors in dealing with their clients' affairs.

Blemishes like these upon the work of the profession obscure but do not efface the public services it renders. Competent solicitors are a blessing to their clients and a necessity for the economic life of the country. Unfortunately, firms have had to face discouraging difficulties in recent years. They have been hit by sharply rising expenses without corresponding rises in income. While the principals are required to confer the benefits of the various employment protection laws upon their employees, they themselves are deprived of any such security, and must pay the special tax for self-employed people masquerading as national insurance, in addition to the insurance premiums needed to provide for retirement or illness. Solicitors also complain of the expense of the practising certificate, the contribution to the compensation fund to recompense defrauded clients, the professional negligence indemnity premium, and the contribution to the Law Society advertisements for the profession. These disbursements do not worry the senior partner in a large firm who makes £30,000 or more a year net, but they fall heavily upon the less successful.

The most profitable part of the solicitor's work is conveyancing; contentious business is inadequately remunerated. But the conveyancing monopoly is under strong attack. Although the non-solicitor conveyancing firms (who use a solicitor only to draw up the conveyance itself) have so far only dented the market, it seems quite likely that the Royal Commission on Legal Services will report in favour of encouraging competition in this area, in which case the cut-price firms may well come to operate more publicly and more aggressively. Again, implementation of the Pearson Report would put an end to many compensation claims handled by solicitors.

Even if these future shocks are discounted, the large increase in recruitment to the profession during the last few years means that new entrants (unless of top quality) often do not find it easy to get started.

Those of my readers who are already in articles will know the technicalities of becoming a solicitor, and I can therefore address myself to those who are not yet in articles but who have or hope to have a University degree. The following account states the position from August 1979 when new regulations will come into force. The Law graduate who has gained full exemption proceeds at once to the Final; this requires attendance for nine months at one of the law schools recognised by the Law Society for this purpose. As with the Bar, many local authorities award grants for maintenance. Two years' service under articles is required, which must be after passing the Final.

A graduate (Law or otherwise) who has not obtained full exemption because he lacks one or more of the "core" subjects in his degree will be required to take the new Common Professional Examination (intended for both barristers and solicitors) before the Final. However, exemption will be granted in respect of particular subjects taken at University, and the requirement of attendance at the lecture course for the C.P.E. can be waived. The six core subjects are: Constitutional and Administrative Law; Contract; Torts; Criminal Law; Land Law and Trusts.

Finding a suitable firm for articles can present problems if you have no friends or relatives who are in a position to help.[13] The Law Society keeps a register for those seeking articles, but many applicants fail to be placed in this way. You can put an advertisement in the Law Society's Gazette or write to firms at random, but if this method produces an offer you will need to take all possible steps to sound opinions upon the standing of the firm. A bad firm can only teach you bad practices. Advice may be obtained from the Law Society or the teaching staff of your law school or your University Careers Service.

Let me now assume that you are being favourably considered by a prospective principal and are seeing him for the first time. A number of important questions need to be asked, with all the tact at your command; some of them may be best addressed to an articled clerk who is already with the firm. Will you be allowed to sit in with your principal or another solicitor, and if so about how often? (A survey showed that only 17 per cent of articled clerks are allowed to sit in often.[14]) Will you have to do your own typing or will you be allowed to use the office typists? Will you be able to

---

[13] For the present chaos see Keith Wallace in 127 New Law Journal 628.
[14] *The Prospective Lawyer—Blue-Print for the Future,* published in 1968 by the Associate Members' Group of the Law Society.

attend courts? (One in three articled clerks never attends court, which implies a serious omission from his training.) If in local government, will you attend committee meetings?

How wide will be the experience you will receive in the firm? The survey already mentioned showed that most prospective solicitors gain some practical experience of: registered and unregistered conveyancing, landlord and tenant, matrimonial causes, probate and succession, family law, criminal law, accident claims, litigation generally and briefing counsel. Most of them never have experience of: town and country planning, administration of trusts, company law, partnership law, tax planning, book-keeping and accounts, commercial law, or (doubtless) advocacy. The law has become so complex that it cannot be expected that the solicitor will be proficient in everything, and we shall undoubtedly move more and more towards the large firm with specialised partners. All the same, it is important that the prospective solicitor should have as broad a base as possible, particularly if he is not certain which field is likely to offer the best opening. Large firms generally arrange for the articled clerk to move around from one department to another—a very satisfactory arrangement.

Will you have the opportunity of spending some time with London Agents, and if so what are the financial terms likely to be? What about holidays and paid sickness leave? Will you be paid while attending an examination course? (Most are not.) If you can attend any practical exercises or advocacy training courses provided for those in articles (*e.g.* in London or Birmingham), do so.

It is probably too delicate to ask the principal the final question: How much of your time will you give to instructing me?—but you may be able to find out the probabilities from any other articled clerks in the firm. Lamentably, one in three articled clerks receives no instruction whatever from his principal, and about one in four receives no instruction from anyone in the office—truly a scandalous state of affairs.[15] Proposals have been made to replace the outmoded system of articles by a proper training course, but they have foundered because no one is willing to put up the funds.

---

[15] A useful summary of the proper training of an articled clerk will be found in 123 New Law Journal 901–902.

An all-round practice gives better training than a specialised one—but it may be well worth taking articles in a specialised firm if you are assured that they are looking out for a bright young man/woman like you to be a partner.

Nearly all firms pay the clerk an allowance, but the 1976 Remuneration Survey found that the average was only £1800,[16] 60 per cent of articled clerks rely on another source of finance apart from their salaries. Generally this is a contribution from parents or spouses. The Law Society administers a number of bursaries to assist articled clerks.

Among the skills that are in short supply are advocacy and probate, so procedure, evidence and wills are good subjects to choose when planning your University course.

Newly qualified solicitors begin as salaried assistant solicitors. Getting a partnership is not easy, and the new partner who cannot provide capital is inevitably burdened with some form of payment for his share. One practice is to establish a retirement benefit scheme, whereby the younger partners, instead of paying an initial sum as their share of capital, contribute to the pensions of the senior partners as they go. Another plan is for new partners to be admitted merely on undertaking to contribute their share of the partnership capital, and this may either be raised by borrowing from a bank or insurance company (with periodic repayments) or be left to be paid over a period of years by deduction from their share of the profits. Either way, the new partner's earnings are greatly reduced, and some legal assistants continue in their salaried position because they cannot afford a partnership.

Instead of going into private practice, or after some years of practice, the solicitor may seek an appointment. The most favourable field is in the local government service, which will be described in the next section. In addition, solicitors are eligible for appointment to the legal departments of Government Departments as described in connection with the Bar, though not always to the head positions. In some cases, by law or practice, the chief appointments are confined to solicitors. Within the judicial system solicitors are appointed as masters and registrars of the Chancery Division, taxing masters, Official Solicitor, bankruptcy

---

[16] £2,300 in Greater London.

registrars, district registrars of the High Court, registrars of county courts,[17] stipendiary magistrates, recorders (and, by way of promotion, circuit judges), magistrates' clerks, and as various kinds of clerk in the Supreme Court, the last with opportunities of promotion (see later, under Civil Service). Then again, various public utility undertakings offer important positions to solicitors. Details of the foregoing can be seen in the *Law Society's Handbook,* or in Halsbury's *Laws of England,* 3rd ed., xxxvi, 52–55. Current vacancies both in private practice (for legal executives,[18] assistants and partners) and in outside appointments are listed by the Law Society's Appointments Registry.

Although both solicitors and barristers may be appointed to positions in industry, there is a tendency to prefer solicitors. Remarks made previously in relation to barristers apply equally to solicitors. Most legal departments in industry merely do the work that would ordinarily be entrusted to a solicitor; sometimes it is largely confined to routine conveyancing and the drawing of contracts, but a much wider field may be touched, including the formation of subsidiary companies, company finance, insurance and employers' liability, patents, trade marks—there is, in fact, hardly any limit to the economic activities upon which a large corporation may engage. Some corporations entrust their routine legal work to outside solicitors, but have legal advisers whose task is to give advice at high level within the industry; these advisers organise the legal work which is to be executed by the outside solicitors—perhaps in many countries. The position of legal adviser to a large and growing industry can be of high importance and interest. At the same time, the highest rewards in industry are not yet available to even the most brilliant lawyer whilst he continues to practise the law.

In view of the difficulty of obtaining articles with a reasonable salary in private practice, the prospect of obtaining a salaried position and free articles in the legal department of a company is attractive. Do not do this, however, unless you are keen to make your career in industry. You will only be taken on if you can convince your employer of this keenness. Articles in industry are in any case not the best preparation for private practice, and

[17] See (1964) 61 Law Society's Gazette 669.
[18] Legal executives (the former managing clerks) have a legal qualification but have not been admitted as solicitors.

unless you have a fairly fixed intention to make your career in industry or commerce you may find it difficult to settle down even for only two or three years in the atmosphere of a company's legal department.

Solicitors are frequently appointed not only in the legal departments but in the secretarial departments of large concerns; but a person who intends to go for a secretarial department would be better advised to obtain a secretarial rather than a legal qualification (to have both would, of course, be best of all).[19] To these possibilities must be added miscellaneous positions not capable of concise description, in building societies, insurance companies, and so on.

It is now quite easy for a solicitor to transfer to the Bar: all he generally needs to do is to spend six months in pupillage. You are much more likely to succeed at the Bar when you have grown a few wrinkles.

A highly specialised profession, open to barristers and solicitors and indeed to those who are neither, is that of Parliamentary Agent, whose work lies in promoting and opposing Bills and Departmental Orders. A description of this work will be found in (1964) 7 The Lawyer 21.

Further information on the technical details of becoming a solicitor can be obtained from the Secretary, Law Society's Hall, Chancery Lane, London WC2A 1PL. The Law Society publish and will supply free two good brochures: *Becoming a Solicitor* and *A Guide for Articled Clerks.* Descriptions of the work of a solicitor are given in a series of booklets published by the Solicitors' Law Stationery Society called *The Doorstep Series,* and in an highly entertaining book by G. A. L. Burgeon, *This Ever Diverse Pair* (1950). See also Michael Gilbert, *The Law* (1977, in the series *The Professions*); Harry Kirk, *Portrait of a Profession* (1976). Fictionalised accounts will be found in the various books by Julian Prescott, such as *Both Sides of the Case* (1958), and in an entertaining story by John Malcolm entitled *Let's Make it Legal* (1966). Other useful hints are given in H. O. Locke's *Advice to a Young Solicitor* (1946) and C. D. Wickenden's *The Modern Family Solicitor* (1975). Elementary advice on litigation is given in Leonard C. Lockwood's *Solicitor's Clerk in Court,* and, on

---

[19] See R. A. Lynex, "The Role of the Employed Lawyer in Industry." (1954) 2 J.S.P.T.L. 214.

conveyancing, in Edward Moeran's *Practical Conveyancing* (6th ed., 1974). In addition to the books on advocacy previously given, there is Sir David Napley's *The Technique of Persuasion* (1970) and F. J. O. Coddington's *Advice on Advocacy to Solicitors* (2nd ed., 1954). Sir Thomas Lund has written a *Guide to the Professional Conduct and Etiquette of Solicitors* (1960).

LOCAL GOVERNMENT

Local government offers a highly attractive field for the lawyer. That local government authorities are profligate with appointments, both in numbers and in scales of remuneration, is a matter of wide knowledge and indignation; and every salary survey during the last few years has shown that their lawyers are appreciably better off, on average, than lawyers in private practice. For example, in 1975 a salary of £7,000 was offered for a conveyancer in a river board, whereas a similarly qualified lawyer could have obtained only £5,500 in private practice. The post of solicitor with a district council was advertised at £6,000, against a salary in the private sector of less than £3,500 for similar qualifications.[20] The salaries paid to articled clerks in local government are also substantially greater; and local authorities are more generous than most private employers in giving paid study leave and assistance for the purchase of books. Lawyers have been conspicuously successful in obtaining the top job of chief executive (the former town clerk or county clerk), where the salary can be as high as £18,000. The valuable pension rights attaching to these posts must also be remembered.

The work of local authorities is wide-ranging; it includes public health in all its branches, education, housing and town planning, maternity and child welfare, public utilities and transport services. If you wish to be articled in local government, you can obtain advice and assistance by writing to that effect to Mr. J. T. Kellet, Hon. Sec. of the Association of District Council Secretaries, County Hall, Chester, or Mrs. M. Mullins, Assistant Secretary of the Society of County Secretaries, Smokey Acre, Broadoaks Hill, Dundrey, Bristol BS18 8NB.

---

[20] 140 Justice of the Peace Newspaper 196.

THE CIVIL SERVICE

For the man or woman with a first-class academic brain the administrative posts in the Home Civil Service have great attraction, above all because they give the satisfaction of doing work of paramount social and national importance. There is the interest of being "in the know" when important governmental decisions are being made, and at the rank of Assistant Secretary there is real governmental power. In order to indicate the importance of this *corps d'élite* of the Civil Service one cannot do better than quote the words of Sir Ivor Jennings, written in 1966.

"The citizen meets it [the process of administration] at many points, the local post office, the telephone exchange, the employment exchange, the office of the inspector of taxes. . . . The most important part, however, is that with which he is not directly in contact but which really influences his environment even more because it assists ministers in reaching the decisions which determine the policy of the country. This 'administrative class,' as it is called, is very small. It contains only about 3,300 people, while Government employees of what are called non-industrial classes number over 600,000 of whom about 250,000 are commonly designated as 'civil servants' by ordinary citizens. These 3,300 men and women, however, occupy the key positions in the administrative system. Some of them are so important that their names get into the newspapers in spite of the service practice of anonymity. These are among the most eminent of the administrative class; but that class includes also the young men and women who came straight from the Universities at the latest examinations."[21]

Since Jennings wrote, the civil service has been reorganised into three groups of staff—the General Category, the Science Category and the Professional and Technology Category. The last, as it affects lawyers, has already been dealt with (p. 173), and we are now considering the General Category, where the prospects at the top levels are distinctly better than in the others. All civil servants, however, have the very valuable privilege of an index-linked pension.

A graduate may join the General Category either as an Administrative Trainee or as an Executive Officer. Selection is by qualifying tests (meant to assess general ability) and interviews.[22]

[21] Jennings, *The British Constitution,* 5th ed. (1966), 131.
[22] The technique of the Civil Service Selection Board interview is explained in a pamphlet entitled *Recruitment to the Administrative Class of the Home Civil Service and the Senior Branch of the Foreign Service,* Cmnd. 232 of 1957.

An alternative mode of entry is available for the Tax Inspectorate. If you are undecided whether to apply, you may visit a government department during vacation in order to see what goes on, your reasonable expenses being refunded.

The mode of entry described above covers not only the administrative class of the Home Civil Service, but also certain clerkships in the House of Commons, the administrative class of the Northern Ireland Civil Service, and the diplomatic service. There is a shortage of suitable recruits in the diplomatic service, which offers varied experience abroad and a good career structure.

Administrative trainees obtain a salary on a par with that obtainable from industry; they enjoy incremental salary scales which ensure progress even during periods of pay restraint, together with virtually complete security, and near-certain promotion within the administrative grade to under-secretary level. Small wonder that industry feels itself to suffer unfairly in the competition for talent.

Intending candidates should obtain further information as soon as possible from the Secretary, Civil Service Commission, Alencon Link, Basingstoke, Hants, RG21 1JB.

Reverting to the Government Legal Service, a new method of entry has been devised by which legal training is obtained after entry. Young men and women with honours degrees or postgraduate degrees can be articled to solicitors in the Legal Service, normally after obtaining exemption from passing Part I of the Law Society examination. Starting salary (in Inner London) is at least £3,330, an appointment as Legal Assistant following admission as a solicitor. Unfortunately, not many clerkships are offered, so competition is likely to be keen. Details can be obtained from the Civil Service Commission.

The various public corporations (such as the National Coal Board, the Airways Corporations, the Railways Board, and the Development Corporations under the New Towns Act 1946) require some lawyers on their staffs, but there is no standard method of recruitment. Vacancies are generally advertised in *The Times*.

FURTHER READING

A good impression of the work of the higher civil service is conveyed in John Carswell's witty book, *The Civil Servant and his World* (1966). See also the volumes in the *Whitehall Series* (published by Putnams), each devoted to a different Government Department, and Frank Dunnill's provocative book: *The Civil Service: Some Human Aspects* (1956).

TEACHING

I need say very little about this, because the kind of life led by a law teacher is well known to the student, and if he aspires to it himself he will not lack advisers. In addition to Universities there are many opportunities of teaching in Polytechnics and Technical Colleges, where Law is taught at every level from "O" level to degree courses.

Research work is an important qualification, and it can be profitably combined with a visit to another University, preferably abroad. Several scholarships and fellowships are available for study in the U.S.A. Some of these require the holder to read for a particular degree; some require assistance with teaching; some are unfettered. The following are bodies offering the main American awards.

American Council of Learned Societies (American Studies Program), 345 East 46th Street, New York, N.Y. 10017, U.S.A. (research in U.S.A.).

English Speaking Union Fellowships (General Fellowships, and University of Michigan Fellowship in Comparative and International Law and post of Instructor); apply to Miss L. Moore, 37 Charles Street, London W1X 8AB.

Harkness Fellowships of the Commonwealth Fund of New York, 38 Upper Brook Street, London W1Y 1PE.

Henry Fund: Secretary, University Chest, Oxford.

Rotary Foundation Fellowships (open to all; inquire at local Rotary organisation).

St. Andrew's Society, New York (for male Scots who are graduates of Oxford, Cambridge or Scottish Universities).

University of California School of Law, Berkeley, Calif., U.S.A. (Fellowships: address to Dean of Graduate Division).

Columbia University, New York, N.Y., U.S.A. (Ford Fellowships in International Law; University Fellowships).

University of Chicago, Chicago, Ill., U.S.A., awards British Commonwealth Fellowships (apply to Secretary of the British Commonwealth Fellowship Program) and Bigelow Teaching Fellowships (apply to Dean of Law School).

Harvard Law School, Cambridge, Mass. 02138, U.S.A. (Graduate Fellowships: address to Chairman of Committee on Graduate Studies. Also Frank Knox Fellowships: address to the Secretary, Knox Fellowships Committee, Association of Commonwealth Universities, 36 Gordon Square, London WC1 0PF).

University of Illinois, College of Law, Champaign, Illinois 61820, U.S.A. (Law teaching Fellowships).

New York University School of Law, New York 10012, N.Y., U.S.A. (Graduate Fellowships).

Northwestern University School of Law, 357 East Chicago Ave., Chicago, Ill. 60611 (Fellowships, and Lectureship for the Legal Writing Program: address to Chairman of the Graduate Committee).

University of Pennsylvania Law School, 3400 Chestnut Street, Philadelphia 19104, U.S.A. (Fellowships). Also Thouron Awards, for which address to the Registrar, The University, Glasgow G12 8QQ, who deals with these awards on behalf of the University of Pennsylvania.

Rutgers University School of Law, 53 Washington Square, Newark, N.J. 07102, U.S.A. (Teaching and Research Associates).

Tulane University School of Law, New Orleans, La., U.S.A. (Fellowships).

University of Virginia Law School, Charlottesville, Virginia 22901, U.S.A. (Fellowships for graduate study; address to Secretary of the Graduate Committee).

Walter G. Meyer Research Institute in Law, 435 West 116th Street, New York, N.Y., 10027 (grants for research in law: address to the Director).

Yale Law School, New Haven, Conn. 06520, U.S.A. (graduate work and visiting research scholars).

Except where otherwise stated, address the Dean of the Law School. State your position, achievements, proposals for U.S. study (research, reading for degree), and whether you would like to teach. If you are contemplating an academic career, say so. Make your inquiries well in advance, otherwise you may be caught by closing dates. The Cultural Office of the U.S. Embassy, 41 Grosvenor Square, London, W.1, will answer most queries. Anyone who has secured dollar support in the U.S. is eligible to apply for a Fulbright Travel Grant, which covers transportation. Apply to U.S. Educational Commission, 71 South Audley Street, London, W.1.

Commonwealth scholarships and fellowships are tenable at Universities in Australia, Canada, Sri Lanka, Ghana, Hong Kong and India; write to the Secretary, Association of Commonwealth Universities, 36 Gordon Square, London WC1H 0PF. Research scholarships are offered by the Australian

National University, Research School of Social Sciences, Box 4, G.P.O. Canberra, A.C.T., Australia.

With our association with Europe, it is vital that some lawyers should interest themselves in the law of the EEC and improve their contacts with European lawyers. A booklet *Scholarships Abroad* is available from the British Council, 65 Davies Street, London, W.1, and details of overseas Universities are given in *The World of Learning,* published annually. There is also a flow the other way: the British Institute of International and Comparative Law, 32 Furnival Street, London, E.C.4, offers Research Fellowships in Public International Law to students from overseas, and lawyers from African and Asian countries may apply for Research Fellowships to the University of London Institute of Advanced Legal Studies, 17 Russell Square, London WC1B 5DR. The University of Cambridge offers Humanitarian Trust Studentships in International Law (write to the Secretary, Faculty Board of Law, The Old Schools, Cambridge). Irrespective of the place of study, senior workers may apply for Leverhulme Research Fellowships and grants, particulars of which may be obtained from the Secretary, Union House, St. Martins-le-Grand, E.C.1. The British Academy, Burlington House, London W1V 0NS awards grants and a Fellowship for research. The Social Sciences Research Council, State House, High Holborn, London, W.C.1, awards studentships for research in socio-legal topics. Oxford also makes awards in this field: write to the Director, Centre for Socio-Legal Studies, 2 Keble Road, Oxford. Lists of other awards in this and other countries are compiled by the Association of Commonwealth Universities (address above).

Experience in the practice of the law is also regarded very favourably by appointing bodies.

In addition to university teaching posts there are lectureships, tutorships and examinerships offered at the Inns of Court School of Law, and tutorships, assistant tutorships, and examinerships at the Law Society's School of Law. Vacancies in the Inns of Court lectureships (which are part-time) are advertised in the legal papers and in *The Times*; they are also announced on the notice boards in the Inns. Vacancies in the Law Society's teaching staff are advertised in the Law Society's Guardian Gazette.

There are many teaching opportunities overseas, where you

will be paid more highly than in England. Certainly go to a teaching post in Canada or Australia or elsewhere if you are unmarried and can easily return to England later on to look for your first post here; or go intending to make a new life in a new country; but do not go, severing your connections with England, intending to make this a step to advancement in England. It is very difficult to transfer to a teaching post in this country from one overseas, because the appointments committee will rarely appoint without interview, and will not be able to pay travel expenses for candidates who are abroad.

ACCOUNTANCY

Few law students go in for accountancy, even though a knowledge of law is useful both for the examinations and for practice. Accountants have become advisers to industry, and many accountants are to be found on the Boards of large public companies. But as many salaried posts are advertised for lawyers as for accountants; and unless you have a special bent for figures you will probably find the law a more interesting profession.

THE SOCIAL SERVICES

You may be interested in a job in the probation and after-care service, or other department of social work. Most social workers have no recognised qualification. The usual qualification of those who have one is a two-year postgraduate course. Graduates in sociology can take the course in one year, but Law graduates are not generally allowed this privilege.[23] Alternatively, would you be interested in the Graduate Entry Scheme in the police force?

OTHER CAREERS

In these pages I have written only of those careers for which a knowledge of law is distinctly a qualification. There are others for which a legal knowledge is no hindrance and may be some help. The *Careers Guide,* published by H.M.S.O., may prove helpful.

[23] See David Carson in 127 New Law Journal 776.

Large industrial and business concerns provide many places for Arts graduates—an expression which for this purpose includes law graduates. One advantage is that salaries are paid even during training; and a career in the world of manufacture and commerce is attractive to those who want to do something "real," to take part in the basic process of creating wealth, to tackle a variety of problems and jobs and to have a chance to organise and administer, and perhaps to travel. The general impression of investigators is that the great majority of the graduates, in spite of certain difficulties, enjoy their work. At the same time, the vast output of Arts graduates from the Universities, coupled with high unemployment, means that competition for vacancies is acute.

A few points on the technique of being interviewed. Before the interview, make sure that you know the details of your own career, and can explain anything requiring explanation, such as the reason why you left your previous job. Find out what you can about the firm offering the job. (Your University Careers Service can probably help). How big is it; what does it make or do; does it operate abroad? And what does the job entail? At the interview, remember that you are a salesman for yourself. Do not answer all questions with a mere Yes or No even if they admit of such answers. Some of the questions are likely to be on your past career as evidenced by your letter of application; so be ready to add explanations when you are given an opening on any item. Explain why you continued your studies for longer than usual; why you changed your course, or your university or college; why you took the vacation job. Be quick to mention what the experience brought you. Decide beforehand what are your best points and try to indicate them; make them as specific as possible. What motivates you? What attracts you about the job? What is there in your background or qualifications that make it seem specially suitable for you? Keep your voice up, and your head up. Look the interviewer in the eye (as you should always do when people are talking to you); and if you can manage a smile now and then, to show what a pleasant person you are to work with, so much the better.

Towards the close of the interview you will probably be invited to ask questions yourself. Consider beforehand precisely what you want to know. Do not commence with enquiries about the salary, holidays and prospects; it gives a better impression to start with questions about the work itself. How has the vacancy arisen? Is training provided for? What will be your relationship to others in the department? Can you meet them before joining? What are the working conditions and fringe benefits? What are the prospects of promotion, and who decides upon promotion? If you are willing to go abroad, you can lead into this by asking if the firm is opening up abroad.

I can say things in print that might naturally give offence (or at least cause distress) if I were speaking to you personally. In print my remarks are obviously indiscriminate. I should not have chosen in a personal conversation to mention the matter of slurred vowels and meaningless noises, as I did on p. 147. Now here are some words of wisdom, after the manner of Polonius, on the delicate matter of your appearance. It is accepted that students can dress comfortably if inelegantly in jeans and pullovers, or in garb expressing a more extravagant fancy. What I want to say is that by the time you are thinking of a career you should be prepared to relinquish these carefree ways. Your acceptance and progress in any walk of life depends upon the judgment of an older generation (to which you will yourself shortly belong), and they will value conspicuous cleanliness, neatness and absence of undue ostentation in dress and hair style. Neither the Sex Discrimination Act nor the Race Relations Act prohibits discrimination on the ground of dress, and, to most members of selection committees, "dress' means approved European business or professional dress. So, if you are a man, buy a single-breasted suit, dark blue or dark grey, of conservative cut. Avoid wide lapels, buttons on pockets, fancy trimmings. Take a friend with you when you buy the suit, to assure you that the collar fits snugly. If there is any suspicion of the suit not fitting well, have it altered; see particularly that it is not too small. Women, similarly, should dress conservatively, without sexual display, in a way that betokens quiet efficiency rather than fashion. Remain a conformist when you start your job. It is a folly to let your appearance handicap your career.

On a less personal subject, why not learn to type? Admittedly, you may be given a secretary to whom you can dictate, and this is a great convenience; but often you will find that the draft you want in a hurry is still in her notebook or on her tape. Anyway, it is much easier to compose a difficult draft by typing it yourself than by dictating it. You can learn to type by touch in only one day, as I did. I bought an instruction book with a chart of the keyboard showing the proper fingering, and I tied an apron round my neck and over the keyboard so that I could not see the keys. (This is essential.) Then I practised the exercises for one day. After that I could remove the apron without having the temptation to peep, and I knew all the finger-stretches and could type by touch. It was far and away the best day's work I ever did. I grievously lacked accuracy at first, but that improved with practice.

For general advice I have seen nothing better than some remarks of Mr. A. D. Bonham-Carter.

"I would say to every ambitious and able young man who is choosing to make his career in industry: first, you must realise that the way to the top is something which has to be worked out with your employer, and although you have to fight your way up in the face of keen competition your employer is not one of your competitors but is just as keen that you should reach the top as you are. Secondly, you will best get there by squeezing all you can out of every position you hold and out of the experience of every man you serve or meet: pick their brains, study their successes and their failures; never be afraid to ask questions or put new ideas, but do not get upset or angry if they are not accepted at first, and do not assume that the other man's judgment is wrong. Maybe it is, but it is just as likely that your idea was not quite right. Finally, look after your health—if you are really going to the top enormous demands are going to be made on your time and strength and you cannot afford to be careless."

GENERALLY

The University student should not neglect his University Careers Service, which can often give him valuable assistance. Solicitors can obtain help from the Law Society's Appointments Officer. Anyone looking out for a public appointment should keep his eye regularly on the Public Appointments column of *The Times*. There is a useful annual publication by the Cornmarket Press called *Directory of Opportunities for Graduates,* which not only provides details of the major employers but gives valuable advice. Read, particularly, the advice there given on the wording of your application.

CHAPTER 14

GENERAL READING

> A lawyer without history or literature is a mechanic, a mere working mason; if he possesses some knowledge of these, he may venture to call himself an architect.
>
> —Scott, *Guy Mannering*

No one wants to read law all the time; but some of the hours not spent on serious legal reading may be devoted with profit and pleasure to lighter literature touching upon the law, and to works that set the background in which the lawyer lives. The following, which is hardly more than a list, may be of assistance not merely to the beginner at law but to the practitioner in his leisure moments. What is offered is a collection of titles that may come the reader's way at intervals during his life, and that are worth reading if they do. Not all the books included are in print.

DRAMA

The number of legal references in Shakespeare has given rise to a theory that he was a trained lawyer. This thesis would be more attractive if the internal evidence had not also been used to assign him to a number of other walks in life.

> The bard play-writing in his room,
> The bard a humble clerk,
> The bard, a lawyer, parson, groom,
> The bard, deer-stalking after dark,
> The bard a tradesman—and a Jew—
> The bard a botanist—a beak—
> The bard a skilled musician, too—
> A sheriff and a surgeon, eke![1]

In fact, modern research has shown that there are as many

[1] W. S. Gilbert, *The Bab Ballads*.

references to legal concepts among the lesser Elizabethan dramatists as in Shakespeare, and that there is no reason to suppose that Shakespeare possessed any unusual knowledge. Much the best discussion of the plays from the legal point of view is G. W. Keeton, *Shakespeare's Legal and Political Background* (1967). See also the very learned study by Professor O. Hood Phillips, *Shakespeare and the Lawyers* (1972). A specialised work comes from America, entitled *The Law of Property in Shakespeare and the Elizabethan Drama,* by Paul S. Clarkson and Clyde T. Warren (1942). It need hardly be added that, as any commentator will allow, the plays themselves are worth a shelf-full of commentaries; commentaries are for those who know the plays. There is endless fascination in picking out the legal allusions in Shakespeare without the help of commentaries.

Among dramatists of the present century, three of Galsworthy's plays have a direct interest for lawyers—*The Silver Box, Justice* and *Loyalties,* the last involving a strict application of professional etiquette. A performance of *Justice* was witnessed in 1911 by Mr. Winston Churchill, then Home Secretary, and he was so moved by it that he made a long-overdue reform in prison administration by drastically curtailing the period of solitary confinement.[2] It is of interest to note that Galsworthy was called to the Bar in 1890; but he never practised.

FICTION

Dickens started life as (among other things) a lawyer's clerk and court reporter, and most of his novels contain legal characters or legal references. The famous trial scene in *Pickwick* (written when the author was only 24) shows the working of the system of advocacy in a common law court at its worst. We have moved far since those days, not least because, since 1851, the parties to the suit have been allowed to testify on their own behalf. Students of the reports may like to know that Dickens's Mr. Justice Stareleigh

---

[2] He reduced it to one month for all but recidivists. Such a reform had been advocated by a Departmental Committee as long before as 1895. See S. and B. Webb, *English Prisons under Local Government* (1922) 223, n. 1.

was modelled upon the real Mr. Justice Gaselee, while Serjeant Buzfuz was Serjeant Bompas.[3]

Less widely read but even more engrossing for the lawyer is the description of the appallingly inefficient proceedings of the Court of Chancery in *Bleak House*. Space forbids extended discussion of Dickens's works, but a good commentary is Holdsworth's *Charles Dickens as a Legal Historian* (1929).[4]

An earlier writer, Henry Fielding, must occupy a special place in the esteem of the lawyer and the law-abiding citizen, for it was he who, with his blind half-brother, sitting as London magistrates, founded the Bow Street Runners, the ancestors of our present professional police.[5] His *Tom Jones* deserves to be read for its own sake, and not merely for the incidental legal allusion.

Thackeray entered the Middle Temple (though he did not get much further), and his experience there is pictured in Chapter 29 of *Pendennis*.

The name of Samuel Warren is no longer known to the general public. He was a snob and often a bore, but withal quite a sound lawyer, and his legal novel, *Ten Thousand a Year,* is assured of immortality within his own profession. It is somewhat over-long, and may be commenced without loss at Chapter 7. The plot involves an action in ejectment which succeeded because the judge refused to admit in evidence a deed on which there appeared an erasure (Chapter 13). The refusal was based on the ancient rule that a material alteration in a document after execution renders it void. Unfortunately Warren is guilty of bad law in this particular: the rule is that there is a presumption in the case of a deed or other document *inter vivos* that any alteration appearing in it was made before execution; and on the facts supposed in the novel there was no evidence to rebut this presumption. Also, the rule avoiding deeds for material alteration does not apply to deeds of

---

[3] For a legal study see Percy Fitzgerald, *Bardell* v. *Pickwick* (1902). It is pointed out in (1923) 1 Can. Bar Rev. 631 that in *Brooke* v. *Pickwick* (1827) 4 Bing. 753, 130 E.R. 753, the defendant was the coach proprietor of Bath from whom Dickens took the name of his hero, and one of the judges was Gaselee J. The legal purlieus of London as they survive since Dickens's time are described in 120 New Law Journal 492.

[4] See also T. A. Fyfe, *Charles Dickens and the Law* (1910): Sir Gerald Hurst, *Lincoln's Inn Essays* (1949) 109.

[5] Anthony Babington, *A House in Bow Street* (1969).

conveyance,[6] as the deed in Warren's novel was. It is said that the character of "Mr. Sterling" was intended to represent Pollock C.B.; Mr. Subtle was Scarlett, Mr. Quicksilver was Brougham, Mr. Crystal and Mr. Lynx were Cresswell and Wightman, Mr. Chaffanbrass was Serjeant Ballantine, Sir Charles Westenholme was Lord Lyndhurst, Lord Widdrington was Lord Tenterden, and Mr. Justice Grayley was Bayley J.[7] To Warren and other legal writers of the ninteenth century belongs the credit of inventing the detective novel.[8]

Galsworthy's *Forsyte Saga* has a solicitor as one of the principal characters, a libel action conducted on somewhat irregular lines,[9] and a will that neglects the Thellusson Act. Someone brought the latter mistake to the author's attention, and in the sequel, entitled *On Forsyte 'Change,* the point is admitted but ingeniously evaded.[10]

Outside the field of English law there are the works of Sir Walter Scott and Honoré de Balzac—both lawyers, and both prolific in legal allusion. Scott combined novel writing with the practice of a busy Scottish advocate and judicial duties. His rather boyish romances do not appeal to all; but the reader may like to know that the two with the strongest legal flavour are *Guy Mannering* and *Redgauntlet.* Students of Scots law will find instruction in *Sir Walter Scott and Scots Law,* by David Marshall (1932). R. L. Stevenson became qualified as a Scottish advocate, though he never practised. His unfinished *Weir of Hermiston* gives an arresting picture of a coarse and cruel Scottish judge, Lord Braxfield (in the story called Lord Hermiston).[11]

It is not only the lawyers, real or nominal, who have written novels with a legal angle. Trollope is best known for his

[6] *Bolton* v. *Bishop of Carlisle* (1793) 2 H.Bl. 260 at 263–264.
[7] See J. B. Atlay in Cornhill, October, 1907.
[8] 139 Justice of the Peace 572, 605.
[9] See (1927) 5 Can. Bar Rev. 500.
[10] (1931) 50 Law Notes 68.
[11] The number of novelists with legal connections is surprising, and it may be of interest to add a note on two others. Charles Reade was a barrister and read in chambers (though he never practised); but although he wrote novels bearing upon the law they are disappointing. His only worthwhile novel (*The Cloister and the Hearth*) is non-legal. Wilkie Collins, another nominal barrister, is notable as one of the forerunners of the modern detective novelists.

descriptions of ecclesiastical life in the *Barchester* series; but
lawyers will remember him for his account of their own profession
in *Orley Farm*.[12] Emily Brontë's *Wuthering Heights* shows an
accurate knowledge of the law of entails fifty years before her own
time.[13] George Eliot's *Felix Holt* has an ambitious legal plot
turning on a base fee—though the legal reader will want to know
why the owner in possession of a base fee, with constant legal
advice, did not take steps to bar the remainder.[14]

Modern novelists deserve a paragraph to themselves. Judge
Gordon Clark wrote detective novels under the pseudonym of
"Cyril Hare," and the plot of several of them turns on a point of
law. Thus his *Tragedy at Law* involves an unobtrusive subsection
(now repealed) of an Act of 1934; it is of interest for its detail of
circuit life. *That Yew Tree's Shade* requires for the solution of the
mystery a rule of law stated in Chapter 7 of the present book.
When the Wind Blows is inspired by a bad old rule of the law of
marriage. English law is steadily becoming more rational, and the
rule in question was abolished in 1960. All these novels were
reprinted as Penguins. Another former County Court judge, H. C.
Leon, wrote under the pen-name of "Henry Cecil." My own
favourite is his first book *Full Circle*; but he wrote many other
humorous best-sellers about judges and lawyers. Lawyers
currently writing detective novels include Michael Gilbert and
Michael Underwood.

BIOGRAPHIES

From the many biographies of lawyers one should perhaps put
first the lives of two great reformers: C. H. S. Fifoot's *Lord
Mansfield* (1936) and Mary L. Mack's *Jeremy Bentham* (Vol. 1,

---

[12] Those who wish to pursue the legal errors (which do not spoil the tale)
will find them unsparingly attacked by Sir Francis Newbolt, k.c., in
(1924) 95 Nineteenth Century 227, reprinted in his *Out of Court* (1925).
Trollope's views on the ethics of advocacy are discussed in E. B. V.
Christian's *Leaves of the Lower Branch* (1909), 65–66. See also Henry S.
Drinker, *The Lawyers of Anthony Trollope*; Hugh Cockerall in 127 New
Law Journal 1252.

[13] See C.P.S[anger], *The Structure of Wuthering Heights* (Hogarth Essays,
1926).

[14] Earlier, Jane Austen had got into trouble on a similar point, in *Pride
and Prejudice*. See 124 New Law Journal 375, 446.

1962). The achievement of Sir Samuel Romilly can best be read in Sir Leon Radzinowicz's monumental *History of English Criminal Law*, Vol. 1, Part V. Romilly and Bentham figure, with Beccaria, in Coleman Phillipson's *Three Criminal Law Reformers* (1923). Mention may also be made of Lord Birkenhead's *Fourteen English Judges* (1926), and Catherine Drinker Bowen's biography of Coke C.J. called *The Lion and the Throne*.

The interest in these works is largely historical, and many readers will be more attracted by biographies of successful lawyers living nearer to our own time. The apex of success is traditionally the Woolsack, and the careers of those who have reached it are given by R. F. V. Heuston in scholarly detail in his *Lives of the Lord Chancellors, 1885–1940* (1964). Edward Marjoribanks's *Life of Sir Edward Marshall Hall* (1929)[15] may be recommended for its portrayal of the last of the flamboyant advocates, and the same writer's *Life of Lord Carson* (1932) is fit to take its place among the best modern biography.[16] Derek Walker-Smith's *Lord Reading and his Cases* (1934) and H. Montgomery Hyde's *Norman Birkett* (1964) are also worth reading.

There is a plethora of autobiography. The late Lord Justice MacKinnon, in his book *On Circuit* (1940), said that most books of legal reminiscence are bad; and he named only two exceptions, in which I hesitate to follow him.[17] My own list of the best legal autobiographies would include one by a successful advocate of the last century, one by a judge who made his name on the criminal side, and one by a country solicitor. The first of these is *Some Experiences of a Barrister's Life*, by William Ballantine (1882)—better known as Serjeant Ballantine's *Experiences*. Its gossipy pages are crowded with Victorian personalities who are

[15] Reprinted in condensed form by Pelican Books.
[16] The author had written the first of what were intended to be two volumes when he died, and his work was then published. It was later completed in a further two volumes by I. Colvin; but those who have only Marjoribanks's volume will find that it gives a satisfying account in itself.
[17] The two exceptions made by MacKinnon L.J. were *"Pie-Powder,"* by "A Circuit Tramp" (J. Alderson Foote, K.C.) (1911), and *As I Went on My Way*, by Arthur J. Ashton, K.C. (1924). The former is little more than a collection of anecdotes (chiefly humorous), though the anecdotes have merit.

still alive to students of the law reports. Ballantine was retained on behalf of Orton, the false claimant in the Tichborne case, and his books gives shrewd advice on advocacy. Two generations on comes Sir Travers Humphreys (Humphreys J.), *Criminal Days* (1946). This is an autobiography full of good stories, with reflections upon the criminal law. Reginald Hine's *Confessions of an Un-Common Attorney* (1945) is a revelation of the interest that can be won from life by a country solicitor who observes his fellow creatures and is an antiquarian and *littérateur* to boot. Not one of these is a "must" book, though each is good in its own class.

Finally, it is convenient to mention here the remarkable *Pollock-Holmes Letters* (2 vols., 1942), the correspondence of two men who became the *doyens* of English and American law, carried on over a period of 58 years. This may well be read with Mark deWolfe Howe's two-volume biography, *Justice Oliver Wendell Holmes* (1957, 1963).

TRIALS

The historian, the devotee of detective fiction, the student of advocacy, and the novelist in search of a plot, should not ignore the very full collection of trials that may be found in some libraries. Cases of historical interest are reported at length in the 34 volumes of Howell's *State Trials,* such, for example, as Coke's virulent prosecution of Sir Walter Raleigh (vol. 2, p. 1). A selection from these trials was published in three volumes by J. W. Willis-Bund. Other series are the Notable British Trials Series, the Famous Trials Series, and the Old Bailey Trials Series; all these give a full transcript of the cases, so that each step in the evidence can be studied. The series presently running is called Celebrated Trials. Perhaps the most remarkable of the nineteenth-century *causes célèbres* was that of *The Tichborne Claimant*; Douglas Woodruffe's book under that title is noteworthy. Illustrations of the technique of famous advocates are given in Edgar Lustgarten's *Defender's Triumph* (1951). There is also an inexpensive series of Famous Trials in Penguins, each volume containing condensed accounts of a number of trials.

As a matter of interest it may be recorded that R. L. Stevenson's *Kidnapped* is based in part on the famous Appin murder case—*R. v. Stewart* (1752) 19 Howell's State Trials 1. This is itself the subject of a study by Sir William MacArthur (*The Appin Murder*, 1960). The *Annesley Case*, retold in the Notable English Trials Series (a series that later became Notable British Trials), supplied material for parts of three novels.[18] Another novelist who used these Trials was Nathaniel Hawthorne.[19]

ESSAYS

It would be possible to compile an anthology of essays bearing upon the law, beginning with Bacon's essay "Of Judicature," and passing through Selden's *Table Talk*, Lamb's "Old Benchers of the Inner Temple,"[20] Bagehot's "Lord Brougham,"[21] Hazlitt's portrait of Eldon,[22] and several by Maitland, to modern examples such as John Buchan's "The Judicial Temperament" (in his *Homilies and Recreations*), Lord Justice MacKinnon's *Murder in the Temple* (1935), Theo. Matthew's *For Lawyers and Others* (1937), and Lord Macmillan's *Law and Other Things* (1937). (John Buchan, be it noted, started at the Bar and wrote a book on the taxation of foreign income). Some of the best legal essays are to be found in no other place than the law reports, in the judgments of such men as Mansfield, Bowen, Macnaghten and Sumner. The speech of Lord Macnaghten in *Gluckstein* v. *Barnes* [1900] A.C. at 255 is a brilliant example of pungent wit, which was thought worthy of inclusion in the *Oxford Book of English Prose*; and Atkin L.J.'s judgment in *Balfour* v. *Balfour* [1919] 2 K.B. 571 also deserves honourable mention. Mr. Louis Blom-Cooper has published his own selections of best legal writing under the titles *The Law as Literature* (1961) and *The Language of the Law* (1965).

---

[18] Tobias Smollett's *Peregrine Pickle*, Chap. 98; Scott's *Guy Mannering*, and Charles Reade's *The Wandering Heir*. See David Marshall, *Sir Walter Scott and Scots Law*, 48–57.

[19] See Alfred S. Reid, *The Yellow Ruff and the Scarlet Letter* (University of Florida Press, 1955).

[20] Included among the *Essays of Elia* and republished with notes by MacKinnon L.J. in a limited edition (1927), and again in the same writer's *Inner Temple Papers* (1948).

[21] Republished in *Collected Works*, ed. N. St. John-Stevas (London, 1968) iii, 159.

[22] Included in his essays entitled *The Spirit of the Age*, first printed in 1825.

HUMOUR

Collections of anecdotes are usually poor things, but exceptions are Sir Robert Megarry's *Miscellany-at-Law* (1955), and *A Second Miscellany-at-Law* (1973), both including many specimens of judicial wit and wisdom. The best book of humorous reminiscence comes from Ireland: it is Maurice Healey's *The Old Munster Circuit* (1939). W. S. Gilbert's libretto to *Trial by Jury* is a joy to read: but then, Gilbert was by training a lawyer! The *Complete Forensic Fables* by "O" (Theo. Matthew) is well known. Sir Alan Herbert's even more famous *Misleading Cases* are now cóllected together under the title *Uncommon Law* (1935) with its sequels *Codd's Last Case* (1952) and *Bardot, M.P.?* (1964).

HISTORY

Legal histories are generally outside the scope of this chapter, but three are so clearly entitled to rank as literature that mention may be made of them. They are Maine's *Ancient Law* (which should be read in Pollock's edition), Maitland's *Constitutional History,* and Holmes's *The Common Law.*

The lawyer must feel a sense of shame about the part played by the legal mechanism in repressing the poor in the eighteenth and nineteenth centuries. J. L. and Barbara Hammond's *The Village Labourer* (Pelican ed.) is good and necessary medicine to cure us of too much professional pride, and from the literary point of view it is by no means unpalatable. It is a study in the government of England before the Reform Act, the impoverishment of the agricultural labourer through enclosures and the Game Laws, and the use of poor relief as a means of avoiding reform. In their book *The Bleak Age* (Pelican Books, 1947) the same writers give an arresting account of conditions in the towns in the thirties and forties of the last century. A reading of it will give colour to the study of local government and town planning, because it shows the needs that called the modern machinery into existence.

It is true, of course, that industrialisation increased wealth, and that without private enterprise there would have been no industrialisation. The points are well made in *The Long Debate on Poverty,* edited by Arthur Seldon (1972). But the fact remains that our Victorian ancestors did far too little to mitigate the inequalities of the system. Those who think that Dickens exaggerated the social evils of his time should read the appalling evidence related in *A People's Conscience* by Strathearn Gordon and T. G. B. Cocks (1952). E. S. Turner, *Roads to Ruin* (Pelican Books, 1966) is an entertaining history of the lamentations that greeted attempts to pass obvious reforms.

Lawyers and the Courts, by Brian Abel-Smith and Robert Stevens (1967), covers the engrossing history of the legal profession to the year 1965, omitting none of our blemishes and indeed giving a general picture of selfishness, chicanery and corruption. This and its companion volume, *In Search of Justice* (1968), should take away any remnants of professional self-esteem left after reading the Hammonds. But the last work should not be read without the counterblast from E. J. Cohn in his review in (1969) 32 M.L.R. 336.

THE CONSTITUTION

Every lawyer will take delight in Sir Alan Herbert's *The Ayes Have It* (1937)—an account of the passage of the Matrimonial Causes Act—and *The Point of Parliament* (1946). If you feel that your knowledge of the working of government is deficient, read S. A. de Smith's vastly informative book, *Constitutional and Administrative Law,* which is available in paperback.

Sir Geoffrey Vickers's *The Art of Judgment* (University Paperbacks) is a classic on policy-making not only in government but in industry.

JURISPRUDENCE, LOGIC, PHILOSOPHY AND ECONOMICS

Selection becomes more difficult when one turns to the theoretical treatment of the law. Much has been written on this, but not of a character to appeal to the general reader. A simple and readable account of juridical thinking is Lon L. Fuller's *Anatomy of the Law* (Pelican). Judge Jerome Frank's *Law and the Modern Mind* (reprinted 1951) is a pungent and provocative book, with which may be coupled Thurman Arnold's *The Folklore of Capitalism* (1937). A classic by a great American judge is Cardozo's *Nature of*

the Judicial Process (1921).[23] All four of these books are
American. Sir Carleton Allen's *Law in the Making* and Julius
Stone's *Legal System and Lawyers' Reasonings* are heavier going,
but every lawyer should read them.

From time to time judges and even Law Lords tell us that logic
is not compulsive in legal reasoning. In this they merely betray a
lack of understanding of what logic is. A good simple account is
Anthony Flew's *Thinking about Thinking* (Fontana 1975). Other
popular expositions of practical logic are R. H. Thouless's
Straight and Crooked Thinking (1930, later published in
paperback) and E. R. Emmet's *The Use of Reason* (1960)
Chapter 9.

People are slowly becoming aware of the effect of language
upon thought, and Stuart Chase's *The Tyranny of Words* (1938) is
a racy primer of the subject. It has a chapter on law, but the
possible applications that suggest themselves go much beyond
that chapter. Readers who feel inclined may proceed from Chase
to the strong meat of Ogden and Richards's *The Meaning of
Meaning,* one of the most influential books of our time.

If anyone wants an acquaintance with Hegel, Marx, the
utilitarians, and other political theorists, he cannot do better than
start with Professor K. B. Smellie's *Reason in Politics* (1939), a
readable account from a modern point of view. The liveliest
history of philosophy for the general reader is Will Durant's
Outlines of Philosophy (available as a paperback), after perusing
which the student will be ready for Bertrand Russell's *History of
Western Philosophy* (1946). Antony Flew in his *An Introduction to
Western Philosophy* (1971) combines extracts from the classical
philosophers with his own comments on the issues.

Nineteenth-century Liberalism and economic *laissez-faire* have
moulded the outlook of lawyers more than they themselves
realise. In their application to constitutional law the classic is, of
course, Dicey's *Law of the Constitution* (10th ed. by E. C. S. Wade,
1961); on the wider aspects there is the same writer's *Law and
Opinion in England during the Nineteenth Century* (reissued as a
paperback in 1962). A continuation volume, *Law and Opinion in
England in the 20th Century,* was produced by a group effort

---

[23] Now available in a collected edition including other works of the
author: *Selected Writings of Benjamin Nathan Cardozo,* ed. Margaret
E. Hall (New York, 1947).

under the editorship of Morris Ginsberg in 1959. It has become the fashion to decry Dicey's Rule of Law as well as Adam Smith's economics: before finally subscribing to the current opinion the student should read Professor Hayek's defence of these doctrines in his book *The Constitution of Liberty* (1960), followed by his important trilogy on *Law, Legislation and Liberty* (1973–). This is an attack upon Socialism, written by a distinguished economist but employing chiefly political arguments which all can understand, whether they agree with them or not. Lord Robbins's powerful dissent from Hayek can be read in his *Politics and Economics* (1963). We must not leave the philosophy of Liberalism without mentioning J. S. Mill's famous essay "On Liberty."[24] This is not only a classic but one that can still be read with keen enjoyment. H. L. A. Hart's *Law, Liberty and Morality* is in the same tradition.

If you are going to practise at the Bar or as a solicitor you must be able to understand a balance-sheet. *How to Read a Balance Sheet* (I.L.O., Geneva, 1966) is a programmed book; you learn by answering questions.

CRIMINOLOGY AND PENOLOGY

All those concerned with the administration of the criminal law should make some effort to keep abreast of the work done by criminologists and penologists. Such knowledge is needed not only by the judge or magistrate in the interests of society but by the defending advocate in the interests of his client. When the defendant has pleaded or has been found guilty the question of punishment or treatment arises, and with the width of choice now open it is most important for the defendant that his advocate should know the possibilities and be able to make proper representations on his behalf. Further, it may be said to be the professional duty of every lawyer to educate himself in these topics in order that he may help to spread enlightenment among the lay community.

The best introduction is Nigel Walker's *Sentencing in a Rational Society* (Pelican, 1972). Detailed surveys of sentencing

---

[24] Reprinted in Fontana Philosophy Classics (paperback) together with the same writer's "Utilitarianism" and "Essay on Bentham," ed. by Mary Warnock.

possibilities are: J. D. McClean and J. C. Wood, *Criminal Justice and the Treatment of Offenders,* and J. E. Hall Williams, *The English Penal System in Transition.* Good introductions to the modern attitude to crime are D. J. West's *The Young Offender* (Pelican Books, 1967), Howard Jones's *Crime in a Changing Society* (Pelican Books, 1965) and Sir Leo Page's *Justice of the Peace* (3rd ed., 1967). A masterly exposure of the limitations of the present science of criminology is Lady Wootton's *Social Science and Social Pathology* (1959). Hugh Klare's *Anatomy of Prison* (Pelican Books, 1962) is a sober and readable statement of the prison system.

INDEX